THATCHER
· The First Term ·

THATCHER
· The First Term ·

PATRICK COSGRAVE

THE BODLEY HEAD

LONDON

*This one is for
Ralph and Constance Ward
in whose home
Stonelynk Farm
the writing of it was begun
and finished*

British Library Cataloguing
in Publication Data
Cosgrave, Patrick
Thatcher: the first term
1. Great Britain—Politics and government—1979
I. Title
354.4107'2'09 JN231

ISBN 0-370-30602-3
© Patrick Cosgrave 1985
Printed in Great Britain for
The Bodley Head Ltd
9 Bow Street, London WC2E 7AL
by Redwood Burn Ltd
Trowbridge, Wiltshire
First published 1985

Contents

Preface

Una femina nobis cunctando restituit rem.
— adapted from Ennius on Quintus Fabius Maximus,
as quoted by Cicero.

I had not thought to return, at least in book form, to the subject of Margaret Thatcher for many years, if at all. The book about her and her ideas which I published in 1978 — *Margaret Thatcher: a Tory and her Party* — was necessarily more than ordinarily one of its time. It was written in the aftermath of a heated struggle for the leadership — and perhaps for the identity — of the Conservative Party in which I had played a small, but highly partisan, role. Its merit, if it had merit, seemed to me to lie in its immediacy, in what it managed to convey of the sheer and passionate excitement of political debate within the party between, say, the opening of Edward Heath's final and disastrous conflict with the National Union of Mineworkers in 1973 and his replacement by a very different kind of leader in February 1975. Professor John Vincent, in the *Times Literary Supplement*, was good enough to say that my account of the battle for the leadership itself — between November 1974 and its conclusion on 11 February 1975 — would be required reading for future students, and so far as reporting or scholarship were concerned I was more than content with that verdict. I did publish, in 1979, just after her first general election victory, a somewhat expanded edition, taking account of the period leading up to the election, and the campaign itself. But the very nature of the product, it seemed to me, excluded revision or rewriting.

Not long before the 1983 general election, however, David Machin, managing director of The Bodley Head, suggested quite another kind of book, a study of the first term, with an introductory account of the period between 1975 and 1979, which account forms the first two chapters of this volume. It says a great deal, I think, about the civilised approach both of David and his firm to political writing that they wanted the book whether or not the Prime Minister won an election which we felt could not be long delayed.

Anyway, this is the book. It is emphatically in no sense an updating of its predecessor on the same subject. I hope it is a good deal more objective, as it is certainly calmer in tone. There is, however, one aspect of it which represents a development from the earlier book. In exploring it I am indebted to a number of those who had written more recently on the subject of Margaret Thatcher's career, notably Russell Lewis in his revision of his 1975 biography, Peter Riddell in *The Thatcher Government*, and William Keegan in *Mrs Thatcher's Economic Experiment*.[1] Before I describe this aspect, however, I should say that in mentioning these three writers I do not mean to disparage such a fine book as George Brock's and Nicholas Wapshott's *Thatcher*. But it is a narrative, whereas Mr Lewis, Mr Riddell and Mr Keegan are concerned with arguments of authority, rightness in policy, and legitimacy.

I call my first chapter 'The Quest for Legitimacy'. This was something I touched on in my earlier volume, but I did not then fully understand its implication, nor possess the information required to examine it fully. It is now broadly accepted that Margaret Thatcher became Leader of the Conservative Party after a campaign which was characterised by boldness (her own) and cunning (that of Airey Neave). Her team took full advantage of the mistakes and failures of her predecessor, the clumsiness of his electoral machine, and the deep sense of unease which the general election campaigns of 1974 had left in the Parliamentary Party. But she was, at the outset, an improbable candidate and, even towards the end, an outsider. What was quite clear then, and is clearer now, was that many of those who voted for her on the first ballot (when she defeated Edward Heath by 130 votes to 119 and established an impregnable position for the second ballot) did not do so with any clear consciousness of the radical platform she subsequently adopted.

Mr Keegan calls what happened in February 1975 — in the words of an unnamed dissident Conservative — 'the hijacking of a political party'. Mr Keegan is hostile to Mrs Thatcher and all her works and pomps, and he wishes particularly to emphasise that her party victory in 1975 conferred on her no mandate to break with the post-war consensus on economic policy (usually described as 'Butskellism') which she promptly shattered. Even given the frequent harshness of his language, however, Mr Keegan's point is not an unfair one. And there is, even, another point to add.

All writers on the subject of the 1974–75 leadership campaign, whatever their point of view, pay tribute to the brilliance of Airey Neave's management. I emphasised in my book, as Brock and Wapshott do in theirs, Neave's last stratagem — to maximise the profit to be gained for his candidate from the widespread disillusionment and unease with the Heath leadership by suggesting, particularly on the night before the first ballot, that she was in a weak polling position *vis-à-vis* her opponent. Certainly, a number of backbenchers — we can definitely identify sixteen, under the chairmanship of Sir John Rodgers — did not want a thoroughgoing Heath victory on the first ballot, where 139 votes would have assured him continued tenure. But they did not want a Thatcher victory either: they wanted her to damage Edward

Heath sufficiently to allow the entry of further candidates the second time around. It was because she did more than damage him — she destroyed him — that she was unbeatable by anybody else. For, said the press — notably the *Daily Telegraph*, in a leading article entitled 'Consider her Courage' — after that opening débâcle, she was the one who had had the courage to engage Heath in a head-on struggle, knowing that her political career would be over if he won. Why should others, less courageous, perhaps even pusillanimous, benefit from her famous victory, even if it had been at least partly won by sleight of hand? It was only later that the fact that there *had* been sleight of hand led to mutterings about her moral authority.

The vital point to emphasise is that for some time Margaret Thatcher herself shared these doubts, and one cannot understand the early years of her leadership without appreciating that fact. For a long time the existence of such doubts vitiated her leadership.

It is these facts, and the fact that the whole bid for the leadership was an improbable business, to be likened to the Duke of Wellington's campaigns — whenever the rope broke, the duke once said, he tied a knot and went on — that renders quite valueless the contribution to Thatcher literature of Mr Bruce Arnold in *Margaret Thatcher: A Study in Power*. Mr Arnold is an attractive writer and — as he has shown in Ireland in his battles with Mr Charles Haughey — a brave journalist. But to make his thesis depend, as he does, on the proposition that (with my aid, incidentally) Mrs Thatcher developed, between 1974 and 1975, a coherent and Machiavellian strategy for gaining the leadership in collusion with the intellectual New Right (the monetarists of Mr Keegan's demonology), a strategy which involved running Sir Keith Joseph as a stalking horse for herself, is arrant nonsense. It has no roots in what happened at the time, and while it is true that I advocated her candidacy from an early stage, I did so against her most emphatically declared wishes, and her campaign did not become a going concern until Airey Neave volunteered to run it. Even at that stage, moreover, Neave was not a Thatcherite but a man on the lookout for somebody who could beat Edward Heath.

It is, in my judgement therefore, vital for any understanding of the first term to know in exactly what circumstances, and under what constraints and pressures, she worked between 1975 and 1979. Indeed, even after that date, her legitimacy was more than once called into question, though, naturally, that is no longer something which concerns her.

In the preparation of this book I have been helped by a number of political friends, some of them currently ministers of the Crown but including many who could by no means be described as Thatcher supporters. In the tradition of these things many wished to remain anonymous, so it would, I believe, be invidious to name any: this silence should not suggest that my gratitude is other than massive. However, and although the book is, I believe, in no sense uncritical of her record, I think it proper to express my thanks to the Prime Minister for the insights she has given me over the years, as well as the opportunity to see high politics close up. Finally, my wife Shirley was a tower of strength throughout.

CHAPTER ONE

The Quest for Legitimacy

'Trust the people' — I have long tried to make that my motto;
but I know, and will not conceal, that there are still a few in
our party who have that lesson yet to learn and have yet to
understand that the Tory party of today is no longer
identified with that small and narrow class which is
connected with the ownership of land; but that its great
strength can be found, and must be developed, in our large
towns as well as in our country districts. Yes, trust the people.
You, who are ambitious, and rightly ambitious, of being the
guardians of the British Constitution, trust the people, and
they will trust you — and they will follow you and join you in
defence of that Constitution against any and every foe. I have
no fear of democracy.
— Lord Randolph Churchill in Birmingham 16 April 1885

At eighteen minutes past ten on 28 March 1979 the result
of a vote of confidence in the House of Commons was
announced. Three hundred and eleven members had no confidence in Her Majesty's government; three hundred and ten
had.

The evening at the end of which that vote was taken was
disfigured in many ways. The most disfiguring moment was
when Michael Foot, the Leader of the House, and the
supposed paragon of parliamentary democracy, approached
the gentle Gwynfor Evans, Leader of the Welsh Nationalist
Party, and told him that, after many refusals, the government

could see its way to putting £60,000 into a fund for Welsh miners suffering from the dread disease of pneumoconiosis. Evans said, quite simply, that he could not be bribed. He voted against the government.

When the result was announced — to the expected roars — the Prime Minister uncoiled his substantial frame from his seat. He said,

> Mr Speaker. Now that the House of Commons has
> declared itself, we shall take our own case to the country.

Both the Prime Minister and the Leader of the Opposition behaved on that evening with dignity, while Labour members sang the 'Red Flag' in as uncertain chorus as Conservatives sang 'Land of Hope and Glory'. Margaret Thatcher went to the office of her Chief Whip, and said, 'At last.' None the less, to understand what happened that night, and to understand her, requires retrospection. She was about to go on to a general election with a majority of more than forty seats, and the biggest swing to her party since before the Second World War. But one has to look back and ask — what made her?

There was a feature of even the friendly reviews of my earlier book which at the time I found puzzling and which, in retrospect, I find interesting and instructive in trying to arrive at a rounded understanding of the phenomenon that is Margaret Thatcher in British politics. My first chapter was entitled 'The Woman' and was an attempt to describe, principally by way of personalised anecdote, her nature and character. I had been constantly surprised by the failure of press and public — particularly the public that had watched her on television — to see behind the facade of her battling public image the warm, humorous, amusing and, above all, kind woman I had known (by then) for some six or seven years, and I strove to redress the balance. Mr Peregrine Worsthorne most notably, but other reivewers as well, disliked (perhaps detested would not be too strong a word) this chapter, even when they were kind to the rest of the book, taking it to be, in Mr Worsthorne's formulation, redolent of women's magazine gossiping at its worst.

Perhaps I did not do the job as it should have been done. But I was then, and remain, convinced that the story I had to tell, and the characteristics the anecdotes revealed, were important to any right analysis of the significance of her election to the leadership and important, too, for any prediction that might be made about what — or how — she would do. Finally, it seemed to me, the very fact that she was a woman was of considerable moment.

This was not a generally shared view. Mr Bernard Levin, for example, writing in *The Times* before the election process was concluded, advised Conservative MPs not to be put off voting for her because she was female: if they elected her they would find, he argued, that being led by an intelligent and able woman would be no different from being led by an intelligent and able man. This was, of course, the conventional moderate feminist point of view: in circles where the continuing emancipation of women was favoured it was *de rigeur* to insist that no discussion of gender should enter into the matter of suitability for a particular position. I thought that view mistaken then, and I think it mistaken now. Certainly, in the early part of her leadership in particular, the fact that she was a woman made a marked difference to the course and outcome of many debates, though when assessing her record it is difficult to apportion weight between that fact and two others — that she was an individual with a notably definite, and perhaps even simple, character, and that she was, in 1975, wholly lacking in experience of really high office.

In any event, it made a difference. There were a great many reasons for this, and not all of them reflect credit on those who were influenced by them. From the moment of her election — and perhaps even before her triumph over Edward Heath — the words (spoken invariably with vehemence) '*that woman*' prefaced practically any remark critical of or derogatory to her from opponents within as well as outside the ranks of her own party. The older males in her Shadow Cabinet, even when, like her deputy William Whitelaw, they were supportive of her, found it very difficult effectively to adjust to so novel an authority. Even today, after she has led the Tories to two general election victories and the nation to a military triumph, political conversation around Westminster reveals a certain continuing unease or incomprehension based on gender. And then, on a much more mundane level — but imposing, on the individual concerned, tiresome pressures — a woman in public life is treated to a great deal more tedious attention from the popular press and television than is a man. It is, possibly, high-minded reaction by fastidious writers like Mr Worsthorne and Mr Levin to such frivolities as the *Daily Mirror*'s 'investigation' into whether the Prime Minister was or was not, on a particular occasion, wearing a wig, that prohibits the discussion of matters relevant not only to her performance, but to her character. That that character is directly and immediately relevant to her achievement is sufficiently demonstrated by a Market Opinion Research International poll of March 1983 showing thirty-three per cent of a sample giving her strength of personality as the principal reason for voting Conservative. This admitted strength bedevils and often obscures the vital questions of whether or not her policies are well-judged, and even what tradition of politics those policies inhabit.

Coming to a satisfactory conclusion on these questions is not helped by the Prime Minister's own reaction to them. From her reply to a question about her attitude to Women's Liberation at her first press conference as Leader — 'What's it ever done for me?' — to a much-publicised 1984 interview with the BBC's World Service in which she paraded her desire to have grandchildren, she has played the matter of being a woman, and that of woman's place in modern society, in a variety of not always very clear-cut ways. She almost invariably refuses entry into any abstract discussion of women's role (as, of course, do a great many women highly successful in public life who simply do not wish to spend time and energy on the merits or otherwise of the theoretical formulations of the feminist movement in any of its manifestations), but much of her rhetoric is suffused by appeals, arguments and propositions that could only be uttered by a woman, and to which only a woman could lend authority.

In 1976, after studying a certain amount of psephological material of general relevance I came to the tentative conclusion that there was a significant female constituency to which she could make a particularly important electoral appeal. I identified (again, tentatively) this constituency as being composed of young or youngish married working women whose husbands were Labour voters with old-fashioned views on the place of women. These ladies, I concluded, had been touched by the Women's Movement, to the extent of feeling some discontent with their lives, but they were not radical feminists in the sense of being prepared either outrightly to assert themselves in the home, or to break it up. I thought that the new Leader, being herself both a successful career woman and an assiduous wife and mother with, generally, traditional views on family life, might strike a particular chord with them, and bring to the polls to vote Conservative people who otherwise might not vote at all — for I concluded that the women I had in mind were in general politically apathetic. It seemed to me both legitimate and desirable to undertake an opinion research survey designed to identify the constituency and explore the aspirations of its members. Since, however, my draft idea for a poll depended on an emphasis on her sexual identity, she turned the scheme down flat, dismissing it as yet another example of an irrelevant and rather academic preoccupation with matters which were of no concern to her.[1]

In November 1982, however, she spoke at a banquet given by the Confederation of British Industry. The speech she made there is highly typical of many of her utterances, and I choose it as an example largely because it was delivered at a time when criticism of her for equating national and household economics was particularly strong, the critics believing, like John Maynard Keynes, that the two systems were quite different. She said she had been attacked for

> talking about the principles of financial management of a nation as if they were like those of a family budget. Some say I preach merely the homilies of housekeeping or the parables of the parlour. But I do not repent. Those parables would have saved many a financier from failure and many a country from crisis.

It is not unimaginable that a male politician would speak in the same general terms, but the precision of the imagery is entirely female and it would now, I think, be generally acceptable that those images are very real to the Prime Minister, and a vital part of her moral nature. What is more, she glories in their use.

What is beyond question is this: as a woman the new Leader was quite isolated from the distinctive and historically conditioned male camaraderie of Conservative politics at Westminster. At the same time, the fact that she was a woman gave her a novelty value — tongue to which was given by the popular press internationally as well as at home, by radio and television, and by the people — which imposed severe and unexpected strains upon her. Thus, just two weeks after her election as Leader she fulfilled a long-standing engagement in Glasgow. The Glasgow police had provided no more than minimal coverage, and found it difficult to cope with a crowd of some thousands. It was not an unfriendly nor a hostile crowd, such as she has become accustomed to over the years since 1979. It was, above all, a curious and interested crowd, one attracted most of all by her novelty value, and perhaps by something that she had stirred in them. It was emphatically not — though one of her subsequently most influential advisers on public relations thought it was — a demonstration of endorsement for her views on any aspect of public policy. It illustrated, however, her problem of how to interpret, and to make use of, the intense public reaction to her in the weeks and months following her election, particularly given the fact that there was no immediate likelihood of a general election. She simply did not know how to handle what seemed to be adulation, but might merely be adulation covering frenzy; nor did she have anybody close to her with the requisite experience to advise her.

Her remark at her apparently highly self-assured first press conference as Leader has been much quoted. 'To me,' she said, 'it is like a dream that the next name in the list ... is Margaret Thatcher.' It is a characteristic — perhaps an unfortunate one — of her personal style to sound certain, even when she is uncertain. All of the journalists who heard her expatiate on her dream, and all of the film cameras which recorded her doing it, conveyed the impression of an exceptionally self-confident woman paying courteous obeisance to the proposition that she should be surprised at what had happened. To Neave, earlier in the afternoon, she had said, 'Me? Good God.' And then, 'Really?' She may have appeared triumphal in public; in private she was dumbfounded.

Nor did anybody close to her have any experience in handling a problem even more important than the instant hysteria of press, radio and television. That was the matter of her relations with her senior colleagues in the parliamentary party. Certainly, Airey Neave was a parliamentarian of great distinction; but he had never held high office. Of the entire

7

complement of the Shadow Cabinet only one — Sir Keith Joseph — could be said with certainty to have voted for her. Others have since said that they supported her on the second ballot, but the only one she could be sure of on the morning of 12 February was Joseph; and he, ally and friend that he was, had, to put it mildly, no great reputation as a political manager. And a political manager of proven seniority was what she needed.

Worse, from her point of view, was the fact that so many of her colleagues were as outraged as she was dumbfounded by her success. There were intellectual reasons for their outrage, and I will shortly describe them. But, for the moment, everything happened on a personal level. Mrs William Whitelaw, for example, advised her husband to refuse to join the Thatcher Shadow Cabinet just as Mrs R. A. Butler had, in 1963, counselled her husband to refuse office under Lord Home. In both cases the impulse was similar: it rested upon a feeling that the victor had won by a trick, that there was something unnatural about the succession. In Margaret Thatcher's case there was the added feeling, still vague, but none the less palpable, that she represented a break in the natural order of things, not merely in terms of personality, but in terms of policy. Although throughout her leadership campaign she had been studiously indefinite about specific policies, she had gathered to herself an assemblage of the right wing of the party. And if — so the argument of her critics ran — you wanted to see what she would do or try to do in power you had only to look at the speeches of what one critic called 'her bloody John the Baptist', Keith Joseph, who was to write, later in the year, 'It was only in April 1974 that I was converted to Conservatism. I had thought I was a Conservative but I now see that I was not one at all.' He had already, by February, made many speeches in a similar vein and, for all the evident agonising that went into them, they were understood not as the emotional self-analysis of a philosophically troubled and questing man, but as the throwing down of a gauntlet to the past.

'These people,' Michael Wolff, Edward Heath's senior speech writer, and the fallen leader's chosen overlord at Conservative Central Office, said to me towards the end of February, 'want to wipe out the past. It can't be done, and it shouldn't be done.' There was a sense, therefore, which I will analyse more fully later, in which the hostile reaction to Margaret Thatcher was not merely personal but based on an understanding — accurate as it turned out to be — that she wanted to repudiate practically everything that had been done during the Heath government, and not merely to repudiate it, but to expunge it.

For the moment, however, the feeling that there was a doctrinal sea-change in the air was inchoate. The focus of resentment was on her personality, and on the very fact that she was there. The goodwill towards her from the press and the public was not mirrored in the Shadow Cabinet.

However much she wished, at least tactically, to placate the vanquished, however, she knew that the new age had to be signalled in some way. Out, therefore, went Heath's campaign manager, Peter Walker and out, too, went Geoffrey Rippon. Before many weeks elapsed out went Michael Wolff, and a number of more junior functionaries from Central Office. A gesture of some kind had to be made to Heath, and she called on him at his house in Wilton Street. While there has been a good deal of controversy over precisely what passed between them, I am satisfied that she did, albeit in the most general terms, offer him a Shadow Cabinet post, though she was greatly relieved when he turned her down. The only posts commensurate with his dignity would have been the Shadow Foreign Secretaryship or the Shadow Chancellorship. But since it was in the areas of economic and foreign policy that her differences from her predecessor were expected to be most marked, to have allowed him control over either area would have made her leadership impossible.

There were several surprises in her appointments, but three were dramatic. Lord Thorneycroft — who as Peter Thorneycroft had resigned as Chancellor of the Exchequer from the Macmillan government on the issue of excessive public spending — was recalled from retirement to take over as Chairman of the Party and hence her chief executive at Conservative Central Office. The post of Shadow Chancellor went, not as expected to Keith Joseph, but to Sir Geoffrey Howe, one of the battered contestants in the second leadership ballot. And Reginald Maudling was brought out of the wilderness to assume the job of Shadow Foreign Secretary, once she had assured herself that the business involvements which had led to his departure from the Heath Cabinet would have no unpleasant legal repercussions.

'You may not see the change,' Neave said, 'but I assure you it is there.' In truth her appointments occasioned a great deal of speculation. That there was no Heath, Rippon or Walker showed, it seemed, that there were to be radical new departures. But the return of Reginald Maudling, so much a part of the post-war Conservative tradition in economic and social policy, so much a part of the Heath view of things, so representative of what she was supposed to be setting out to overthrow, indicated that perhaps the change was not going to be so dramatic after all — particularly as it quickly emerged that Maudling's views on foreign policy were very different from hers, and that he intended to speak on economic matters in the Shadow Cabinet, in opposition to both Howe and Joseph. It was evidently going to be a good deal less than easy to produce agreement on policy among the group that she gathered about her.

I discussed these matters with her in her office in the House of Commons towards the end of February 1975, and expressed a certain perturbation which, indeed, reflected the unease of many on the right who had supported her. It was all very well to seek a balanced Shadow Cabinet, and the party's senior body should not be allowed to become the property of a sect, however much one felt oneself to be a member of that sect. But there was another view to the effect that a reforming leader must act with speed and audacity during that period when his (or her) authority is at its height, that is, in the period just after he has been chosen. I quoted Churchill to this effect. Neave, who had taken over responsibility for Northern Ireland, as well as becoming Head of the Leader's private office, merely observed, 'Oh, she'll make the policy herself.'

It was, of course, precisely that which her critics feared. And here was a paradox.

Those in the Shadow Cabinet who were critical of Margaret Thatcher personally, or fearful of the directions in which she might lead the party, were in the main supporters of Edward Heath. Yet, in style and conduct Heath was one of the most authoritarian of modern political leaders. Those who regretted his departure — or, perhaps, were simply deploring the fact that the parliamentary party had chosen a replacement of a different philosophical mode — sought to deny to his successor, as a matter of principle, the full authority of her office. Yet, there is an authoritative view[2] supporting the proposition that the Leader of the Conservative Party is the fount of all authority in the making of policy. Far from being revolutionary, the view that Neave expressed to me is merely a repetition of an old Conservative maxim — that policy is what the Leader says it is, no more and no less.

What gave colour to the view expressed by so many of Margaret Thatcher's critics from 1975 onwards — to the effect that policy should be the expression of the collective view of the Shadow Cabinet — was the change that had come about in Conservative politics in 1965, when the parliamentary party elected a leader for the first time. Hitherto leaders had 'emerged', a euphemism for saying that they were chosen by a handful of senior members of the party, that choice being endorsed both by the acclamation of the whole body of back-benchers and a summons from the Palace to form a government — for, it should be remembered that on only two occasions this century before 1975 did the party change leaders while out of office. The election of Edward Heath as Leader in 1965 heralded — or was supposed to herald — the beginning of the democratisation of the party. It was supposed to usher in a new age, in which the leadership was less shrouded in awe and even mysticism than before. It was therefore, on the face of it, plausible to assert in 1975 an extension of that process. If the leader was elected, and did not 'emerge' by some arcane procedure, if his selection was an expression of the collective will of the parliamentary party, surely it was logical to suppose that policy should be an expression of the collective will of the Shadow Cabinet?

There was, however, another consideration. Tory tradition dictates that other things — such as health — being equal the only ground for refusing to serve in a Shadow Cabinet or Cabinet is a serious difference of policy. In 1911 there was such a difference between two contenders for the leadership, Walter Long and Austen Chamberlain. The matter was resolved by both men standing down in favour of Andrew Bonar Law. Subsequent changes in the leadership were effected without open conflict: Chamberlain succeeded Law and Law then succeeded him, after a difference of opinion within the party on the question of whether the coalition government led by David Lloyd George should continue in existence. Baldwin followed Law, Neville Chamberlain Baldwin, Churchill Chamberlain, Eden Churchill, Macmillan Eden, and Home Macmillan. In all these cases the departing leader and his successor supported each other. In the cases where there was a contest the man beaten served his rival, however bruised his ego might have been. The strength of this tradition was most marked in 1963 when although two of his followers — Iain Macleod and Enoch Powell — refused office R. A. Butler accepted the offer of the Foreign Office from Lord Home. In 1965 there was, for the first time, an open contest for the leadership. But the two candidates defeated on the first ballot — Reginald Maudling and Enoch Powell — immediately withdrew, and put their services at the disposal of Edward Heath. Macleod, indeed, at the time declared that his preference for Heath over Maudling simply rested on the belief that Heath would be more energetic. Powell, the candidate whose victory would have represented a radical change in policy — and probably the outbreak of doctrinal warfare — collected only a derisory number of votes.

The rule on these matters was very well expressed in a letter Lord Dilhorne, the Lord Chancellor, wrote to Butler just after Home's appointment:

> By your action you have held together the Tory party at a very critical time. I do not doubt that if you had refused to serve, Alec would have failed to form a government and if you had then been sent for, which seems most likely, I think you would have started under very heavy criticism, for it would indeed be hard to justify a refusal to serve on a ground of policy — for there was no difference of policy — and differences of policy are really the only justification for refusing to serve a colleague.

It was not, however, any distinct consciousness of fundamental difference between Edward Heath and Margaret Thatcher over policy matters — which differences did not, in any event, clearly emerge until later — that conditioned press, public and wider party reaction to his conduct after her election. It was, rather, comparison between his conduct towards her in 1975 and Lord Home's conduct towards him ten years earlier.

Home was immensely popular as a man, but less than a complete success as a leader — that is, he failed to win the

1964 general election, although he came astonishingly close to doing so. His defeat by Harold Wilson, however, fed doubts about his legitimacy, those doubts being focused on the method by which he emerged as Leader in 1963. Under astutely organised pressure from a group of MPs, principal among them Humphry Berkeley, Home undertook to provide a system whereby Tory members could, in future, elect their leaders. The method adopted had one glaring deficiency: it made no provision for more than the one choice. That is to say, the party had no means of getting rid of a leader with whom it had become discontented. This omission was, however, repaired before the 1975 election, by a committee appointed by Heath under Home's chairmanship. As things have stood since that day the leader submits himself (or herself) for re-election each year. Since 1975 there has been no opposition of that kind to Margaret Thatcher, but the machinery remains ready for use.

Home's admirers — and there were many — urged him after the 1964 election quickly to introduce a system of election and to offer himself again as Leader under its provisions. This advice he declined, for he is one of those rare politicians who does not much mind whether or not he holds the top job. 'I like being Leader,' he told the late George Hutchinson, 'but not enough to fight for it.' However, immediately upon Heath's victory he offered his services to his successor, eventually served again as Foreign Secretary and announced in 1975 that he was supporting Heath against Margaret Thatcher.

As Home's supporters advised him in 1964 so Heath's advised him after the October defeat of 1975. Heath procrastinated, thus making it less, rather than more, likely that he would retain the office of Leader. And, of course, he both refused to serve the new Leader and denied her more than the barest line of congratulation on her triumph. The press knew that their meeting at Wilton Street had been glacial. Later in the year, at Blackpool, during her first conference as Party Leader he twice snubbed her in public. He declined to have his photograph taken with her, and in the course of the conference he spoke to three journalists — Peter Jenkins of the *Guardian*, Christopher Hitchens of the *New Statesman* and Ula Terkelson of Scandinavian radio and TV — in the bitterest tones of reproach and condemnation both of his successor and of Sir Keith Joseph. It was thus easy for her supporters — and, for that matter, the party in the country — to deride him as a bad loser, and to point the stark contrast with Home's behaviour.

And yet Heath had a point, and it was her awareness, as she told me in the summer of 1975, of that point that made her question her own legitimacy. There were real differences between them and they could, in principle at any rate, justify both his refusal to accept membership of her Shadow Cabinet and the other posts — the Secretary Generalship of NATO (which was to all intents and purposes within her gift at the time) and the British Embassy in Washington among them — which she was prepared to offer him. His petulance, however, caused his still-substantial support in the House of Commons to wane, to the point that, in advance of the party conference of 1976 his remaining supporters urged upon him the absolute necessity of making a speech of reconciliation. This he attempted to do, though when the fine print of the speech — on economic affairs — was scrutinised it was clear that his support for the new regime was highly qualified. Neither party to the dispute was satisfied and, over the years, the conflict has become exacerbated, even though Heath, through intermediaries, expressed a willingness to serve in a Thatcher government after the 1979 general election.

In 1975 Heath was in an exceptionally difficult position, one that would have required the diplomacy and guile of a Talleyrand to resolve successfully. And he was bitter and hurt personally. According to his friends, while he condemned both her and Keith Joseph for consigning overboard so readily the whole record of a government — that of 1970–74 — of which they had apparently happily remained members, he condemned himself for having underrated her, and given her a position — that of second Treasury spokesman — from which she could launch a successful assault on the citadel of his office. The self-reproach was, I believe, as great, and ran as deep, as the resentment. However, because that resentment was so publicly evident it embarrassed his allies, and made it easy to shrug off his criticisms. Early in 1984 I asked somebody who had served in both their governments how he now regarded Heath, particularly in the light of the argument about the Prime Minister's proposed reforms of local government. My interlocutor was, as it happens, sharply critical of the government on this issue, and the differences between him and Heath were insignificant. But he made it plain that he regarded the support of his former leader as embarrassing. 'Once you have Ted on your side you're lost,' he said, 'because everybody believes that he personalises every issue that comes up.'

It should, however, be mentioned — even emphasised — that during the crucial months of his battle to survive as Leader, and in the aftermath of his defeat, Heath was suffering from a thyroid deficiency so serious that at one stage the gland ceased altogether to function. The principal characteristics of his condition were an extraordinary, though intermittent, physical lassitude and an acerbity of temper marked even in a man not hitherto noted for the benevolence of his manner.

However, the decline of Edward Heath as a force in the House of Commons, inevitable as it may seem in retrospect, was not at all predictable in 1975, particularly by a new and untried Leader, with no previous experience of high office.

George Brock and Nicholas Wapshott put it well in their book when they quote a source as saying of this time,

'Edward Heath had a loyal Cabinet and a wobbly Party, Margaret Thatcher was the other way round: she had a loyal Party and a wobbly Shadow Cabinet.' Indeed, one of her great advantages in the early days of her leadership was the way in which the party and the country took to her. This was in part probably because they shared the delight of the general public with the novelty of a female leader; but it was certainly in part due — as she believed herself — to their awareness of the fact that she shared their simpler values in a way that her critics and rivals did not. None the less, as Peter Riddell observes, she appears 'unassailable only in retrospect'.

There were two other factors working against her. The first was her ignorance in so many areas of high policy, particularly foreign affairs. The second that in Harold Wilson she was up against one of the great masters of parliamentary combat, and even if he was well past his best, he was a formidable opponent at the despatch box for an untried and uncertain adversary. She began to read, and she began to travel (though even this aroused criticism, Harold Macmillan making a caustic observation on the inadequacy of travel as a means of learning about foreign policy). In her battle with Wilson — particularly in the Tuesday and Thursday gladiatorial exchanges politely referred to as Questions to the Prime Minister — her natural combativeness and quickness of wit came early to her rescue. The particular Wilsonian ploy was to play on her inexperience which, after the initial euphoria, became a preoccupation of the press as well. 'What the Prime Minister means,' she observed of one Wilsonian essay in reminiscence about the great days, 'is that he's been around a long time. And he looks it.' It was at that moment, Lord Wilson told me later, that he began to take her seriously.

None the less, the early days in the House of Commons were difficult. To this day the Prime Minister excites rage and abuse from the opposition Labour benches in a measure not seen since the war. However, there is now an extent to which, after two general election victories, they fear her. At the beginning there was a liberal admixture of contempt in their hostility. Lady Falkender — then, as Marcia Williams, Harold Wilson's political and personal secretary — recalls in her latest book[3] with what joy Labour leaders received the news of the Thatcher victory. Apart, she says, from herself and Peter Shore there was a universal belief that the Conservatives had delivered themselves into Labour hands, partly by choosing a woman, partly by choosing a woman who combined inexperience with certitude in such full measure. Lady Falkender, on the contrary, reckoned that Mrs Thatcher would prove a doughty opponent.

The Prime Minister reads extraordinarily — indeed abnormally — fast, and her first months as Leader required a great deal of application. 'It was like,' she said to me, 'being back at school and having to prepare against time for important examinations.' With all the problems she had on her plate — with the House and with the Shadow Cabinet in particular — she had also to make up for the experience she lacked through study. Her method of preparing a speech — which has not changed significantly to this day, though, of course, the exigencies of prime ministerial life allow less time — was revealing of the way she went about the job. There were several stages. The first was the acquisition of an idea, as it might be simply a theme.

Once she seized on the idea or theme she began both to read, and to trawl for information and suggestions. The first session with a speech-writer consisted of her dilating on the way she approached the subject and what material she wanted to include. She provided a summary of all she had been reading, passing flagged and copiously annotated photocopies of sections from books and magazine articles across all the time. Frequently, the speech-writer would be instructed to get in touch with a particular writer to explore with him some perhaps under-emphasised theme. It was then necessary for the speech-writer to read and digest whatever she had read and digested. The next stage was a detailed analysis of his draft, possibly a redraft, and perhaps the entry into the act of other writers. When the product was near to satisfying her she would take it away, and work on it herself. The sheer intensity of this process was remarkable, as was the physical energy she displayed during discussion, pacing her room, gesturing with animation, from time to time dashing out by herself to the House of Commons Library to hunt down a reference. Of course, as time went by, and her own knowledge and confidence increased, and as subjects were returned to for the fourth or fifth, or perhaps the umpteenth, time these sessions became less frenetic. But her vibrancy and enthusiasm is, I think, something anybody who worked for her in the early years will remember with pleasure and affection.

She was hungry for knowledge and argument, and infectious in the animation with which she pursued a subject. This was not, it goes without saying, how her Shadow Cabinet colleagues found her. To them, or to some of them, she seemed overbearing, her words rolling like a tide over the rock of opposition or reservation. That there should be this contradiction between different perceptions of her was not surprising. Shadow Cabinet colleagues of far greater experience than herself knew much more than she did about many of the subjects under discussion, and had taken up firm positions on most of them. They did not come to meetings with her to learn, nor to explain, still less to justify: they came to restrain. This she found intensely frustrating, not merely because they would not debate with her in the way in which she chose to debate, but because they seemed to her to be — and were — antipathetic to the instincts and insights she brought to political problems.

On the other hand — and this was the greatest source of strength for her in the years of opposition — there had grown up in Britain a whole school of right-wing thought. This school is usually referred to as the New Right, to distinguish it from the Old Right which, while assertive in foreign — and especially in colonial — policy tends to be paternalistic on every domestic subject except immigration. One of the major preoccupations of the New Right was the overthrow of practically all the domestic assumptions about economic policy which had, generally, prevailed among politicians of all parties.

The lineaments of New Right policy, particularly in its distinction from the Butskellite consensus, will become apparent in later pages, when the details of individual choices are discussed. For the moment it is sufficient to state what is widely known. The old order in the Conservative Party — the order which opposed the Thatcher bid for the leadership — assumed a beneficent nature on the part of the state. Where inequality or poverty or unhappiness existed, the assumption was that the government of the day should do something about it. The New Right, on the other hand, argued that the reverse was true. Whatever the initial impact of any social programme funded by government, it was unlikely to fulfil its no doubt laudable ambitions over a period. Further, it brought evils in its train. The bureaucratic machine required to implement it would grow larger and larger; the freedom of the citizen would grow smaller and smaller; and happiness would not be reached at the end. Many a time and often the New Right's propositions were put in terms of cold logic. To Margaret Thatcher they were intellectual structures corresponding to her deepest personal instincts. At its simplest level — in economics — they supported her equation between household and national finance. This was the revolutionary change she was to bring, first to her party, and then to the country.

The stage was thus set in February 1975 for the first ideological conflict in British politics since the arguments over Free Trade and Protection which bedevilled public life in the late years of the nineteenth and the early years of the twentieth centuries, a conflict which was one of the major causes of the destruction of the old Liberal Party, and came near to destroying the Tory Party as well.

Unlike Keith Joseph, Margaret Thatcher is not naturally an intellectual politician. However, in the period before she became Leader there was coming to fruition a whole system of thought which corresponded to her instincts. Foremost among the organisations propounding the economic ideas of the New Right was the Institute of Economic Affairs in Lord North Street, part of her debt to which was subsequently paid by the ennoblement, in her first Honours List, of its Director, Ralph Harris (now Lord Harris of High Cross). The work of Harris's Deputy Director, Arthur Seldon, on welfare matters was at least as cogent and important. For years the IEA had ploughed a lonely furrow in its espousal of capitalist ideas 'in conditions,' as Hugh Stephenson put it 'of near exile in a kind of intellectual Siberia.'[4] After the defeat of February 1974 Keith Joseph founded the Centre for Policy Studies, in alliance with Margaret Thatcher. In essence, the CPS was a politicised version of the IEA and, under its Director of Studies (now Sir) Alfred Sherman it produced a veritable cascade of brilliantly argued polemics for the replacement of the post-war economic and social consensus with a new, vigorous and aggressive free-market philosophy. The New Right had mounted a formidable intellectual argument which required answers which the Butskellites were quite unable to give, at least for the moment.

The way the whole climate of political life had changed was well put by Lord Blake, Provost of Queen's College Oxford, historian of the Conservative Party, and a peer who owed his title to Edward Heath, in an essay in 1976:

The Conservatives did not go into the election of 1970 devoid of policies, but they did go into it without the sort of freshly articulated doctrinal support which they had enjoyed twenty years earlier from such diverse thinkers as Hayek[5] and Lord Hailsham. The outlook of commentators, economists, intellectuals, journalists — the opinion formers in general — was anti-Conservative. The accepted 'philosophy' was still *dirigiste*. Planning, high public expenditure, high taxation, a rising role for the State remained the accepted shibboleths, however doubtful some people may have become about their practical manifestation during the last years of Harold Wilson's first administration. There was no serious challenge in intellectual circles to this orthodoxy. The Conservatives did not win the election because they had won 'the battle for the mind', rather because of a general discontent about high prices and sheer governmental incompetence.

But, Lord Blake went on, after saying that the atmosphere of politics had changed:

If this assessment of a changing intellectual climate is anywhere near to reality, then the Conservatives have an excellent chance of recovering power, and of doing so on the basis of a new orthodoxy replacing the old one created in the war years, a new concept of the relationship between government and people. How this might be done was broadly adumbrated by Mrs Thatcher in her splendid keynote speech to the 1975 Conservative Conference in Blackpool, when she urged the case for less government, less interference, more freedom for the ordinary person to get on with his work unhindered by bureaucracy, and more freedom for him to do what he wishes with more of his own money. Mr Heath said just the same in his day. The difference is that the climate of opinion has changed. What could plausibly, though wrongly, be dismissed in 1970 as 'reactionary' amidst giggles from Hampstead cannot be laughed off today.[6]

This analysis, broadly and pungently true as it is, still requires one qualification, if we are to understand the intellectual battlefield of British politics that Margaret Thatcher has made her own today. The intellectual climate — though not necessarily the political — was more favourable to her in 1975 than it was to Edward Heath in 1970. The free-market philosophy on which he was elected in 1970 was not all that dissimilar to the one on which she was elected in 1979. But Heath changed — indeed, reversed — his policies in 1972, because he had become convinced that they did not work. Between 1975 and 1979 it was a constant theme of her critics that what she was advocating had been tried before. 'We tried all that stuff,' Peter Walker said scornfully to me in 1982, when the prestige of the Thatcher government was low, 'and it just didn't do.' In Chapter Four I will discuss what happened when the Prime Minister faced the kind of dilemma Edward Heath faced in 1972. Suffice it to say for now that there was a difference of character between them.

The policies Edward Heath adopted between 1965 and 1970 were adopted in a managerial spirit. He was concerned less with what might be called their moral value or weight than with the mechanistic question: will they work? By 1972 Heath reckoned that he had given the policies a chance, and they did not work. So he changed them, thus returning himself to the mainstream of post-war paternalistic, statist Conservatism, where he has remained ever since. When in 1981 and 1982 Margaret Thatcher seemed to face a similar difficulty (in part, as I shall argue, of her own making, and her failure to make the most of her opportunities between 1979 and 1980) she held on. And she was emboldened and empowered to do so because the policies over which the new wave of right-wing intellectuals had laboured so long in the barren days of the 1960s and the early 1970s appealed to something very deep in her own nature.

'Am I really the leader of this party, or not?' she asked rhetorically at the beginning of the 1975–76 parliamentary session. The tone was aggressive, the thought was not. It was part of a perennially expressed worry about what she had to do and how long she had to do it. 'We must win the argument,' she would say again and again, in what was first an unconscious, and then a conscious repetition of the analysis just quoted from Robert Blake. And again, a favourite theme, reiterated and reiterated over, in only very slightly different words, 'I know I'll be given only one chance at this thing' — that is at winning a general election — 'so I must do it properly.' She went about her task in the only way she knew how, by using her instinct and buttressing it with her studies.

In this time, as I will shortly show in detail, she developed a practice which she has continued as Prime Minister — that of making policy without reference to her Shadow Cabinet. That such a practice has perfectly respectable antecedents Robert McKenzie has already shown. But for her it was a necessary resolution of a dilemma.

She felt herself to be living on a knife's edge of possibility and the threat of disaster. She felt that the strength she had — the strength that might again carry her through to a victory — lay in her instinct about things, an instinct, she believed, she shared with the people who would, one day, sooner or later, lift her up or cast her down — the electorate. On the other hand she could as a matter of course command the unstinting support of only a section of her Shadow Cabinet and only a section of the parliamentary party. Some of the things she felt she needed to do, some of the aspirations and fears she felt she needed to express, some of the policies she had to articulate, to gain and keep the support of the people, were ones she could not depend on being able to carry through the Shadow Cabinet. Yet these things had to be done, these aspirations and fears had to be expressed, these policies had to be articulated, if she was to gain the vital electoral support she needed. So she went, as Neave had predicted she would, and did it herself, a process described by her critics variously as 'shooting from the hip' or 'making policy on the hoof'.

There was something else as well. The world which supported her — the intellectual New Right — and the world about whose support she was doubtful — the parliamentary party and the Shadow Cabinet — met at very few points. There were, of course, some politicians wholly conversant with, and socially at home with, her intellectual spear-carriers, but they were few. There were some right-wing intellectuals who had an easy acquaintance with the general world of politics; but these, again, were few. So, for a time, she lived in two worlds — the world of the management of politics, and the world of the discussion and propagation of ideas. In the latter world she found the justification for her instincts that she needed for propounding her instincts as public policy. In the former she sought the legitimacy that only the political world could confer.

As long as she was denied — or felt she was denied — that legitimacy she was from time to time uncertain. I do not mean that she would have been incautious or even reckless if the legitimacy was felt to be fully conferred on the night of 11 February 1975, for there is an element of caution in her — an element of responsibility, if you like — which is ingrained. But from 1975 to 1979 she felt — and the feeling was often enough expressed to a sufficient number of people for there to be no doubt about its existence — that her moral right to be in charge of a great party at a time of crisis in the nation's fortunes was uncertain, and this governed a great deal of what she did. More: even when she won the general election of 1979, and won it with a handsome majority, she was still uncertain. Partly this was because of her complete lack of knowledge of the world of patronage and power into which she suddenly entered, but partly it was because of a feeling that even the kind of second triumph that she had just enjoyed did not confer full legitimacy. It was not, in my judgement, until the budget of 1981, that pivotal point of the first term, that Margaret Thatcher felt she was truly in charge.

None of the doubts and hesitancies, none of the fears which I have described make up much part of the general picture of the Prime Minister which most of those who observe her in action see. But they were, and to an extent still are, there all the same. 'It is like a dream ...' to quote again her remark on becoming Leader. For a very long time it remained a dream to her, a dream which sometimes seemed to take on the shape of a nightmare. She is so compounded of certainty and uncertainty as to be resistant to full rounded explanation. In many respects she is at her best when things and people seem most set against her, and at her worst when things are going too well and people are too agreeable. But these facets of the fissures in her nature were, I believe, made more significant, more cragged and more dangerous by the important, but minor, fact that in 1975 she was inexperienced; and by the major fact that she was a woman. Just as Edward Heath's serious differences from her on policy could be quite readily obscured by her partisans on the grounds that he was a bad and disappointed loser, so her proposals for a new future for Britain could, if they did not please her critics and enemies, whatever popular support they enjoyed, be explained away on the grounds that she was a tiresome female.

Perhaps—to express it in general terms, and without reference to whether given policies were right or wrong, wise or foolish — the most remarkable thing she set out to do in 1975 was to make the Conservative Party a radical one, *the* party of change, the party which was going to break a consensus. It seemed an affront to the very name of the political organisation of which she had become Leader. Through all her hesitancies, her retreats, her covering with peace-making words of serious fissures, she remained true to that commitment. Perhaps she was sometimes inclined to exaggerate it. When, in 1977, I asked her what she thought she had changed she said she had changed everything. She had not, of course, for she did not yet have power, and had not proved herself. But there are few, friends or enemies — there are only a tiny handful of the politically interested who are neutral on the subject of Margaret Thatcher — who would, in 1985, deny that she has changed a great deal. For how long, and to what end, and in what manner, remains for examination.

In the meantime, while it is clear that her 1977 judgement on herself was precipitate, it was not unreasonable. The very choice of a woman as Leader of the Conservative Party was a fundamental change. That a woman should have put herself forward for the leadership at all meant that there was an exceptional (I use the word with no normative connotation) female around. By standing for the leadership she had changed things. By winning she had changed more. Whether she had changed 'everything' has still to be proven.

CHAPTER TWO

The Apprenticeship

It is not unknown to me how many men have had, and still have, the opinion that the affairs of the world are in such wise governed by fortune and by God that men with their wisdom cannot direct them and that no one can even help them; and because of this they would have us believe that it is not necessary to labour much in affairs, but to let chance govern them. This opinion has been more credited in our times because of the great changes in affairs which have been seen, and may still be seen, every day. Sometimes pondering over this, I am in some degree inclined to their opinion. Nevertheless, not to extinguish our free will, I hold it to be true that fortune is the arbiter of one half of our actions, but that she still leaves us to direct the other half, or perhaps a little less.
— Niccolò Machiavelli, *History of Florence*, 1513. I have followed Luigi Ricci's translation, published in New York in 1901

'The duty of an opposition,' ran Lord Randolph Churchill's dictum, 'is to oppose.' But there is rather more to it than that. Only during such times as those of the second Attlee government, from 1950 to 1951, or the fag end of the Conservative thirteen years — between 1963 and 1964 — can an opposition enjoy the luxury of outright attack, because the government of the day is seen to be, or is, punch drunk, confused, or simply tired. The Labour government which

Margaret Thatcher had to tackle in 1975 was by no means in good shape. However, it seemed to improve, a year later, when James Callaghan succeeded Harold Wilson and brought his own bluff manner to the management of Britain. The government, it is true, was in a tight parliamentary situation: its majority was vestigial, and the business of government was bedevilled by the minority parties — Liberals, Official Ulster Unionists, Democratic Ulster Unionists, (Ulster) Social Democratic and Labour Party (only one member, but a hyper-active one, Gerry [now Lord] Fitt), Welsh Nationalists and Scottish Nationalists.

The majority in due course disappeared, due to failure at by-elections, but Callaghan, with the indispensible aid of Michael Foot, was both able to cobble together the Lib–Lab pact which — though it did not give power to the Liberals, brought them into consultation on various matters of policy — and to procure the parliamentary support of other minorities in return for concessions on specific issues.

Of the other groups the most significant was the Scottish National Party with eleven seats. The condition of their support for the government was two-pronged. First, they required legislation allowing for a directly elected Scottish Chamber; second, they demanded that the Prime Minister ensured that the assent of the Scottish electorate was procured by his own wholehearted commitment. The second point was vital: no excuses would be accepted if the referendum failed. In due course, on 1 March 1979, the referendum did fail and in due course again, on 28 March the Scottish National Party voted to bring the government down.

Devolution is now an an almost forgotten issue, and most students of Margaret Thatcher's career virtually ignore the tortuous battles fought over it. I will, however, return to the subject because of the fascinating insights it offers into her political tactics — the fashion in which she uses advance, withdrawal and cunning to achieve her aims.

For the moment, from the opening of the parliamentary session in the Autumn of 1975, her tactics towards the government were simple — to harry them at every opportunity.

A number of her colleagues — not all of them opposed to her — doubted the wisdom of this. After all, the Conservative Party was itself in bad shape, not least because of the divisions exposed by her election. Over-aggressive opposition might well expose those divisions further. 'What is your answer?' said a senior Tory former Cabinet minister. 'That will be Wilson's question all the time. What is your answer? Just now we haven't any answers. This government is more secure than it looks. Don't forget that. There's nothing in battle for us just now. For God's sake persuade her to keep a low profile until we've sorted ourselves out.'

But that was not her way at all. She was fully aware that if there was one single act which won her the leadership it was her destruction of Denis Healey in the Finance Bill debate earlier in the year. She also felt — rightly — that the party in the country could only be kept in good heart by constant action. At the same time she would move with all possible speed behind the scenes to 'sort ourselves out', while developing a public image of her own.

Over everything else loomed the grand question: what was now to be Conservative economic policy? There were many aspects to that question, of which the most important were: how high a priority was the conquest of inflation to assume? What was to be done about policy on the trade unions? And, was there to be a Conservative incomes policy? Each one of these assumed agonising prominence, not merely because they were major problems for any government, or whatever party, but because they were precisely the questions which excited most division in Conservative ranks.

To the Leader and her closest advisers the answers were clear-cut. Attacking inflation was *the* priority, and if the cost was to be higher unemployment that would have to be accepted. It was desirable, further, to make another major attempt to reduce the power of the trade unions — the last attempt, by Edward Heath, having dismally failed, its measures repealed and replaced by a mass of pro-trade-union legislation by Labour. And, finally, there would be no incomes policy, statutory or otherwise.

The economic policies favoured in the Thatcher circle had, in fact, been outlined by Sir Keith Joseph in a speech at Preston the previous September. Then, for the first time, a major British political figure had endorsed the doctrine — or heresy, according to orthodox economists — of monetarism, according to which the only method of curing inflation was strictly to control the amount of money in the economy, as a consequence of which both public spending and government borrowing would have to be severely reduced. An apparently — though not actually — paradoxical result of the adoption of this policy was the not infrequent parliamentary alliance in the following years of Labour left wingers and Tory right wingers. The left resisted any attempt to impose control of incomes, because the trade unions were opposed to such control. The right opposed income policies because of the belief that high wage claims were a symptom rather than a cause of inflation — quite apart from their being unworkable in practice. Their view was that if the government refused to supply credit then the ineluctable consequence of excessive wage claims would be higher unemployment, and that would be the responsibility not of government but of irresponsible trade union leadership.

Thus were the battle lines drawn, not only between opposition and government, but within the Conservative Party itself. Having made her disposition, Margaret Thatcher discovered that she had one rather unexpected ally, and one powerful opponent. The ally was her Shadow Chancellor, Sir Geoffrey Howe, whose experience in the later stages of the Heath government had led him to the judgement that price and wage controls were impracticable and even dangerous instruments of government. The opponent was the Shadow Secretary of State for Employment, James Prior, who was determined to resist all proposals for further legislation of a radical character on trade unions. All proposals for such legislation were, as a general rule, enthusiastically supported by party activists in the country, but greeted with scepticism or hostility in Parliament, for the simple reason that the Heath experiment in this area had signally failed. As Sir Ian Gilmour wrote, 'The voters do not want perpetual confrontation between government and unions, any more than they want the unions to be the effective government.' Adding to the potential confusion in the Shadow Cabinet, Gilmour was later to support the Leader's hard line on relations with the Soviet Union in opposition to the Shadow Foreign Secretary, even though Maudling was on the side of Gilmour and Prior when it came to economic and trade union matters.

The opposition to the emerging ideas of the Thatcher group was a combination of principle and pragmatism. The very idea of controlling the economy through the control of the money supply (oddly, detailed policy on industry was little discussed between 1975 and 1979) was repugnant to such as Prior, Maudling and Gilmour because of the social results that seemed likely to flow from it, including high unemployment and a conceivably drastic reduction in welfare provision. It seemed unlikely, further, to have electoral appeal: it was a fundamental piece of so-called political wisdom common to both parties that a government could not be re-elected if it were presiding over large-scale unemployment; it was a corollary that an opposition which seemed virtually to be courting unemployment could not achieve victory at the polls either. Finally, as regards trade union legislation, it was pointed out that Edward Heath had spent years in opposition preparing the most elaborate schemes for trade union reform, and they had all failed. From this flowed another piece of conventional wisdom — that industrial relations could not be improved by legislation and were not susceptible to governance by the courts. It is possible to argue, therefore, that those who sought to restrain the instincts of the new Leader were not simply harking nostalgically back to the days of Edward Heath: they believed as practical men that some of the solutions being proposed were at least similar to ones that had been tried, and had failed.

The conflict at the top was mirrored in that between the Conservative Research Department — still at this stage, as it had been historically, largely independent of Conservative Central Office — headed by Chris Patten, and the Centre for Policy Studies, under Martin Wassall, Gerry Frost and the formidable Alfred Sherman. The Leader's Private Office in the House of Commons, headed by Neave, was tiny. It consisted for a time of Gordon Reece (who later moved to Central Office as Director of Publicity); Richard Ryder, her Political Secretary; Derek Howe, in charge of relations with the press; and a handful of secretaries. It also included, when required, part-time consultants and volunteers, such as myself and the playwright Ronald (now Sir Ronald) Millar. In general, it may be said that the Private Office, while it existed to furnish a technical service rather than to provide ideas, sympathised more with the CPS than with the CRD. (It is important to remember that whereas the CRD is a section of the party, and paid for out of party funds, the CPS is separately funded.) Broadly, again, the CRD was regarded as the intellectual repository of the old Conservatism, and it was constantly under budgetary and other attack (which has finally led to its absorption into Central Office and the loss of the kind of substantial influence it enjoyed in the years of opposition before 1970) while the CPS was the home of the New Right. In illustration, I may perhaps mention that during my time as a special adviser attached to the Private Office I never once consulted the Research Department, although I had once worked there and its Director, Chris Patten, was an old friend. I spent much time, on the other hand, with the CPS. In part this reflected my own sympathies, but there were occasions when I was actually discouraged from making use of the CRD's resources.

All this activity, this potential and actual conflict, had as its apex the mind and personality of the Leader herself. 'Her rhetoric is radical,' Hugh Stephenson wrote in *Mrs Thatcher's First Year*, 'even reckless. But from the start her deeds have shown a politician's instinctive caution.' The caution in the years of opposition came above all from the feeling that she was not wholly in control of events and that, as I wrote in the last chapter, her legitimacy was not assured. In consequence, she would from time to time reassure herself by speaking out directly to the public, either from a platform or through radio or television, to assure herself of general support, if she could not enjoy the particular support of her Shadow Cabinet.

One example will, for the moment, suffice. The tussle over what measures of trade union reform the Conservatives would propose continued up to the end of 1978 when the events of the 'winter of discontent' so turned the public mind against the trade union movement that it became possible, with only the minimum of dissent, to insert in the manifesto ringing promises of reform. During that period complex issues and questions boiled down to one simple question. It was this: given that the trade unions simply refused to obey the Heath legislation, and broke it through their resistance, what would you do in the event of your new laws being similarly flouted? The question was asked many times, in many places, and under many guises. In the spring of 1977 she was due to appear on Brian Walden's 'Weekend World' programme. Walden was known not only for his searching questions, but for the time that his producers allowed him to develop a particular line of questioning on a given subject.

On Saturday, the day before the live transmission, she was

going over her briefing material and discussing topics and questions likely to be raised. It was put to her that Walden would certainly raise the matter of trade union disobedience. She thought about it, and announced that in such a case she would hold a national referendum to ascertain the state of public opinion (there having been a precedent in the referendum on continued membership of the Common Market). In due course Walden put that question and she gave that answer, implying that expressed public support for the legislation (whatever it was) would empower her to take draconian measures of enforcement, such as Heath had pulled back from. Not a single member of the Shadow Cabinet, except Neave, had been consulted, and the reaction among its members was one of confusion, bewilderment and outrage at not being consulted. In the event, nothing came of the referendum proposal, but the incident was typical of her tactical methods in policy-making without consultation.

If this suggests the reckless politician of Stephenson's judgement — and if it suggests ruthlessness and unscrupulousness as well — it should be emphasised that she showed quite other qualities consistently in opposition, the most vividly expressed of them being a conviction and idealism that Riddell calls mesmeric. I mentioned earlier that in Parliament she pursued a policy of harrying the government at every opportunity. On 9 March 1976 the Wilson government was badly damaged in a vote on its Public Expenditure White Paper, through the abstention of a number of members of the Tribune Group. She immediately put down a vote of no confidence in the government. She did this against the wishes of more cautious colleagues who distrusted her liking for these set-piece battles, and feared the devaluation of the whole process of attack by constant repetition. She insisted on going ahead: 'I will bang on that door again and again until it is opened.' In order, however, to justify a vote of no confidence, which had to be taken the following day, she had to argue that the government should have resigned, given the wide-open divisions in the Labour Party on a central issue of policy. She sought historical precedents and urgent telephone calls were made up and down the country to historians known to be sympathetic to her cause. The general argument was that there were no true precedents. It was possible to contend, none the less, that Balfour in 1905, Baldwin in 1923 and Chamberlain in 1940 had all resigned when they did not need to do so, because of division in party or country. She was enamoured of these examples, and began to build them into her speech. At a meeting to discuss the text, however, William Whitelaw cautioned her, 'Don't go too far along that line. After all, you may find yourself in a similar position one day when you're Prime Minister.' She looked around the table and said slowly, 'If I found myself in that position I should resign.' The gathering was quite large, and not everybody was a Thatcher partisan, but I do not believe there was a single man in the room who doubted her for a moment.

People who met her for the first time during this period of opposition were almost invariably struck by her personal conviction. Paul Johnson, for example, the former editor of the *New Statesman* who had just begun his march along the road from socialism to right-wing Toryism, thought her 'wonderful. Too wonderful. This wretched country will end up by breaking her heart.' Others were less ecstatic. A senior British diplomat, having heard her speak at Dorking on the Soviet threat in 1976, said to me afterwards, 'Your woman's mad.' The fervour of her personality either attracted or repelled. The evident sense of mission seemed to many men, both politicians and reporters, altogether improper in British politics. Yet many who shared her views and beliefs, who, even, thought her the last, best hope of British politics, were concerned by her bursts of caution and doubt. She would not, thus, move James Prior from his position as Shadow spokesman on employment and resisted, eighteen months before the general election of 1979, a formal appeal from the executive of the 1922 Committee to undertake a drastic reshuffle of the Shadow Cabinet, if only to give new men experience of the responsibilities of the front bench and give her a wider choice of postulants from which to choose a Cabinet in the event of an election victory. Yet again, when John (now Sir John) Hoskyns was introduced to her by Alfred Sherman in 1977 she was enthusiastic. Hoskyns was a self-made millionaire who had sold his own computer business to give himself time to think seriously about politics and the machinery of government in the aggressive and radical mode that she favoured. He subsequently became one of her chief advisers at No. 10 Downing Street, resigned after finding her insufficiently revolutionary, and became head of the Institute of Directors.

She set Hoskyns on to Prior. He undertook — with the aid of Norman Strauss, a Unilever graduate who also, later, was to become a denizen of No. 10 — a wide-ranging series of commissions, to look afresh at pretty well anything from public-sector pay to welfare benefits. But he was particularly charged to come up with proposals on the reform of industrial relations, to which Prior would have to respond. A courteous but sustained siege of Prior's position — called by Hoskyns, with scorn, 'minimalist' — ensued. However, though it was clear where her sympathies lay, she never moved formally against Prior. Indeed, for all her injection of some hard phrases on reducing trade union power into the 1979 manifesto, she remained cautious on the subject until well into her first term, imposing a settlement of which he disapproved with the National Union of Mineworkers on her Secretary of State for Energy, David Howell, in 1981, and balancing it by the exile of Prior to the Northern Ireland Office in the same year.

She was sometimes baffling, even to her closest adherents. Pressed, occasionally, to explain why she seemed so tough and daring in some areas — as when she dismissed Reginald

Maudling in 1976 — and so hesitant in others — as when she refused to make any overt move against Prior — she would talk quietly and abstractedly about 'getting the strategy right' and 'winning the argument'. Still, the outline of the strategy seemed often obscure. 'Think of her like a tennis player,' said one of her colleagues — a man who has distinctly mixed feelings about her. 'She's absolutely brilliant at the net. She can handle any fast ball that comes her way. But she's nothing like so good from the baseline. She builds a game in fits and starts. She *knows* she's naturally impulsive, just like a woman. She *believes* her impulses are right, but she has so many of them that the cautious side of her mind makes her act only on some. In that sense she's not really rational or considered at all. The solvent for the whole thing is her extraordinary willpower and self-belief — which is not at all the same thing as self-confidence. The other thing is that she has a fantastic capacity for waking every morning to a new day, a day that she is perfectly willing to believe will be quite unlike any other day in history. If the day before was lousy there will be no hangovers from it, no worries, no depression. *This* day, the one she's starting on, is going to be a great day. Yet, because she's the same woman today as she was yesterday, some of the impulses will still be there, going bang, bang, bang. So a lot of what she wants to do gets done. She just wears everybody down eventually.' And Enoch Powell, when once I asked his opinion of her, observed more crisply, 'When she trusts her instincts she's almost always right. When she stops to think she's all too often wrong.'

Indeed, many of her actions seemed arbitrary, or, at least, she refused to spell out the reasoning behind them. The reasons for firing Reginald Maudling were obvious. He had reacted quite violently to one of her anti-Soviet speeches (in an episode which I will describe shortly) and, in general, did not like her foreign policy line. But he was also a former chancellor of the exchequer, and could pull his weight against the emerging monetarist view on economic policy in the Shadow Cabinet. There were thus two separate, and not unreasonable, grounds for getting rid of him. However, according to his memoirs (and there is no reason to disbelieve what he said then) she gave a third. 'She said that there had been a lot of pressure from Central Office because I was not making enough speeches for the Party.' And then he showed his hurt:

> I must admit it was rather a shock, after more than twenty years on the front bench in one capacity or another, as Senior Privy Councillor on the Conservative side of the House, and with an experience of government and a record of service much longer than Mrs Thatcher's, to be summoned and dismissed without any prior criticism or warning from her of any sort whatsoever . . .

There, indeed, was the rub, felt by many of her colleagues other than Maudling: she was so comparatively inexperienced. How dared she be so confident, how dared she not take advantage of their experience? How dared she throw her weight about?

The fact is, of course, that in the view of some of her acolytes she threw her weight about far too infrequently. The moods of uncertainty were as regular, and as prolonged, as the moods of assertiveness.

Over the period between the autumn of 1975 and the winter of 1979 the combination of impulse and considered objective resulted in the creation of what might also be called a parallel opposition. In considering its character it is important to bear in mind what I stressed earlier: the Conservative Research Department, so far as its finance and administration were concerned, came under the aegis of Conservative Central Office. It was a party body. The Centre for Policy Studies — in terms of its permanent staff, incidentally, a much smaller body — was funded from outside, and responsible only to its board of directors, most important among them Margaret Thatcher and Keith Joseph. There were many complaints, both from Central Office and from the Research Department, that the funding going to Wilfred Street would have been more usefully spent on a party headquarters already suffering from the straitened times and the recession. But the Leader would neither move to make Central Office over in her image (which she would have been perfectly entitled to do, given the constitutional point that Central Office *is* the Leader's private office) nor absorb the CPS into the machine.

Further: whereas Central Office (or, more properly, the party) receives many donations from businesses as well as individuals, it insists on its own right to appropriate such gifts exactly as it pleases, in the service of the general administration of the party. The CPS was much more narrowly conceived, had a specific intellectual mission in life — the changing of the general climate of politics to make it more habitable by the New Right and specifically by its economists — and naturally therefore attracted not just businessmen who had a generalised goodwill towards the Tories, but businessmen with specific ideas of their own about the direction in which policy should move. It was natural, therefore, that alliances should spring up between the Centre's permanent staff, like-minded politicians and businessmen with ideas, and a host of outsiders, journalists, academics and other intellectuals. These alliances had social foci, both the lunch table at Wilfred Street and the monthly lunches at l'Escargot in Soho (those gathering there being dubbed the Argonauts). Collectively the shifting groups surrounding the Centre were more experienced, more formidable and more thrusting than anything the Research Department could muster, consisting as it did of some old party hands and some bright young men and women recently down from university and using it as a sort of political finishing school. The left of the party might (and did) dub the Wilfred Street *galère* cranky, fanatical, obsessed by monetarism, or wildly reactionary. But the plain fact of the matter was that they possessed a far greater intellectual punch than could be mustered on the other side. It was not long before *Politics Today*, the admirable regular publication of the Research Department which has both the job of providing a comprehensive summary of what is going on in politics and presenting party policy in an attractive and stylish fashion, began to look grey compared to the published output of the CPS, to the publications of which were often attached the names of outstanding businessmen or weighty academics.

It was almost inevitable, therefore, given the divisions in the Shadow Cabinet and Margaret Thatcher's own attitudes, that the CPS became the centre of a vast network of committees — sixty in all at one stage — producing the fine print of increasingly radical policies. Politicians were not invariably excluded from these gatherings — Barney Hayhoe, one of James Prior's closest allies, and subsequently his junior minister at the Department of Employment, sat on one committee run by John Hoskyns — but there their influence was relatively insignificant. A system grew up — it would be exaggerating vastly to say that a system was designed — which in many ways by-passed the whole structure depending on the Shadow Cabinet.

To illustrate: the Conservative Research Department and its officers have two distinct responsibilities — apart, of course, from the undertaking of any task for which the Leader of the party may call upon them. Each individual desk officer is responsible to a shadow minister or, in government, a minister. His, or her, job is to act as a research assistant and (depending on the extent to which they get on together) adviser to their politician. Each officer will probably act as secretary to a backbench committee or even a policy research committee. He, or she, will in addition be responsible for generalised briefing of all Conservative backbenchers on a particular subject of the moment — say, an important debate. A tremendous amount of the work is routine, and whether the Department in general, or any officer in particular, enjoys influence in the higher councils of the party depends on a variety of considerations. But there is always the burden of generalised routine. The Centre, having no routine responsibilities, and enjoying the goodwill and voluntary energy of a great variety of outside talent, could concentrate its forces and direct its talent. Although until 1979 Chris Patten, CRD's director, continued at the centre of high politics — assisting, particularly, in the drafting of such important documents as *The Right Approach* and *The Right Approach to the Economy* (both mid-term policy documents) as well as the 1979 manifesto — the significance of his office steadily declined throughout the period of opposition.

In 1976, moreover, the IMF came to Britain. The economy was in such disarray that the Chancellor of the Exchequer, Denis Healey, was forced to call on the International Monetary Fund for aid. The Fund attached stringent conditions to that aid. In particular, it insisted on stern curbs in public expenditure and a great tightening up of national housekeeping. All this was a severe blow to the morale of the Labour Party, and of the nation. It was damaging to the prestige of Prime Minister, Chancellor and Cabinet. But it had to be accepted, and virtually full acceptance was signalled in a speech by the Prime Minister, James Callaghan, to the Labour Party Conference that year. 'You cannot spend your way out of recession,' he told his followers in a speech partly drafted for him by his son-in-law Peter Jay, a convert to monetarism. This, of course, was precisely what the monetarists on the Conservative right had been saying. And it is another adage of British politics that when a government starts imitating an opposition it is in trouble.

At the same time the conversion of Geoffrey Howe was

being completed. Howe had been an unexpected choice as Shadow Chancellor. Had Mrs Thatcher been as doctrinaire as her closest supporters would have liked, Sir Keith Joseph would have been the choice. Had she lent her ear to those voices pleading with her for restraint — that combination of continuity of policy and freshness of image which might have cemented an alliance between old Toryism and new ideas — she might have chosen Gilmour (who had begun reading about economics with almost the same intensity as she had herself),[1] Prior or, even, Whitelaw, a man with no pretence either to knowledge or judgement in matters of economics, but who could be relied upon to follow the centrist judgement which decreed that social expenditure was a political and moral necessity and the harsher disciplines of the control of the money supply were things to be rejected. 'She would never give the job to me,' Ian Gilmour told George Hutchinson, 'but I pray she may give it to Willie.' Ian Gilmour has since written two books explaining why she should have given it to him.[2]

Joseph, I believe, declined a chalice that might well have been poisoned. For all of that alliance between himself and Margaret Thatcher, which amounts to friendship, he did not feel he had the resolution to pursue in detail the insights he believed he had into economic policy. He was in doubt whether he could serve either her, or his ideas, as well as he, with his commitment to excellence, thought they should be served. He has a self-lacerating conscience, and he is a man of the most precise honour. A different kind of politician would have insisted on the Shadow Chancellorship and, possibly, would not have needed to insist on it. Joseph declined it in advance. The choice fell on Geoffrey Howe. It seems certain that — Joseph being out of the reckoning — both Airey Neave and Peter Thorneycroft recommended Howe. Their reasoning was pellucid:

However logical the reasoning of the New Right it seemed to lack heart. It was all very well to say that if there was a tight control of the money supply, subsequent unemployment was the fault either of inefficient industry or the abuse of the virtual monopoly power of the trade unions. That was a doctrine without appeal. On the other hand was the powerful proposition that thriftless spending of public money, and thriftless requisitions on the credit of government were unacceptable, because they seemed to lead the nation ever further into a tangled jungle of inflation. Thorneycroft predicted, in 1974, that the International Monetary Fund would have to be called in, to rescue the oldest industrial nation from bankruptcy. In 1975, just over a year before that dire prediction came true, he reckoned that the Conservative Party under its new Leader, who had just rescued him from political oblivion, whose first meeting when she was Secretary of the Oxford University Conservative Association he had spoken to as the honoured guest, needed a shadow chancellor who had a rigorous mind and a social conscience as well.

Howe is a deceptive politician whose mildness of manner hides sternness of will. Initially, he confused critics: how could the emerging hard monetarist be the same man as the Geoffrey Howe who had written all those socially compassionate articles in *Crossbow* (the journal of the Conservative Bow Group) some years previously and who had been chosen by Richard Crossman (at the time a Labour government's Secretary of State for Social Services) as chairman of a committee of inquiry into inadequacies at Ely Mental Hospital? Howe denied — and denies — that there was any contradiction, maintaining that an efficient economy provided the necessary basis for a compassionate social policy, and that the necessary condition for an efficient economy was adoption of the monetarist policy of which he now became the chief exponent.

Again, whereas in public relations terms the Conservative opposition was given a high profile by the rhetoric of its Leader, the Shadow Chancellor was publicly an entirely subfusc figure, certainly overshadowed by his opposite number, Denis Healey, who once compared being attacked by Howe to being savaged by a dead sheep. Certainly the courteous reserve that Howe invariably maintained in the face of all questioning and adversity, the almost soporific peacefulness of his manner, the capacity effortlessly to absorb rhetorical punishment, did not appear coherent with the activity of a restlessly aggressive opposition. It was not until Howe himself became Chancellor that it was seen, first, how strong his nerve was and, second, what an advantage with the public his lapidary quietude of manner gave him, at a time when the decibels of political argument were rising daily.

Given that Keith Joseph, in his role as overall spokesman on policy, and interpreter in detail of the philosophy that Margaret Thatcher painted in broad brush strokes, was Chairman of the Advisory Committee on Policy, through which all the contributions on policy formation were channelled, it soon became apparent that Howe was a crucial figure in the reconstruction of the identity of the party. In any government the Chancellor of the Exchequer is, more often than not, the most powerful figure after the Prime Minister. His department says 'nay' far more often than 'yea' to the proposals of the departmental ministers, and he wins far more battles than he loses in the annual round of argument over departmental budgets. A shadow chancellor remains a shadow, but he is a true simulacrum of his opposite number in power. Howe's economic reconstruction group was more nearly independent of the rest of the policy-making apparatus than any other. With the help of such as Professor Alan Walters, Professor Brian Griffiths, and a whole clutch of radically minded stockbrokers (one of whom, Peter Lilley, has since become a Conservative backbencher) he steadily shifted the party to the right in economic terms.

The control of public expenditure was, probably, their chief concern, and here another important influence was a junior Treasury spokesman, Nigel Lawson, who has since ascended to the heights once occupied by Howe himself, in what is probably the most daring appointment ever made by the Prime Minister. Above all Howe committed himself to a steady contraction of the money supply and, so far as pay in the public sector was concerned, he believed he could reduce demands partly by a process of education and partly by cash limits, the idea behind which he explained in a speech in May 1976:

> In the nationalised industries the main discipline should come from the imposition of strict cash limits on any funds available from the Exchequer and from the enforcement of strict commercial targets. But in the directly employed public sector we also stand in need of some more coherent bargaining arrangement than the series of ad hoc solutions.

Need was no longer to be met by open-ended provision: the extent to which it would be gratified was to be defined by the amount of money made available.

It is still open to question how effectively and thoroughly the reforms implied by this rigorous attitude were carried out in power; but it is undeniable that a serious attempt was made to carry them through, and this attempt in itself provoked the deepest and most acrimonious debate about economic policy in Britain since the war. Indeed, it may be said that it continues into the second Thatcher term. What happened by way of the endless and multifarious committee meetings, through the long and often tedious discussions, throughout exchange after exchange, was the execution of a pincer movement against the traditional (or, in the parlance subsequently established by Margaret Thatcher, 'wet') Tories. On one side was the Leader herself, launching initiative after initiative by way of the exploitation of her personality, and through the newspapers, radio and television. On the other was the steady sapping against the positions held by the Heath supporters of 1975, by a handful of members of the Shadow Cabinet, and by the various outside groupings I have described. It was a prolonged operation, far from complete by the time of the general election of 1979, and it was often performed with brilliance. It may be that the whole thing could and should have been done with much more speed and panache — that, for example, Margaret Thatcher gave an unnecessary hostage to fortune by inviting Reginald Maudling to join her Shadow Cabinet — but when one contemplates her steady progress towards both legitimacy and dominance, through private caution and public *bravura*, one contemplates a supreme piece of political siege warfare. If William Keegan was right — or, at least, not unfair — in describing her capture of the leadership as a 'hi-jacking', then the consolidation of her hold on it must merit more considered adjectives.

Central though the development of economic and industrial relations policy was, however, there were many other matters to be taken account of, particularly given the necessity of achieving the public ascendancy of Mrs Thatcher as Leader, not just of the Conservative Party, but of the opposition, and as an alternative prime minister. Opportunities and possibilities were considered and discarded. For example, when the time came to hold a referendum on Britain's continued membership of the European Economic Community, she preferred to take a comparatively modest part. To some extent this was because it was 'Ted's issue', and it was felt that her predecessor would more fittingly take the lead for the Conservatives on it — though she was driven to a pitch of real anger when she saw him, on the early evening TV news, being accompanied on his rounds by a Conservative Central Office official. 'He [the official] surely has better things to do.' She paid her obeisances to the Tory commitment to the European involvement, but in a manner that irritated the supporters of the Community (dubbed by her staff 'Eurofreaks') and encouraged the small remaining band of Conservative parliamentarians who opposed Britain's continued affiliation to the Community. (Though it was small, incidentally, this group was not unimportant: in the middle of the referendum campaign Edward du Cann came out as an opponent of membership.)

Again, late in 1977, with the public opinion polls suggesting that the Labour government was standing relatively well with the public on economic issues, a decision was taken to concentrate during the New Year on social affairs. On 30 January 1978, on Granada's 'World in Action', in a repeat of a television interview given to a local Manchester current affairs programme, she discussed immigration in stentorian terms, saying that '... if there is any fear that it [the British nation] might be swamped people are going to react and be rather hostile to those coming in'. And she added, '... we are not in politics to ignore people's worries, we are in politics to deal with them'. Unexceptionable though her statement of the case might seem, again it was something said quite without reference to her senior colleagues, and it caused them (and especially William Whitelaw who, in his capacity as Shadow Home Secretary, was immediately besieged with inquiries) considerable embarrassment. The hostile reaction among senior Conservatives was particularly strong, and Edward Heath accused her of provoking 'an unnecessary national row'. The public response, however, as evinced in her correspondence and in the opinion polls, was massively favourable. Three months before the general election, what is more, she repeated her assertions, denied she had ever modified her position and added, 'Of course people can feel they are being swamped.'

In 1968, in a speech that had procured him dismissal from the Shadow Cabinet of Edward Heath, Enoch Powell had proved there was no issue which demonstrated so great a fissure between public opinion and the opinion of the political establishment as immigration. Nearly ten years later Mrs Thatcher made it clear that the fissure had not been closed. At the moment when she first spoke the opposition were preparing proposals for the reform of British nationality law, a tighter definition of which, it was assumed, would reduce the pressure of immigration. But public discussion of the subject was to a certain extent still taboo; and she had, it quickly appeared, offended against the taboo.

There was, however, a wider significance to the whole episode. For all that she no more than expressed a feeling, for all that what she said was obvious, the various reactions to the interview convinced Margaret Thatcher of one thing she had long scarcely dared to believe: that she had a capacity to communicate directly with the public not possessed by any other senior politician in either party; a capacity to express and define those feelings, and to respond to them, which nobody else had. Her growing awareness that she had what one critic scornfully called 'a line to the people' led to a change in her style which has since been greatly developed in character. She began to distance herself in public, and in private conversation, from the Shadow Cabinet, increasingly referring to them as 'they', just as, in office, she has referred from time to time to the Cabinet as 'the government', as though it were a body of people for whose actions she had no responsibility, and who were continually getting in her way. Her perception of the difference in impulse between herself and her colleagues was to have importance for the manner of her conduct of government.

While this tortuous and internecine process went on Mrs Thatcher (American journalists, on her first visit as Leader to the United States, were quite at a loss to know whether to address her as 'Mrs' or 'Ms', and she told them, 'I am not sure I fully understand the significance of your question') had become a figure of interest to the outside world. Initially, the interest was, in large part, a function of the fact that she was female. For the first time a major political party in a Western country had chosen a woman as its leader. Was it possible that this woman might become Prime Minister?

This natural interest — or gossipy curiosity — was further fuelled by her decision to make good, in part at least, her evident lack of knowledge of foreign affairs, by a series of trips abroad. These trips, especially that to the United States in September 1975, when President Carter, acting against his principle of not meeting foreign opposition leaders, did receive her, made for excellent publicity at home. But, gratifying though overseas interest in her might be, and useful, too, though it might be in persuading a domestic audience that she was being taken seriously on the world stage, she was already, in the autumn of the year of the leadership election, preparing to make a more substantial impact.

There is, always, a tussle in her nature between things that she regards as matters of principle, and things that she regards as matters of political tactics. Something may be right: she wishes to declare that it is so; but she is prepared to bide her time. The urge to speak out is, however, always strong, and it has not often betrayed her.

She had had, from the moment she first read a Solzhenitsyn novel, *One Day in the Life of Ivan Denisovich*, on a flight from Zurich (when she was Secretary of State for Education) a consciousness of, and a repugnance towards, the practical policies of the Soviet Union. There was nothing remarkable about that in a woman of her background; and it was, in any event, a view shared by most of her acquaintances. She gave, however, a passion to it, as she does to any subject which excites her close interest. Then, in 1975, her reading and, even more particularly, her conversations with Robert Conquest — one of the finest scholars of the history of the Soviet Revolution, a virtually life-long Labour Party supporter, but now a convert to Conservatism — and the South African writer, Laurens van der Post, led her to a sharper perception of the capacity — and perhaps willingness — of the USSR to present a military threat to the Western world. She was influenced, further, by the Western German Defence White Paper of 1975, which concluded that a Soviet thrust in the central plain of Europe could be expected to reach the English Channel in a matter of days. She saw herself, as Leader of the Conservative Party, and putative Prime Minister, as having a duty to speak out on these matters, particularly as so few politicians and journalists seemed to understand the danger as she did herself.

It is impossible to know, let alone describe, all the thoughts and influences that chased one another across her mind on this subject from August 1975 to the end of the year. It may be that she could not trace the process of thought herself: she has said that she is more likely to write a novel about her life than a volume of memoirs, because all that has happened to her, and all that she has done, is too improbable to be contained within the borders of a politician's reminiscences. In any event, in the winter of 1975, she made a speech to the Chelsea Conservative Association expatiating on the Soviet threat.

It was given very little notice by the Press. 'And thank God for that,' said her Shadow Foreign Secretary, Reginald Maudling, who had not known she was going to make it. The Western and Eastern powers were about, in Helsinki, to come to a series of agreements (collectively generally known as the Helsinki Accords) which ushered in the period (it was then assumed that it would be an 'age' or maybe an 'era') of détente. In the event a quite bewildering number of documents were signed by all the participants. Hope was in the air in international relations: it seemed that there would be a vast number of contractual entanglements between the Soviet Union and its satraps on the one side, and the United States and her allies on the other which would build confidence, encompassing as they did both arms limitations and cultural and economic exchanges of a kind that, with the passage of time, would bring East and West together. So far as British foreign policy was concerned there was also a technical problem with regard to her expressed hostility to the Accords. Maudling explained it in an article in *The Times* when he said that 'The broad stream of British foreign policy should not be sharply diverted with every change of government...' He did not, in a word, want his Leader and his party to seem to be too much out of step with the British government of the day — as, he would hope, a Labour opposition would not diverge too far from the foreign policy of a Conservative government. This was an honourable position to occupy: in 1964 a Conservative Prime Minister, Alec Douglas-Home, had suggested an agreed foreign policy to the Labour opposition, and regular, formal talks to bring such a consummation about. There was then — as there is now — a serious difference on the question of what ought to be done in foreign and defence affairs between opposition and government, and Harold Wilson refused Home's offer. The difference then as now concerned the wisdom of retaining an independent British nuclear deterrent.

Some of Margaret Thatcher's most loyal supporters were as relieved as was Reginald Maudling that the Chelsea speech went off as quietly as it did. It was not that they differed from her in her analysis. It was, rather, that they saw the whole world arrayed against her, just at the moment when she was beginning the effort to make herself credible as a proponent of a domestic policy alternative to that of the government. Others of her advisers — and, particularly because of his special knowledge, Conquest — took a quite different view. It was not ignoble, they concluded, to *hope* for something from the Helsinki Accords, but it was impractical. The fact of the matter, as they saw it, was that the Soviet Union (to quote one note she received at the time) 'was offering promissory notes on human rights in the future, while the West was delivering limitations on its own arms now'.

Inter alia at Helsinki the Soviet authorities undertook to provide freer distribution of Western newspapers throughout their dominions, freer use of their airwaves by Western broadcasters and — most crucial — freer movement of people across borders between East and West. In return, the Western powers, having nothing to offer on similar cultural matters — since Soviet literature is readily available in the West, Soviet citizens wishing to emigrate are, in general, welcomed and Soviet radio stations are not jammed — undertook to delay the development and deployment of certain weapon systems. Particularly under the influence of the Carter government in the United States — though American policy was the creation of an earlier American administration — the Western powers kept their collective word. It was always possible that the love of peace, and the development of such cultural and political affinities as there were, would blunt weapons. It was common both to Margaret Thatcher's supporters and critics that, if the Soviet Union kept its word on human rights and cultural exchange, then swords might be turned into ploughshares. It was not until President Brezhnev enunciated the Brezhnev Doctrine — to the effect that nothing done at Helsinki would in any way restrict the activity of the Soviet Union in spreading world revolution, nor inhibit the government of that Union in the discipline it imposed on its own people, that scales began to drop from eyes.[3]

For the moment, however, at the end of 1975, Margaret Thatcher would have none of it, and nothing of these complicated arguments. At Kensington Town Hall in January 1976 she returned to the charge: the Soviet Union presented a serious threat, both military and political, and it was vital that the West responded with strength and confidence. She was strongly advised against making this speech. The first speech on the same subject had had no useful impact. Not merely Britain's European allies, but the government of the United States — than which, she had said herself, there was no more important ally — were supportive of what had been agreed at Helsinki. If the speech was noted she would have very few friends.

The speech was not merely noted: it received attention across the world. She had, in less than forty minutes of delivery, secured more international headlines than most politicians could expect to receive in a lifetime. With very few exceptions editorial comment was unfriendly, when it was not blatantly hostile. The patient arguments of the academic critics of the Helsinki Accords were brushed aside. She appeared to many commentators who had hitherto seemed interested in and even sympathetic to her to be staking out an extremist position, and her Shadow Foreign Secretary was, naturally, given his previously expressed views, upset. Finally, she received what she has always since called an 'accolade', but which the vast majority of those who commented on the speech at Kensington Town Hall regarded as an extremely worrying reaction: the description 'Iron Lady' from *Red Star*, the official journal of the army of the Soviet Union.[3]

Sotto voce there was a certain amount of support for the logic of her position. 'I know there's a lot of truth in what she says,' observed one Shadow Cabinet member who had been perennially critical of her position on economic policy, 'but I wish she wouldn't say it so loudly.' The loud tone — which her friends called firm, her enemies strident — had gained an effect, of what value, in policy or in electoral terms, nobody could tell. After the international outburst following the Kensington speech, however, she fell silent, and concentrated on economic policy, the work of many committees, the weekly Shadow Cabinet meetings, and the hammering away at the government in the House of Commons. Questions of foreign policy seemed laid aside.

Then, at a weekly meeting to discuss her diary she told her staff that she wished to make a speech on the anniversary of the Helsinki Declaration. The anniversary was only four days away; it was on a Saturday; she had no engagements on that Saturday. It was what was designated in the diary, in perhaps unconscious remembrance both of schooldays and of business conferences, a 'free day', when she could read, and potter, and be with her family. Since her words and attitude made it clear that she intended to make a major speech, the technical problems attending the organization of such a speech — given the furore that had followed the speech in Kensington — flew into several minds. There had to be a suitably large audience; one had to be found. The newspaper reporters — but, much more important, the television news producers, accustomed to easy weekends so far as politics were concerned — had to be alerted, for she was quite clearly determined to make headlines on the same subject again.

Then there was the problem of a text. There was no problem about the broad thrust of the argument: that would be as it had been at Kensington, with the added and sharply phrased conclusion that, a year on, all the evidence suggested that the Helsinki Declaration had been a failure. She had read everything recent on the subject, but she wanted to know from everybody who kept up with what was called 'implementation' what was happening, minute by minute. Cautionary words were uttered, but she made manifest her determination to go ahead. There was, however, one *caveat*: her staff were to have no consultation with the Conservative Research Department, nor with the Shadow Foreign Secretary, for the moment at any rate.

After frantic telephone calls, a Conservative Association reasonably adjacent to London — that of Dorking — was found. Its executive could not only provide a large hall and fill it, but arrange for all the technical facilities which would be required by television cameramen. Work on the text went ahead, to the exclusion of almost all other work. A rumour was spread that there was to be a major speech on foreign policy on the Saturday. On Thursday Reginald Maudling was sent a copy of the text she had approved. He was, and very understandably, angry. He told friends in the press that he would see that it was 'toned down'. He wrote to her — and had delivered by hand — a letter of rebuke, accompanied by a draft prepared by himself and the Conservative Research Department of what he thought she should say. A part of his letter went as follows:

> I understand that the draft [the one sent to him] was produced by Lord Chalfont and Mr Patrick Cosgrave. I have no ideas of their views on foreign policy, or their reasons for them.

He went on to say that he was her principal adviser on foreign policy, and stood ready, always, to advise her. He expressed a reserved hurt that neither he, nor the Research Department, had been informed that the speech was to take place, much less consulted about its content. And he gave, then, his reservations about it on a point of principle:

> No doubt a violent and sustained attack upon the Soviet Union may have some political advantage within our own ranks. But I am doubtful as to what long term purpose it is intended to serve, not only in opposition, but more important, in Government.

He suggested that the draft she had sent to him implied a programme of rearmament: 'Maybe we should adopt this as a policy, but I think we should consider it carefully and at length in the Shadow Cabinet before we do.'

He was making a point that was relevant not only to this particular speech, but to the general argument about how the business of opposition should be conducted. He gave his personal advice on the merits of what she was going to say, but he also put forward the view, as a matter of principle, that the agreement of the Shadow Cabinet should be procured for any major political statement the Leader was going to make. That evening she dined with, among others, the Shadow Defence spokesman, Sir Ian Gilmour — in all other respects an ally of Maudling — and procured his agreement to the draft she preferred. The journalist to whom Maudling had confided his intention of having that draft 'toned down' subsequently observed, 'If that was toned down, I'd like to see the original.' Not only did she say what she had originally wanted to say, she interpolated a passage designed especially for the television cameras in which she referred to herself with pleasure as the one dubbed Iron Lady by the Russians, and she ignored every one of Maudling's reservations. Shortly afterwards, she dismissed him from the Shadow Cabinet.

The problem of the right foreign policy for Britain is still with us. Her method as an opposition and party leader is to be seen even more clearly than in the formulation of foreign policy in the way she dealt with a subject which was then a paramount one in domestic policy but which is now virtually forgotten.

In the handling of Conservative Party policy on the issue of devolution for Scotland and Wales, she inherited a commitment. It was not simply a commitment made by Edward Heath personally, though he had given it a particular personal sanction by allowing a speech of his (in 1968) to the Scottish Conservative Party Conference, to be dubbed the Declaration of Perth. It was a commitment, to state it simply, to give the people of Scotland and the people of Wales much more say in their own affairs, much more independence from what, in the debate on these matters which ran for so many years, was called the 'imperial' Parliament at Westminster. It was assumed, moreover, that the say in question could be provided only through the setting up of Scottish and Welsh assemblies, or sub-parliaments. The only question to be resolved — and it was admitted by all except such out and out

Scottish and Welsh nationalists as wished to sever all legislative relations with Westminster that it was technically a very difficult one — was that of the precise balance of power between Westminster and any initially subsidiary assemblies which were created. In December 1973 I asked her what she thought about devolution. She answered: 'I'm worried about it.' In January 1975 she told a Scottish Conservative member, 'It must be stopped, really, or it will break up the kingdom.' He was horrified, for he was one of the many Scottish Tories who believed that, with the electoral rise of the Scottish National Party, devolution was the only method of preserving the United Kingdom — this time by consent, rather than through legislative fiat from Westminster.

Hard though it is to recall the fact now, in 1975 devolution was one of the major political issues of the day, and had been so for years. It was virtually axiomatic that, in some form, devolution would come. The only question was, what kind of devolution? Since the 1960s, indeed, the Liberal Party had been advocating something far more extensive than elected assemblies in Scotland and Wales; they wanted mini-parliaments in the English regions as well. First George Brown, as Deputy Leader of the Labour Party and then Edward Heath, as Leader of the Conservative Party, committed their respective organisations to the idea of devolving at least some of the functions of government away from Westminster. Only a handful of politicians of any consequence remained opposed to the idea root and branch.

No doubt there were many who took up the devolution banner because they felt that government was too big and too centralised, and carried it because they believed in the principle of local democracy. There was also, as an influence, however, the uncomfortable fact of the advance of the Nationalist parties, the Scots holding eleven seats by 1978. Nationalism, so the argument ran, could only be killed by kindness, in the form of devolution. In the upper reaches of the Conservative Party in Scotland the conviction that Nationalism had to be appeased ran particularly strongly: 'The lairds are dead scared,' said Teddy Taylor, Tory member for Glasgow Cathcart (and now for Southend), contemptuously. He was one of the very few Scottish Conservatives who was an out and out opponent of devolution. All through the first phase of Margaret Thatcher's leadership the argument ran on to a crescendo, its climax to be provided eventually by Scottish and Welsh referenda on whatever proposals the government eventually put to Parliament.

From the very beginning she set out to scupper the whole project. She was convinced that nationalism could not, ultimately, be appeased, and that devolution was merely the first step down the road to the break-up of the United Kingdom. She was convinced, moreover, that if only the whole business could be protracted, and a suitable mechanism built into the referenda arrangements, then disaster could be averted. But she would not tackle the issue head on, nor as a matter of principle. When I presented her with a draft speech for her first Scottish Tory Conference as Leader which expressed unequivocal opposition to the whole business of devolution she rejected it, saying, quite gently, 'No. I will retreat, but I do not want to bang the drums too loudly.' What she did at that conference — which was in Perth — was assent in the most general terms to the principle that people should have more control over their own affairs, inveigh against the wickedness of over-powerful government, and conclude with a ringing peroration on the greatness of the United Kingdom.

After that, everything was tactics. She changed her spokesmen in devolution debates with bewildering regularity. First William Whitelaw enjoyed (if that is the right word) responsibility for the subject, then it was Francis Pym. But Teddy Taylor, as Shadow Secretary of State for Scotland, also had a right to a say, and she regularly intervened in debates herself. The general line was invariably to oppose the government on the technicalities, never on the principles, of its proposals.

Moreover, she watched with care the evolution on the Labour side of a substantial body of opinion hostile to the whole idea, the most prominent members of which were George Cunningham and Tam Dalyell. (It is ironic, in view of her later battles with Dalyell over the sinking of the Argentinian battleship *Belgrano* during the Falklands war, how vital their subterranean alliance with one another was during the constitutional crisis which the devolution debate represented.)

The greatest care was taken not to offend the susceptibilities of potential Labour rebels against the Callaghan government and thus, when Dalyell made it known through unofficial channels in advance of one particular debate that some Labour members who were hesitating over how to use their votes would, because of personal dislike for both of them, be irritated into the government lobby by the appearance either of Margaret Thatcher or Teddy Taylor as speakers, both the Leader of the Opposition and the Shadow Secretary of State for Scotland stood down, giving their places to their more emollient colleagues. Finally, George Cunningham produced an ingenious amendment to the government's proposed legislation which would require forty per cent of the qualified electorate — not just of those voting — to support devolution in the Welsh and Scottish referenda before the measures proposed took effect. With Tory support it was carried.

It was too much to ask. In March 1979 devolution was destroyed both in Scotland and Wales. Mrs Thatcher had demonstrated a hitherto unsuspected capacity to play a waiting game. The SNP became unremitting enemies of James Callaghan, and on 28 March were instrumental in bringing down his government. 'They will melt like snow in the sunshine,' she had said of the Nationalists when a colleague propounded the supposed necessity of appeasement. The Nationalist vote of no confidence in the government on 28 March was, said Callaghan, repeating an old adage, like turkeys voting for an early Christmas. The Prime Minister and his principal opponent were both right: in the ensuing general election the SNP representation in Parliament was reduced to one member; and no sign of recovery was evident in the general election of 1983. She had played a long hand with great skill and nerve, and had taken the vital trick.

The conventional wisdom is that what finally destroyed the Callaghan government was the winter of discontent of 1978–79. In the autumn of 1978, in contrast to the spring of 1979, the Callaghan government seemed to be getting on top of things. True, Britain had been subjected to the humiliating discipline of the International Monetary Fund. True, the incomes policy showed signs of strain. True, there was a constant seething discontent evident on the part of left-wing Labour backbenchers. And, true, sympathetic trade union leaders had advised ministers that they could not hold the line against their restive members much longer. Whether the perilous equilibrium that had been established — both inside and outside Parliament — could be made to last was a question nobody could answer. But it seemed certain that James Callaghan would seize the moment to call a general election, and there were a number of Conservatives — though not Margaret Thatcher herself — who feared that he would win it on his avuncular image alone. In the event he flinched from the challenge of an October 1978 poll. The trade unions threw off the displeasing burden of wage restraint, and a host of official and unofficial industrial disputes broke out; disputes which the government was very evidently unable to control.

In my own judgement it would have made very little difference whether the election was held in October or, as happened, in April. The tide of events had been moving in the opposition's direction since 1976. With every move Denis Healey made under constraint, and notably in the multiple ministerial warning about public expenditure levels, it seemed that Labour was being forced to do, grudgingly, what Mrs Thatcher and the Tories would do thoroughly.

At the same time, Conservative discontents were kept tightly under wraps. In 1976 a mid-term manifesto, *The Right Approach*, appeared. In 1977 it was followed by *The Right Approach to the Economy*. The only difference of note between the prescriptions of these documents and those of the general election manifesto was the promulgation in the last of the three of a promise of tough policies towards the unions. So unpopular had the winter made trade unions and trade unionists that the old fears of the inefficacy of legislation in industrial relations were, for the moment at any rate, removed.

Further, while all the policy struggles, nationally and within the party, had been continuing, the presentation of Margaret Thatcher to the public by Gordon Reece, and of the Conservative Party by the advertising agency Saatchi and Saatchi, had achieved streamlined perfection.

Reece was prodigal with her time for popular newspapers and radio and television programmes, like 'The Jimmy Young Show' and 'Jim'll Fix It' which, to say the least, were not designed for audiences with a serious interest in politics. He was positively niggardly with her time, on the other hand, for the more heavyweight newspapers and the more prestigious current affairs programmes. He was accused (as were Saatchi and Saatchi) of trivialising politics in general and the issues in particular. 'Rubbish,' he said in answer to one such criticism. 'Did you notice how hard Denis Healey tried to get on "Jim'll Fix It" after she had appeared? I simply encourage her to appear everywhere she can appear to the best advantage. It's the most ludicrous intellectual snobbery to say that a politician should not appear on general interest programmes because the listeners are supposed to be on a lower level of humanity than the people who watch "Panorama". They have votes too, and if she talked down to them they'd soon rumble her. The others are just jealous because they just couldn't do these programmes.'

Certainly, it was Reece's intention that she should avoid major political confrontations except at times, and on ground, of her own choosing. The election campaign itself he planned down to the last and most trivial detail. Her meetings were all-ticket affairs (though this was as much at the request of the police and the security services as a result of tactical political choice), and most of her supposedly informal meetings with the voters were minutely stage-managed. For this reason the press found hers an immensely dull campaign, for nothing, from beginning to end, went wrong with it. Yet, while the understandable journalistic response to this unwontedly smooth state of electoral affairs was to send up the campaign, and to make fun of her elaborate stage management, it was evident that the Thatcher message of self-sufficiency, self-reliance and national renewal was getting through to the voters. What Reece had done was to devise a mechanism by which her individual sense of identification with the electorate could best express itself.

An enormous amount of critical attention was then, and has since been, devoted to the mechanics of the Conservative campaign. I fancy, however, that the importance of those mechanics to her victory has been greatly over-rated, partly because the techniques employed, at least to the degree that they were employed, were new to the British scene. There can have been very few voters who, on the morrow of her victory did not realise — perhaps with a certain trepidation, perhaps with delight — that the nation had chosen something and someone different. As she put it in her speech at Cardiff Town Hall in the second week of the campaign, attacking the Callaghan rhetoric of the search for a national consensus:

The Old Testament prophets did not say 'Brothers, I want a consensus.' They said: 'This is my faith, this is what I passionately believe. If you believe it too, then come with me.'

CHAPTER THREE

The Lost Year

I shall not be understood, my dear Marquis, to speak of consequences, which may be produced in the revolution of ages, by corruption of morals, profligacy of manners, and listlessness for the preservation of the natural and inalienable rights of mankind, nor of the successful usurpations, that may be established at such an unpropitious juncture upon the ruins of liberty, however providently guarded and secured; as these are contingencies against which no human prudence can effectually provide.
— George Washington to the Marquis de Lafayette, 7 February 1788

Only one thing disfigured Margaret Thatcher's first victorious general election campaign. That was the murder, on 30 March, two days after the fall of the Callaghan government, of Airey Neave, by the Irish National Liberation Army. It was not merely the brutality of the act that was shocking, or the fact that it took place within the environs of the House of Commons, nor the fact that the victim had come through the tribulations of a distinguished war unscathed, but the plain evidence it provided that terror could readily reach into the heart of the political system. For herself, Neave's death meant not just the loss of somebody she had known for years — she had been a junior barrister in his chambers — but of somebody who had become, over the period since 1964, a friend and counsellor.

Indeed, Neave was as nearly indispensible to her as any one individual could be. She was as fond of Keith Joseph, but she — rightly — distrusted his judgement. She trusted the judgement of William Whitelaw, but there were too many barriers of experience and attitude between them for the kind of friendship she had had with Neave to blossom. From the very beginning of her leadership she had to a great extent been dependent on Whitelaw's loyalty, and she was to continue from time to time to be dependent on it throughout her first term, but there was little of the personal intimacy between them that there had been between herself and Neave which, perhaps, she needed to make the same kind of sure-footed start as Prime Minister that she had made as Leader. One of her staff who was devoted to both of them put it this way: 'The relationship with Airey was the kind of relationship every prime minister needs. She had enough trust in him to follow his advice even against her instincts, and not to resent the fact. He also had a kind of touch in his judgement of people that she does not herself have. He could predict what people would do and what they were capable of doing, so little in politics ever surprised him. She is always being surprised, and she is often disappointed. He cushioned surprise and disappointment for her, and he could make her relax.'

There had been certain indications, before his death, that Neave was of a mind to advise her to be more daring than she turned out to be in the selection of her first Cabinet — one that was to survive without alteration until January 1981. There was, however, the fact that, having rejected the advice of the 1922 Committee executive eighteen months previously — to give experience of Shadow office to a wider variety of members — she was to some extent limited in what she could do. It would have seemed odd to reshuffle the pack drastically when she had lived with it (or at least its main components) for so long. So, there were few surprises.

One or two choices had to be made. There was, for

example, the question of who should be Foreign Secretary. Lord Carrington, in opposition the Leader of the House of Lords, coveted the position ('the only job I have ever really wanted') and so, naturally, did Francis Pym, who had had the Shadow responsibility. Her choice fell on Carrington, who was allowed his own choice of Ian Gilmour as his Commons spokesman, with Gilmour to enjoy Cabinet rank as Lord Privy Seal. Pym went to Defence, the victim of this shuffle being Tom King, who had been Shadow Defence Secretary, and now had to content himself with the number two job at the Department of the Environment, under Michael Heseltine. A few eyebrows were raised at the return of Lord Hailsham to the Woolsack as Lord Chancellor, at the appointment of Christopher Soames (who had last held ministerial office under Harold Macmillan) as Leader of the House of Lords, and at the occupation of the Northern Ireland Office by the Chief Whip, Humphrey Atkins, who had never been known to betray the slightest interest in the subject and did not seem (to his critics at least) to have the robustness required for the administration of that troubled province.

Two appointments shocked, and two pleased, her most radical supporters. Peter Walker was recalled from the wilderness and, though he received only the Ministry of Agriculture (where he was to perform with some style) it seemed an unnecessary gesture to the acolytes of her predecessor. Then, Mark Carlisle was confirmed as Secretary of State for education, something which might have been expected, since he had held the Shadow post, but which offended the right, who had hoped for a minister who would take a more stringent line than Carlisle was likely to with the comprehensive school system. Insult was added to injury here, for Rhodes Boyson, though appointed a junior to Carlisle, was excluded from responsibility for schools. The former headmaster of Highbury Grove School, he had entered the House in 1974 and was one of the most abrasive of educational thinkers, being one of the authors of the famous Black Papers that had caused so much fluttering in progressive educational dovecotes in the 1960s and that had contributed to the withdrawal from public life of Sir Edward Boyle, a Secretary of State for Education who had once been thought of as a potential Tory leader.

On the credit side, there was the return of John Biffen, as a Treasury Minister with a seat in the Cabinet. Biffen, a man of modesty, charm and considerable intellectual power, had been one of the few Conservative backbenchers who had had the courage consistently to oppose Edward Heath during the life of the Heath government — on public expenditure and membership of the Common Market among other things. Though possessed of sometimes almost ferocious views, his diffidence was such that he had never cut the kind of figure that had been cut by his friend Enoch Powell. He had been one of Margaret Thatcher's more imaginative appointments — as Shadow Secretary of State for Energy — in 1975, but had withdrawn from the Shadow Cabinet in 1977 for reasons never very clearly explained, but which were supposed to have to do with health. He was held in universal esteem and was reckoned, as one colleague put it, to be 'just the man to put the intellectual stuffing into Geoffrey [Howe]'. Finally, Angus Maude, one of the most curmudgeonly and yet charming intellectuals of the old right — who had been dismissed as a Shadow spokesman by Edward Heath in 1967 — a man of formidable mind and great intelligence, but questionable energy, returned to high office as Paymaster General. To her most fervent supporters, however, the balance seemed tilted the wrong way.

To most commentators, on the other hand, it seemed just about right. There was, as in everything else, a tradition in these matters and, until the leadership of Edward Heath it was taken for granted that prime ministers, and especially

Conservative prime ministers, took great trouble to balance their cabinets between the different sections of the party. Heath had, in this respect, been unusual in his exclusion of dissent throughout the 1970–74 period. On the other hand, there is a general case to be made for a prime minister bent on radical reform at least initially excluding opponents, in the interests of action. And, after all, she had told Kenneth Harris of the *Observer* on 25 February 1979, 'As Prime Minister I couldn't waste time having arguments.' She was to find herself having a great many, some of which she did not win. It seems, however, that she may have hoped that the very completeness of her victory — which came, it must be remembered, after a long period in which the general assumption was that Britain faced a long period of minority governments — would dissipate opposition to her policies, at least within the party, and that it was this that encouraged her to enter No. 10 Downing Street with the unlikely words of St Francis of Assisi on her lips.

The new government faced one immediate task, the urgency of which derived from the date of the general election. When the Callaghan government fell Denis Healey had been preparing his spring budget. By agreement with all parties he instead introduced, on 3 April, a caretaker budget, which ensured that revenues continued to be raised and bills to be paid while the politicians were off fighting an election campaign. It now fell to Sir Geoffrey Howe to prepare a budget — a process normally taking months — in double-quick time. This he presented on 12 June, the government's general aims having been set out in the Queen's Speech on 15 May. In advance of that, however, two decisions with economic consequences were taken, both in fulfilment of election pledges. These were the raising of pay in the armed services by thirty-two per cent, and in the police force by twenty per cent.

The initial omens were not good. 'Simply stated,' as Hugh

Stephenson put it, 'on the basis of pre-election promises, the figures did not add up.'

The difficulty was that, until the middle of 1978, Howe had believed that the reductions in income tax which were a central part of the Shadow Cabinet's thinking would have to come later rather than earlier. This was a rational — but not an electorally attractive — policy, and by the close of the year the Shadow Chancellor found himself committed to early cuts in taxation. There was a certain degree of symbolism about these commitments: a party devoted to the idea of extending the freedom of the individual and reducing the role of government in the life of the nation obviously had to be devoted to making it possible for the individual to keep more of his (or her) earnings. However, with the new financial year already more than two months old on 12 June, the scope for compensating cuts in public expenditure within its duration would, evidently, be small. Further, aside altogether from the immediate pay awards to the services and the police the Prime Minister had rashly given an undertaking to honour the awards of the Clegg Commission on pay comparability. The job of the Commission, which started work on 7 March under Professor Hugh Clegg, was to review and make recommendations upon public sector wage claims. In all the Commission had, by election day, a substantial number of claims under examination — those of local authority and university manual workers, ancillary workers in the National Health Service, ambulance men, ambulance officers, nurses and midwives, university technicians, municipal airport workers, and employees in the supplementary medical professions. To put the matter crudely, Clegg was surveying the ruined remains of the winter of discontent, and since his remit was to ensure comparability of pay between workers without, and those with, industrial muscle the bill for his recommendations was likely to be a highly expensive one. (Indeed, in the budget debate in March 1980 it was computed as £2,000 million.) It was not, however, immediately realised by the government how dangerous a threat Clegg was to the whole structure of its economic policy, and it was to take even longer to get around to abolishing the Commission.

Two other difficulties loomed ahead. The first was the fact that inflation was set to increase world wide, with the likelihood (which was fulfilled) of an increase in the price of oil later in the year. This, of course, was none of the government's making, but ministers failed to take its significance into account, just as, between June and October 1970, the just-elected Heath government utterly failed to take into account the inflationary pressures exerted by the rapid increase in the supply of money caused by Harold Wilson's pre-election spending spree.

For the second difficulty the government — indeed, the Prime Minister herself — was directly responsible. To Howe between May and June it seemed that the circle simply could not be squared. Yet, in addition to his budget and the consequent Finance Bill, Howe had to prepare the annual White Paper on public spending for the following year. This was in any case a difficult exercise, and it was to prove inadequate as an instrument of control over the economy, given the failure to predict some of the forthcoming pressures and the dangers inherent in the budget strategy. Its faults were not, however, quickly to be discovered, for publication was postponed from July to October, her argument for doing this being that once it came out there would have to be a full-dress debate in the House of Commons and this, in turn, would mean postponing the start of the summer recess. She was unwilling to do that, both for fear that it would suggest a hidden crisis which she did not believe existed, and because she had already begun to turn her mind to the forthcoming Commonwealth Prime Ministers' conference in Lusaka where the issue of Rhodesia would be at the top of the agenda.

She was not, however, wholly oblivious to the risks she was

running in the budget. The pure milk of monetarist doctrine would require the balancing of cuts in income tax with reductions in public expenditure. In addition, the fact that the expenditure assumptions of the previous government's White Paper were unduly low, the forthcoming Clegg awards, and the various inflationary pressures already present in the economy, would have required, in a monetarist world, yet further cuts. When at the end of May Howe, Biffen and the Treasury team offered her a package of measures amounting to £500 million, she turned it down flat, insisting on something much larger (the figure was eventually adjusted to £3,500 million, but much of that was notional). Her determination, inadequate though it was, came as a shock to the Treasury, accustomed as officials there were to having to persuade politicians to make reductions rather than the reverse. This initial surprise was a harbinger of things to come, and confirms Peter Riddell's judgement that 'for those outside the Conservative tribe Thatcherism has appeared to be a bogey. The biggest shock has been for the centrist establishment — the world of senior civil servants, lawyers, top bankers, university lecturers and pundits. These have recoiled from the style as well as the content of Thatcherism, from its deliberate rejection of the consensus cherished by so many of them.'

The budget looked both innovative and shocking. The major tax cuts were made at the top end of the scale, the Prime Minister apparently believing (as do some American economists) that tax cuts by themselves would stimulate productivity. But indirect taxes were sharply increased — VAT to what was then an unbelievable flat rate of fifteen per cent, while in an independent move, though one concerted with No. 10 Downing Street, the Bank of England raised its minimum lending rate by two per cent. It all looked dashing, but it was quite simply not enough.

Both the caution, then, of her ministerial appointments,

and the fact that hope rather than rigour marked her opening moves in economic policy (with results that we shall see later) contradicted her self-proclaimed image of ruthless radicalism. Jim Prior, for example, had been quite certain that he would not be appointed as Employment Secretary unless she had a very slender majority indeed, but she passed him quietly into the office he had been preparing for. Her allies and her critics alike expected a far tougher approach to the economy. What she offered instead was a dangerous gamble, an assumption that inflationary pressures, international or domestic, would simply not materialise, that the taxation reductions which were made would encourage the expectation of others, and that that expectation would fuel enterprise and productivity. She asked the City of London, in addition, to accept on trust her determination to cut the rate of growth in the money supply to between seven and eleven per cent. She was not believed.

Why were these her opening moves? There were a number of subsidiary pressures and assumptions at work upon her. The first was an innate caution which, as I suggested earlier, inhabited her personality alongside a tendency to boldness. The second was simply plain inexperience: she did not yet know enough to be able to look at all sides of the economic equation, and she had nobody in her Cabinet with experience of Treasury matters. The third was her continuing, almost subliminal, lack of confidence in her authority: it was not until she acquired the daily habit of taking decisions in power that her confidence matured. A fourth factor was that she decided from the beginning to run No. 10 Downing Street with its existing Civil Service establishment. Although John Hoskyns was, instantly and unexpectedly, moved into No. 10 as head of her policy unit, she made no effort to add to her team any of the monetarists on whom she had in opposition relied for advice, so there was nobody at hand with the requisite knowledge to tell her where she was going wrong. It was not until October that she appointed Dr Terry Burns from the London Business School as the government's Chief Economic Adviser, and not until much later that she brought in Professor Alan Walters (who had been working in the United States) to provide her with personal economic advice. She was, in a word, over-confident of her own mastery of economic policy.

Finally, there was something else. When a prime minister takes office — particularly when it is for the first time — he (or she) has a choice of attitude. It is perfectly possible to start off gloomily and act repressively, blaming the necessity of this on the sins of one's predecessors. It is also tempting to believe that one's very arrival in the seat of power presages better times, and this temptation is understandably fortified by the personal euphoria that attends a general election victory. Margaret Thatcher came to power with substantial moral capital, in part created out of admiration for her seizing of the improbable opportunities that had come her way, in part out of regard for her evident steadfastness. Before the end of her first year a great deal of that capital had to be expended simply in holding on to her position. All this was because she had yielded to the temptation of allowing her personal euphoria to spill over into the public domain.

In the meantime, however, the budget behind her, she turned her eyes overseas. In Rhodesia, that most intractable of survivals from the colonial era, Bishop Abel Muzorewa had preceded her into office on 24 April, the first black prime minister of his country. She had sent Lord Boyd of Merton (a former Colonial Secretary) out to Africa to watch the first election in which the black population would vote, and to report on whether it was free and fair. Boyd was convinced that it was as free and fair as could, in the circumstances, be expected, given that there was a guerrilla war being waged against the government by the forces of Joshua Nkomo and Robert Mugabe, ranged together in the uneasy alliance known as the Popular Front. She was anxious, however, neither to publicise the report nor announce intended action on it during the general election campaign in Britain. She wanted no complicating factors, and the issue of Rhodesia was a highly divisive one. After her victory she could not delay much longer and besides, she had to have a policy view before the Lusaka Commonwealth Conference at the end of July. Thus, on 16 May she formally received Lord Boyd's report.

On 11 November 1965 the white settler government of Ian Smith had issued the unilateral declaration of Rhodesian independence, and the resultant conflict had plagued every British government thereafter. The situation was particularly difficult for a Conservative leader, for there was a great deal of sympathy within the party for the Smith government, and whenever that government made a reformist move, even if that move was purely cosmetic, there was an outcry within the party for recognition and the lifting of the sanctions which Harold Wilson, under the fiat of the United Nations, had imposed in 1965. The sanctions, moreover, had to be renewed annually, and this provided a regularly recurring opportunity to thrash out the whole matter again. There was never any danger that sanctions would be lifted, except at the behest of a Conservative government, for the Labour, Liberal and most other parties would vote solidly for their retention, even to the point of sustaining a Conservative administration facing a major rebellion. Over the years there had been rebellions, but none of them were major, the massive authority of Sir Alec Douglas-Home being invariably employed to keep the troops in line.

In 1979 the situation was different. Not only had Ian Smith undertaken many reforms, the white population had endorsed by referendum a new constitution based on black majority rule, and Muzorewa was its product. True, the constitution had certain entrenched provisions, and these could ensure that the whites held the real levers of power for many years to come. But the principle had none the less been established, and the last of the six conditions (five laid down by Alec Douglas-Home and Duncan Sandys, one by Harold Wilson) which had to be met before recognition and the lifting of sanctions appeared, on the face of it, to have been met. Moreover, both the Prime Minister and the new Foreign Secretary believed that they would find it difficult to carry a renewal of sanctions through Parliament, without a massive split in the party, something that nobody could readily contemplate on the happy morrow of an election victory. It would further probably be correct to say that most of those most closely connected with Margaret Thatcher, even if they had no particular interest in foreign policy, favoured the cutting of the Gordian knot by recognition of Bishop Muzorewa.

Unfortunately, the coloured Commonwealth and Australia did not see the matter that way at all, nor did the United Nations. The Thatcher government was moving towards a very nasty confrontation at Lusaka, and the situation was so fraught that consideration was even given to advising the Queen not to attend the conference, a suggestion which was firmly turned down by the Palace, where sympathy for and interest in the modern Commonwealth was considerable.

Without ever having given the matter much thought, the Prime Minister instinctively favoured recognition. Although a passionate (and frequently voluble) critic of South Africa's apartheid system, Mrs Thatcher was not a politician whose heart beat in time to the tunes of racial equality, nor had she much confidence in nor sympathy towards the leaders of black Africa. Besides, Rhodesia was an entanglement, a complication she could do without, given that she had so much on her hands at home. Nor initially, at any rate, did it seem likely that she would be persuaded otherwise. Kenneth Kaunda, the President of Zambia and, therefore, a leading figure at

Lusaka, she had met once. The occasion had been a frosty one, she being impatient with his socialistic philosophising and the propounding of his humanist beliefs. 'The man bleats all the time,' she snapped contemptuously to somebody who asked her how they had got on.

On 27 June she was in Tokyo for her first Western economic summit. She stopped on the way back at Canberra to confer with the Australian Prime Minister, Malcolm Fraser. Fraser had come to office with policies rather similar to her own, and his methods as well as his philosophy had naturally been of great interest to her staff in the period of opposition. Indeed, Conservative Central Office had invited some of Fraser's people — including his English-born media adviser — to England to try to learn from their experience down under. These visits had been particularly happy occasions but, contrary to what came to be believed, she did not get on well with Fraser himself, although they had both been education ministers in the governments of their respective countries. Moreover, Fraser had what amounted almost to an obsession with racial equality in general, and with the Rhodesian question in particular. He made it crystal clear to her that at Lusaka he would line Australia up firmly with the so-called front-line states, and resist any concessions to Muzorewa and Smith. Perhaps taken aback by his vehemence she spoke at large a little later to an Australian press conference, stressing the difficulty of renewing sanctions and holding out the possibility of recognition. There was an immediate international storm.

We now enter a period the history of which is dominated by the myth that Lord Carrington and the Foreign Office weaned her away from a position that would certainly have isolated Britain both in the Commonwealth and at the United Nations. In truth, the Office was as slow as she — considering its long experience of the whole imbroglio a great deal slower — to come to the view that a settlement directly with

Muzorewa, without a constitutional conference involving all parties, was not the right policy.

Several factors went towards persuading her to change her front. She met Muzorewa, and formed a downrightly unfavourable opinion of him. She had begun to read voraciously on the recent history of Rhodesia, and if that reading did not warm her heart towards Joshua Nkomo and Robert Mugabe, it led her steadily away from sympathy with the bishop and Ian Smith. She had sources of intelligence outside the Foreign Office. I myself, for example, spent several long sessions with Kaunda in July and became convinced of the rightness of his view that a constitutional conference was a necessary preliminary to a settlement. I became convinced, moreover, as did others, that the black states would compel Mugabe and Nkomo to the conference table, and that South Africa would do the same to Smith and Muzorewa. I reported to her to this effect.

After her return from Australia on 3 July she engaged in a long series of consultative meetings with Foreign Office politicians, meetings at which she was irritated by their pessimism. Carrington could see no way out of the impasse, though he could not bring himself to counsel recognition either. It struck her that what concerned the Foreign Office most was the forthcoming series of European summits. Here, they believed, lay the centre of action in foreign policy, Africa being a tiresome irrelevance.

Before she went to Africa she had to speak on Rhodesia in an adjournment debate in the House of Commons, on 25 July. This was one of the most intriguing speeches she has ever made, more significantly evasive, even, than her early speeches on devolution. She had the problem of dealing with a manifesto commitment to the effect that a Conservative government would 'do its utmost' to secure recognition for Rhodesia if the six principles were met. She recognised that they had been met, but she added a seventh — a requirement that any recognition must be international. 'At the same time,' she said, 'because it is in Rhodesia's own interest to be accepted into the international community, we must have regard to the views of other governments.' And she declined to endorse Boyd's judgement that the elections had been free and fair saying, 'That was his view. We have not yet decided on the matter, because we have wanted to go another way — a way that we believe will be better for Rhodesia in the longer run. It is a way that we believe will bring more countries along with us, and if we go along that consultation route it will be to the benefit of Rhodesia.'

At the time, because of industrial disputes, neither *The Times* nor *Hansard* was being printed. No other newspaper noted the shift in the Prime Minister's position, and only Julian Amery (who supported the new order in Rhodesia) of the backbenchers speaking seemed to understand what had happened. But Parliament rose, and by the time she met it again her *volte face* had been institutionalised in Lusaka.

A hostile reception was being prepared for her in Zambia, although a careful study by Kaunda of the 25 July speech resulted in hostility being muted. When I took a copy of the speech out to him he was very nearly ecstatic, but there was still a good deal of suspicion in the Zambian attitude. The Prime Minister took two pairs of dark glasses with her on the flight 'in case they throw acid or something at me'. None the less, to the horror of her security men, she stepped off her plane straight into a milling African crowd without hesitation or nervousness. What followed was a revelation.

She made it clear from the outset that there would be no recognition of the Muzorewa government without a constitutional conference, and that she wanted all parties to the dispute to attend that conference, including Nkomo and Mugabe, as well as such lesser figures as Ndabininge Sithole. However, there were conditions: the reality as well as the form of British responsibility for the colony would have to be observed. A British governor would return to Salisbury, and British soldiers would police the transition to independence, during which time the guerrillas, though not the Rhodesian security forces — who would come under British command — would be disarmed.

These conditions alarmed the African leaders, and a small steering group was set up, the membership of which included Fraser, to hammer out the details of what had to be done. Although this group eventually came to an agreement, there were frequent tensions and on one occasion only the intervention of Denis Thatcher, who persuaded his wife to go to bed, prevented an explosion. The principal bone of contention was African opposition to the exclusively British control of events upon which she insisted. Indeed, her daring as well as her firmness were remarkable: her Labour predecessors had ruled out of hand any suggestion that the British Army should police a fresh election. The situation in Rhodesia was fraught with danger. Whatever form of truce was agreed on between the warring factions it seemed optimistic in the extreme to imagine that it would be kept, and Britain simply did not have the manpower to impose her will on the country.

Partly out of distrust of Mrs Thatcher, however, the African leaders wanted a United Nations force on the ground and, if not that, one drawn from the Commonwealth. The Prime Minister turned down both suggestions, though she did agree to the presence of Commonwealth observers. She was as cool towards the Commonwealth as she was towards the European Economic Community, but she despised the United Nations very nearly totally. 'Heavens, she was mad yesterday,' Kaunda told me after one of the steering-group sessions. 'What is this thing she has about the United Nations?' His remark was made with affection, however, for one of the most improbable features of the conference was the total rapprochement between the two of them, she being 'dearest

Margaret' to him by the end and he being 'a dear, dear man' to her. When I told the President of the soubriquet Norman St John Stevas had applied to her — 'the Blesséd Margaret' — he went on repeating it happily, and when I lunched with him after the conference had ended and the politicians had departed I was quizzed at great length on British attitudes to the new Prime Minister, Kaunda professing himself quite incapable of understanding why it was that some of 'her own people' could bring themselves to be critical of her. In my view this unlikely mutual admiration society came into existence because both he and she have a certain directness and simplicity of nature. Once she assured him that she meant what she said about the future of Rhodesia he accepted her word absolutely. She, on the other hand, surrounded by African politicians suspicious of her intentions and objectives, appreciated his trust. When, at the Conference Ball Mr Thatcher led out Mrs Kaunda, and the President the Prime Minister, a Zambian minister with whom I was sitting offered a spectacle of almost utter bewilderment. 'When I think,' he said, 'of the reception we were preparing for her a few weeks ago. There was not one of us, not one, who could have imagined anything like this. I'm still not really sure it's happening.'

Clouds of mutual esteem, therefore, wafted up from Lusaka as the conference came to an end. But there was still another conference now looming — the constitutional conference to be held at Lancaster House in London. The various Rhodesian parties to the dispute arrived bristling with suspicion, and Carrington did a very nearly marvellous diplomatic job in even getting the conference under way.

The details of that conference need not concern us here. But there are a few things it is important to stress. With both South Africa and the front-line states anxious for a settlement, the combatants had little enough resources behind them. Carrington's position, endorsed by the Prime Minister (whom he twice called down to Lancaster House to read the riot act), was perfectly simple: he hoped for an agreement to hold a fresh election, policed by Britain, to which all the groups were party. If he could not achieve that he would deal with any party which would deal with him. Thus, when Robert Mugabe threatened to withdraw from the conference Carrington simply indicated that he would then settle with Muzorewa and Nkomo. On this shifting formula the Foreign Secretary was absolutely inflexible. And here the intimacy established between Margaret Thatcher and Kenneth Kaunda became important. Kaunda took the trouble to fly to London and explain to Nkomo, whose troops were quartered in Zambia, that he could not continue to support him if he would not work with Carrington. Kaunda also spoke to President Samora Machel of Mozambique, who was Mugabe's most important backer. When Mugabe left the conference to fly to Maputo, therefore, Machel gave him the same message Kaunda had given Nkomo. A settlement there had to be, and anybody who refused to be part of that settlement would be out in the cold.

The results of the Lusaka conference, even before the talks at Lancaster House had begun, and before the general election which gave power to Robert Mugabe was fought in a virtually trouble-free atmosphere under the authority of Lord Soames, who was sent out as Governor, won international acclaim for the fledgling Prime Minister. The Carter administration, for example, which had greeted her arrival in office with an apprehension tinged with hostility (President Carter had liked James Callaghan and, on the evidence of their only meeting, disliked her) was gushing in its praise. The truth had been that there was practically no government which had believed that the Rhodesian dilemma could be resolved except by victory and defeat in open warfare, and her success was, moreover, given a particular savour by the fact that she had succeeded where the immensely more experienced

Harold Wilson and Edward Heath, and even the legendary darling of the Conservative Party, Alec Douglas-Home, had failed. If there remained discontent on the right, and even if less committed observers feared for the future in what was now about to become Zimbabwe, that seemed a small price to pay.

In her first year, however, there was another area of foreign policy in which she did not win plaudits. This was the area of Britain's relations with her partners in the European Economic Community. Initially the other Community leaders welcomed her election, not least because they regarded the Conservatives as the party of Europe and Labour as the party of opposition to European commitment. On 10 May 1979 she received Chancellor Helmut Schmidt of West Germany in London and on 6 June she paid an official visit to France in the course of which she heaped lavish praise on the French nuclear energy programme. Both Schmidt and President Valéry Giscard d'Estaing found much to be pleased with. They found her an attractive woman, as well as being direct, fresh and open-minded. With Giscard she shared a love of opera, though this common taste did not prevent her liking Schmidt rather better.

All three were aware that there were certain difficulties in Britain's relations with the Community, principally those concerned with the size of Britain's contribution to the EEC budget. It was generally agreed, even by the French, that this was too high, although it was in part at least due to the fact that, in the negotiations leading up to the Treaty of Brussels (by which Britain joined the Community in 1973), the Heath government had insisted on maintaining more open trading links with the outside world than was common with the Western European powers. Because the Community is in part based on the idea that it should present a common tariff wall to the outside world, and because impositions are therefore laid upon goods coming in, Britain found herself required to pay for her imports from such countries as New Zealand. In addition, however, there was the fact that Britain, despite being the poorest industrialised country in the EEC, was making an excessively large financial contribution to its expenditure.

These matters were discussed in a general way at her first meeting of EEC heads of government in Strasbourg on 22 June, and on the sidelines at the Tokyo Western summit on 27 June. On 7 June the Conservative Party enjoyed a spectacular triumph in elections (on a very low poll) held for members of the European Assembly, winning sixty seats to seventeen for Labour, only a handful going to minor parties. This was a reason for congratulating her warmly at Strasbourg on 22 June. It seemed to the Europeans that the British electorate had underlined the verdict of the referendum on continued membership in 1975: Britain was in Europe to stay, and her new Prime Minister — if of necessity less warmly regarded than Edward Heath, the pioneering leader of entry into the Community — was certainly more personable than her predecessor. Schmidt, asked about his reaction to her, declared that he had been 'particularly impressed by her knowledge, authority and sense of responsibility...' It was possible to look forward with hope, and even confidence, to the Dublin summit of EEC powers in November, where the question of Britain's budgetary contributions would be a major item on the agenda.

The danger signs were simply not noticed. The continental countries were perfectly prepared to accept that a £1,000 million difference between what Britain paid to the EEC and what she received from the communal coffers was rather excessive, particularly given her own economic position. That was, after all, practical politics. She, like them, had an electorate to please. What they failed utterly to grasp was that she had a very highly developed sense of nationalism, and regarded the budgetary imbalance not as a regrettable problem which could be dealt with through goodwill on all sides but a matter of fundamental difference. She had neither sympathy for nor, probably, comprehension of an idea fundamental to the nature of the Community — that it should, considered as a unit, have its own resources. Without that principle the EEC had no organic existence of its own; it was merely a collection of more or less friendly states.

There were four points on which the continental leaders could see a possibility of progress. First, since Britain was clearly shouldering an unfair burden, something by way of rebate should be done for her. Second, since Britain was the only member country self-sufficient in oil, that oil should be the basic commodity in the evolution of a common European energy policy, one of the great dreams of the original six members. It should in practical terms be possible, through British resources, to make oil available to EEC countries at a cost lower than was being levied by the Organisation of Petroleum Exporting Countries. Third, if British waters were made more readily available to the fishermen of the continental countries a common fisheries policy could be brought into being. Fourth — and as Edward Heath had once promised — Britain should join the other powers in a common monetary system, with the pound linked to other European currencies. (Then, as now, the pound was floating against other currencies, its value fixed by the daily fluctuation of the money markets, something which made centralised planning for the Community extremely difficult.)

It seems, in retrospect, that the President of France and the Chancellor of the Federal Republic of Germany (as well as the heads of government of the smaller powers) were simply existing on a different plane from Margaret Thatcher during the summer and autumn of 1979. They had found her agreeable and friendly. They were sure a deal could be worked out. They were well disposed. But, a week after becoming Prime Minister she had said: 'It has been suggested that I and my government[1] will be a "soft touch" in the Community ... We shall judge what British interests are, and we shall be resolute in defending them.' It was more than a hint; it was very plain. And she rubbed it in in unmistakable terms in Strasbourg:

> I must be absolutely clear about this. Britain cannot accept the present situation on the budget. It is demonstrably unjust. It is politically indefensible: I cannot play Sister Bountiful to the Community while my own electorate are being asked to forego improvements in the fields of health, education, welfare and the rest.

It could all hardly have been made clearer. And yet, just as Geoffrey Howe contrived to forget the Clegg Commission when he was preparing his first budget, the other European governments simply failed to understand what she was saying. Thus, after her first speech as Prime Minister to the Conservative Party Conference in October 1979 I was lunching with a senior French diplomat. When I arrived, a trifle late, I found him studying the text of her speech. In it she had referred to the prospect of the Dublin summit in November. He had underlined and starred a passage in which she said that she expected 'to make very real progress at the next European Council at the end of November'. When I asked him why he had marked that particular passage he explained to me that it was one vital for his report. It was the passage, he thought, which made it clear that Mrs Thatcher would be *communitaire* in Dublin, that she would not be narrowly nationalistic, and that her idea of 'progress' was one of progress for the Community as a whole. Since I happened to know something of the circumstances of the drafting of the speech I tried to disabuse him of this notion, and we embarked on what amounted to a literary critical dissection of the speech. I tried to convince him that when she said 'we' in discoursing on European affairs she meant the British, and when she said 'progress' she meant progress in the resolving of Britain's complaints. He would have none of it.

Yet, on the four points around which a deal might have been devised she was virtually immovable. The very idea of handing as much as a pint of North Sea oil over to Community supervision, let alone Community control, appalled her. She had no intention whatsoever of joining a European monetary union. And protracted negotiations would be required before the formulation of a common fisheries policy. Whatever emerged would have to be justifiable in itself; it could not be part of any budgetary deal. For, to her mind the budgetary issue — the question of imbalance for Britain between payment and return — stood alone and in gaunt isolation. It was not part of anything, and she would not allow it to become part of anything. She wanted her money back, and that was all there was to be said about the matter.

Looking back on it, it seems amazing that the other countries failed to understand what she was saying. But there were circumstances which mitigate their error. The Cabinet was divided, and Carrington in particular, seeing her headed for a confrontation with the other members of the EEC, sought to persuade her to adopt a less rigid policy. In trying to persuade her to be more flexible he was not merely expressing his own views as a convinced proponent of British membership of the Common Market; he was also reflecting the settled and long-held views of his own department. If unease was expressed on the continent about the utterances of the British Prime Minister, reassurance was forthcoming from the Foreign Office. Mrs Thatcher would be restrained. Lord Carrington (and Sir Ian Gilmour, his number two, and Mr Francis Pym, and Mr Peter Walker, the Agriculture Minister) were all doing their bit on the restraining of the lady. She would have to be offered something, certainly, but the top offer of the Council of Ministers — around about £300 million — would almost certainly do very nicely. In the event, at Dublin, £350 million was offered, and flatly rejected in spite of Carrington's protestations. The Foreign Office, in my judgement, bears a heavy responsibility for what became the catastrophe of the Dublin summit, for British diplomats did not take their own Prime Minister's assertion of her government's position seriously, and encouraged continental diplomats to assume that something was going to happen which was *not* going to happen and which, if they had read her speeches and understood her character, they would have *known* was not going to happen.

It should not be assumed, however, that the Prime Minister herself did not realise that there would be storms in Dublin. From the opening of the summit, when she brusquely dismissed any idea that the budgetary question could be linked with any other, she knew exactly what she was doing, just as she had known for some time exactly what she was going to do.

Like the myth about the origins of the change of policy on Rhodesia, there is a myth about the Prime Minister's approach to the meeting in Dublin. According to that myth, much favoured in Foreign Office circles, and given public expression on more than one occasion by Edward Heath, she blundered into a confrontation in Dublin through ignorance and wilfulness. That is quite simply not so. On the Tuesday before her departure for Dublin she told the Conservative Foreign Affairs Committee — 'with relish', as one member put it — that she was going to 'put them on the spot'. Whether the observer thinks her tactics well or ill-judged this is certain: she knew exactly what she was doing.

The other heads of government were outraged by her behaviour. 'She was certainly adamant,' said Mr Jack Lynch, the Irish host and a man of gentle words, 'persistent and, if I may say so, repetitive.' What Lynch meant was not merely that she held to her position on the budget, but that she quite simply refused to discuss anything else. The meeting broke up in deadlock and confusion.

There was to be a further series of summits. An attempt by the Italians to arrange one in January — this was to be defined as an emergency meeting — came to nothing but, after further meetings in Luxembourg and Strasbourg she got most of what she wanted. Six months after the acrid meeting in Dublin the other countries agreed to compensate Britain for her excessive contributions in 1980 and 1981 and undertook to seek a permanent solution to the budgetary imbalance though, if such had not been achieved by 1983, there was provision for a further year of special compensations to Britain. The net result of all this was that in 1980 and 1981 Britain's contribution to the EEC was just under £200 million though, of course, no permanent and agreeable solution had yet been arrived at, and political warfare between the partners was to break out again in 1983 and 1984.

The immediate terms of the 1980 agreement were satisfying to the Prime Minister: she had got back most of the money that she wanted and she had been successful in her rejection of the idea of allying the budgetary question to any other aspect of Community development. As I will discuss in a later chapter, she began from then on to turn the diplomatic tables. It was unsatisfactory to have to accept a temporary rather than a permanent solution of her country's financial relations with the rest of the EEC, but she had seen off those who argued that a compromise on oil, fish or monetary matters should be the price Britain had to pay for a direct rebate. From 1982 onwards, however, she insisted that there should be not only a permanent solution — an inbuilt system not subject to annual renegotiation — for Britain's problems, but that both the Common Agricultural Policy and the general system of EEC financing should be reformed root and branch before she would permit any further serious progress in the knitting together of the Community. In 1982, thus, she was behaving towards her partners exactly as they had behaved towards her at Dublin. 'I cannot see why they made such a fuss,' she said after the interim budgetary agreement, 'I told them in Dublin I was going to stick it out.'

Hugh Stephenson believes that she 'lost face' in Dublin and Peter Riddell deplores the disruption she provoked. Certainly the reactions to the two major foreign policy engagements of her first year were quite different. Among the *cognoscenti*, and from every government in the Western world, there was universal praise for the British handling of the Rhodesia question, even though too much of the credit was often given to Carrington. So far as the European issue was concerned, however, there was an almost equal chorus of criticism from the same sources, while public support for her stand rose in Britain. By the standards of classical diplomatic history, however, she won a more significant diplomatic victory in Europe than in Africa. True, what she achieved was defined as temporary. True, a great deal of aggravation had attended her achievement (which was not true in Africa). And again true, she made enemies of two men — Giscard and Schmidt — who would have been her friends. But she followed — by instinct, for she had certainly not read up on classical diplomacy — the rules of Salisbury and Curzon, Richelieu and de Gaulle. She defined her objective, she chose her method, and she was utterly ruthless and unforgiving in her tactics, being in addition quite uncaring of the opprobrium which was heaped on her head. She followed, indeed, exactly, the rules for a leader laid down by Charles de Gaulle[2] (and that a French President was one of those wounded by her adds a piquancy to the story). She saw, throughout, the consequences of her policy and her tactics, and she was prepared to live with them. It did not matter a jot to her whether she was thought of well or ill in the newspapers, or in the chanceries of Western Europe. Her European *démarche* appealed to the only jury whose verdict she cares about — the British electorate. And she could even argue (though the matter is as yet not resolved) that her intransigence in 1979 and 1980 paved the way for what has often been agreed to be necessary, but what had never been tackled — the serious reform of the financial structure of the EEC. All this she did alone.

The capacity to enjoy being alone is a terrible and formidable strength in a politician as in a diplomat. She cares nothing for praise or approval from her fellow heads of government, from the members of her Cabinet or from the media, save when such praise serves her electoral purposes. It would be incorrect, even, to say that she craves the approval of her electorate: she believes herself to be the same as that electorate or, at least, to feel and react in the same way as they do to every challenge. Since she assumes an identity between the nation and herself no questions need arise in her mind about whether it is proper or improper to do this or that, whether she is acting purely for short-term advantage or not. None of this will change in her character.

She is hesitant — sometimes weak — only when there is a clash in herself between what reason tells her she ought to do, and what instinct directs her to do. Brock and Wapshott, at the end of their chapter preceding the one devoted to the Falklands war, put the matter most succinctly, by combining a quotation from and one about her. They write, beginning with her speech to the Institute of Directors in 1983:

> The comfortable illusions that accompanied our gradual decline have been shattered. The nation had woken up to the reality of the need to earn its place in the world.

And they continue:

> On that priority Thatcher's friends and enemies would agree, her intellect and her emotion send her in the same direction. 'When that happens,' said one adviser, 'she's a pretty irresistible force.'

While she achieved a success in Africa, however, and while she made a stand in Europe, consequences of the first Conservative budget of 1979 were being made manifest and she had, as yet, no answer to the problems they newly posed. In July, the government decided to sell off a large proportion of the British National Oil Corporation (though there had been only one reference, in *The Right Approach*, to what has come to be called 'privatisation', and there was no serious manifesto commitment). News from the industrial relations front was mixed. In September the National Union of Mineworkers put forward a claim for a pay increase of sixty-five per cent. In October a ten-week-long engineering dispute ended. On 5 December, however, the miners voted against a strike, though on 2 January 1980 a steel strike began. Against a cacophonous background of attack and withdrawal, the dangerous nature of the general economic situation became apparent. 'She's kept the home fires burning,' said Geoffrey Rippon, Secretary of State for the Environment in the Heath government, but excluded from both her Shadow Cabinet and her Cabinet, 'and she doesn't realise that they're burning the house down.'

'All right,' said a Cabinet minister well disposed to her. 'She's sorted out the wogs and she's sorted out the frogs. What about us?' The plain fact of the matter was that the budget mixture of June 1979 was not working, and did not seem likely to work. Public expenditure was out of control, partly at least because of the Treasury's system of accountancy which decrees that a cut in expenditure goes into the books as a cut, even if it is made only on projected expenditure.

To illustrate: the Thatcher government inherited as a working document the Labour White Paper on public expenditure of 1978. That Paper made, as I have already observed, unrealistically low estimates of financial requirements. None the less, its estimates of what would be required in the way of spending by the government far exceeded the cash that would be available. All the estimates of Treasury cuts made in the first year of the new government were based on the cutting of projected, not real, expenditure. So the expenditure cuts offered in the June 1979 budget were notional. There had, therefore, been no change in the structure of the economy. But Mrs Thatcher had been elected, in part at least, because she had said she would change the structure of the economy.

'All is show,' said Norman St John Stevas, at a party just before the 1979 Christmas recess, 'nothing is substance.' The Prime Minister's style, especially in international relations, had been effective; but things, it seemed, were going wrong at home.

While on 21 February 1980 the Welsh coalminers refused to strike in support of the steel workers, the steel strike none the less went ahead. On 3 April they were bought off with a sixteen per cent wage increase, one dependent, however, on substantial redundancies in the industry. The money-supply target of between seven and eleven per cent seemed certain to be exceeded; the latest prediction for inflation was that it might well exceed twenty per cent. There was no sign of that increase in productivity on the optimistic prediction of which the argument for the 1979 budget had depended.

From the beginning of the life of the government, moreover, the Cabinet had not had a single discussion of the general nature of economic policy. The Prime Minister had forbidden all such discussions, and all departmental decisions which were relevant to general policy — such as the reference of a pay claim by schoolteachers to the Clegg Commission — were taken by small groups of ministers, meeting informally. At a by-election at Southend in March her former Shadow Secretary of State for Scotland, Teddy Taylor, who had lost his Glasgow seat in the general election, saw a Tory majority of 10,000 reduced to one of under 500. The new government's domestic position suddenly looked fragile in the extreme.

As the second budget of the Thatcher government approached, Denis Healey denounced the economic policy of the government as 'punk monetarism'. In March the Prime Minister herself confessed on the BBC television programme 'Panorama' that things were certainly going to get worse before they got better, and she argued 'that after almost any major operation you feel worse before you convalesce'. The fact which could not be burked, however, was that as a result of the decisions taken on the public economy in June 1979, the general situation of the country had worsened sharply. To her critics in the Conservative Party this seemed to be a direct result of her refusal to continue with the gentle expansion of credit which had been sanctioned by the previous Labour government. To her friends it seemed that the hasty and ill-thought-out economic decisions of the early weeks of her term had imperilled all of the government's bright prospects. 'We are afloat without a rudder,' exclaimed John Biffen.

Keith Joseph subsequently dubbed this period 'the lost year'. What he meant was that the government had lived, between 1979 and 1980, on credit borrowed from an unexpectedly decisive general election victory. If the monetarist prescription had been followed, difficult decisions about public expenditure would have been taken immediately after the general election; and they had not been. In the early weeks of 1980 it became apparent that either they would have to be taken, or the philosophy would have to be abandoned. However, senior ministers would not — so they said — agree to the kind of surgery at the Treasury that monetarist doctrine required without, at least, an open discussion in Cabinet on what appeared to be going wrong. The Prime Minister was by no means certain to win the argument in such a discussion.

What was quite clear was that the economy had not been turned around. Nor was there any serious prospect of a turn-around. Increased inflation and increased unemployment — what Iain Macleod had called 'stagflation' — loomed, and no prospect of the new Britain on which Margaret Thatcher had set her eye yet showed itself. Whatever the effect of her excursions into foreign policy had been, things at home were going from bad to worse.

· CHAPTER FOUR ·

The Battles of the Budget

The point that is relevant for us is that if we are determined not to allow unemployment at any price, and are not willing to use coercion, we shall be driven to all sorts of desperate expedients, none of which can bring any lasting relief and all of which will seriously interfere with the most productive use of our resources. It should be specially noted that monetary policy cannot provide a real cure for this difficulty except by a general and considerable inflation, sufficient to raise all other wages and prices relative to those that cannot be lowered, and that even this would bring about the desired result only by effecting in a concealed and underhand fashion that reduction of real wages which would not be brought about directly. Yet to raise all other wages and incomes to an extent sufficient to adjust the position of the group in question would involve an inflationary expansion on such a scale that the disturbances, hardships, and injustices caused would be much greater than those to be cured.
— F. A. Hayek, *The Road to Serfdom* (London, 1976 edn.)

Sir Geoffrey Howe's third budget, in 1981, represented, at least in the field of economic policy, the true strategic beginning of the introduction of Thatcherism[1] into government. 'Things were to seem very bad later,' said one minister, 'and she had rough times with colleagues, with the press, and with the electorate. But for me the really black period was the summer and autumn of 1980, because everything then was so muddled. Nobody really knew what to do or who was making the decisions. And it was clear that neither the 1979 nor the 1980 budgets were having the intended effect, even though we had to go round defending them.' This defence involved, as William Keegan rightly points out,[2] the rhetorical reiteration of one of the fundamental theses of monetarist philosophy, that government expenditure, not wage increases, causes inflation. Even Nigel Lawson, the Financial Secretary to the Treasury, and one of the most intellectually rigorous of men, was guilty of a defence of government policy which was largely spurious. For when, as in Britain, government is itself an employer on so large a scale that its outgoings on salaries and wages are a crucial part of public expenditure, then such actions as the unthinking acceptance of the Clegg recommendations, combined with the over-eager tax cuts of the 1979 budget, undoubtedly contributed to that steady rise in inflation which it was the Prime Minister's principal and most determinedly held object to reduce.

There were perfectly understandable reasons why, by the autumn of 1980, the government was floundering. Some of them were due less to circumstances — over which no politician can exert more than a certain amount of control — than to its own action and inaction. It is important to remember, none the less, that even in the economic field decisions were taken during the period between the general election and the 1981 budget which did effectively represent and encapsulate both the intentions and the tactics of the Prime Minister and her closest advisers. Indeed, one senior minister believes that, for all the importance of the 1981 budget in the history of the government, and for all that it demonstrated a badly needed recovery (in terms of policy) of ground lost in the first year and a half of office, important things had been done before. 'Nineteen eighty-one,' he says, 'was necessary, no doubt about that. If we hadn't got a grip of things then we'd have been on the run. But implicit or explicit in the seventy-nine

97

budget were the abolition of all controls on prices and incomes, the removal of exchange controls and the long-term commitment, expressed in the dramatic increases in VAT, to shift from direct to indirect taxation. Whatever you think of the merits of these policies they were precisely the kind of thing we had promised, and bang in line with the free-market philosophy.' There is a good deal to be said for that point of view; but the fact remains that towards the end of 1980 the central management of the economy seemed to verge on chaos and there were many — not all, by any means, ancient critics of the Prime Minister — who began to wonder whether she could cope. After all, by May 1980 inflation stood at 21.9 per cent, and by the end of the year unemployment exceeded two million.

There were a number of reasons why this situation had arisen. The world recession proved to be an unexpectedly deep one, and the effect of the government's measures on industry and employment were greater than anticipated, thus making the Prime Minister's critics bolder and her allies more nervous. No matter how reasonable it was to blame a part of their difficulties on the world recession, however, it was not readily acceptable, when offered as an excuse by men and a woman who had so scornfully declined retrospectively to accept exactly the same excuse from the defenders of the record of the Heath government.

Besides the recession there were other reasons why the government, by the autumn of 1980, was, as one of its members put it, 'afloat without a rudder'. They were three in number, and one contained important elements of the paradoxical. The first of these was the absence of detailed commitments in previous policy documents, and particularly in the 1979 manifesto. The second was the continuity of opposition to her within her own party between the period before and then after the election. And the third was her method of running the government and the reaction to that method.

In the first case, the Prime Minister had not, in opposition, thought through in detail the implications for policy and administration of her change of the philosophical direction of the Conservative Party. As explained in the last chapter, she has a capacity to see and accept even the unpleasant consequences of a policy she thinks right, and is thus stronger in crisis than politicians often are: indeed, she was to show this strength throughout 1980 and the early part of 1981. But, in the run-up to the 1979 general election, influenced, perhaps, by the excitement of events, she made promises she should not have made and on the other hand, influenced more certainly by the caution which from time to time afflicts her, she failed to spell out things that should have been spelled out. She was bounced, during the campaign, into her unwise undertaking to respect the recommendations of the Clegg Commission and although David Howell in particular, and others of her advisers less emphatically, advised her to repudiate that rash undertaking once she was in office, she refused to do so. Further, she was never as clear in public as she was in private about the fact that her central tenet of economic policy — the monetarist doctrine of cutting money supply — was even on the most optimistic prediction bound to cause hardship. Within the ranks of the academic monetarists themselves — at the Institute of Economic Affairs, for example, or among those surrounding Professor Milton Friedman in Chicago, the debate was about how long the period of unpleasant impact would be, following the introduction of a monetarist budget. In such circles, however, the debate was sophisticated and impeccably detailed:[3] the argument came down to numbers of months and, in some cases, weeks. In the political arena everything was much vaguer, not least because, however attractive a programme of Cromwellian austerity may sometimes be to an intelligent electorate (and, indeed, the British electorate was about to show its willingness to take massive doses over the coming years) no politician seeking office is eager to describe it in every lineament.

But the failure to spell things out — such as was demonstrated both in the anodyne if elegantly written policy document *The Right Approach to the Economy*[4] and in the 1979 manifesto — had repercussions. It was readily argued, both within and without the party, when some unexpected action was proposed or taken, that there was no mandate for it. 'You didn't tell us that before the election,' was a repeated and often ferocious cry, carrying with it the implication that Margaret Thatcher and Geoffrey Howe had been less than frank with the electorate while seeking power. Conversely, the Prime Minister and her Cabinet allies could not, when doing something that excited particular opposition, appeal to the manifesto as the fount of authority.

Appeals to the manifesto, under governments of either party, have become rather too frequent in recent years, as manifestos, until the Conservative Party's of 1979, have become too long. The process started with Edward Heath between 1965 and 1970. Heath was then embarking on the adoption of a policy quite as radical as that of 1975–79, and it was in his dogged nature to demonstrate to the people that everything had been thoroughly worked out. Policy document succeeded policy document; the manifesto itself was lengthy; and for quite some time the Prime Minister used to take a copy of it to Cabinet meetings where part of the business of the day would be a detailed checking with ministers on how far they had gone in keeping the promises which lay within their remit.

At the same time a similar process was taking place within the Labour Party. A dissatisfaction aroused in the breasts of Labour activists — especially but not solely on the left — with the failure to keep promises of the first two Wilson governments led to a greater and greater determination to tie Labour Shadow Cabinets and Cabinets down to highly specific promises of action to be taken in office. Cabinets felt at least partially hamstrung; they were slow in that reaction to the unexpectedness of events in which all successful governments must be speedy; and when they had to react to events by abandoning or curtailing promises the dissatisfaction of their followers increased.

Margaret Thatcher looked back to the Heath experience and at the continuing dispute within the Labour Party with profound suspicion. It may seem odd that a woman so distinguished in her political working life by an appetite for paper — we know that there is almost no day in which she goes to sleep before digesting every document in her dispatch boxes; her colleagues and advisers know that every brief must be meticulously complete; and anybody who has ever helped her with a speech knows that the reading programme required as background to it may well amount to the equivalent of the research needed for the preparation of a small scholarly book — is so averse to the kind of manifesto detail in which Edward Heath delighted, and which he felt to be indispensable to honest politics. But there it is.

We know that she has been influenced by some writing on the history of manifestos and on their more recent character. But the real reason for her dislike of over-much detail in published policy documents has, I believe, a more personal source. No modern politician is more adept at debate. This was so from the beginning. On her debut in the House of Commons as a junior minister she, as the *Liverpool Daily Post* reported, 'left MPs stunned by statistics'. As Russell Lewis records, they were so stunned that the Speaker had to call twice for further contributions before any member rose to rebut her. But she regards the use of detail in this fashion as a part of cut and thrust. All the speeches she regards as important are notably bereft of detail, and whatever in the way of industry has gone into their preparation, they are marked for being high on generality. Detail she regards as a foundation for the conclusion. The conclusion is what is uttered. In this she conforms, in her political practice, to Ernest Hemingway's artistic dictum that material digested in drafts can safely be left out of the finished product, but that its force will none the less be felt.[5] A policy document, a manifesto, a major speech is and should be, she believes, a distillation: the place for detail is before.

The second point about the difficulties in which the Prime Minister and the government found themselves during 1980 concerns the continuity of the opposition to her within her own party. In the heady days after her victory on 3 May 1979 it might have seemed to the public and to the press that her triumph was absolute: it did not seem so to herself, nor to her Conservative critics for whom, it might be said, the motto was *La lutte continue.*

Their position was all the stronger in that the manifesto commitments were so imprecise; in that her Cabinet appointments seemed to reflect either a desire to balance all factions within the party or her fear of her critics; and in that two at least of her known supporters within the Cabinet, John Biffen, Chief Secretary to the Treasury, and Sir Keith Joseph, Secretary of State for Industry, seemed to hesitate, if not exactly quail, in the face of their responsibilities and the storms blowing up in the national economy.

It is true that her initial Cabinet appointments were at first seen as finely judged. Those members of her Shadow Cabinet — a majority — who had dissented from her developing economic policy were kept away from the major spending departments. On the other hand Francis Pym, the new Secretary of State for Defence, hitherto seen, if not as a Thatcher loyalist at least not as a critic either, was, in November 1980, revealed as a rebel. Peter Walker who as Secretary of State for Agriculture presided over a virtually sacrosanct spending programme and was in any event expected to be fully occupied in negotiations with the EEC, none the less proved able and willing to argue the toss whenever the opportunity arose. And finally James Prior, at the Department of Employment, was a member of the 'E' Committee of the Cabinet — that charged with the general oversight of the economy. He could and did plausibly argue that as unemployment steadily rose he had a duty to concern himself with the argument for policies — of reflation — which might provide amelioration.

None of this would have mattered very much if the provisions of the 1979 budget had been seen to have something of their intended effect. But as 1979 and 1980 wore on it seemed to be evident that there was no trade-off between inflation and unemployment: both continued to rise. This was not what the Prime Minister had intended, or believed would happen.

The opposing propositions may be put quite simply. Traditional thinking about the economy and employment, such as had been dominant in both major political parties since the war, dictated that modestly inflationary policies, involving a relatively high level of public spending, kept unemployment down. The prescription was a formula for juggling with the inflation figures as against the unemployment figures. By 1979, however, both inflation and unemployment were high, and the Thatcher government decided that inflation was at the root of the problem. The Prime Minister willingly — indeed, delightedly — accepted the conquest of inflation as the first charge on her and the government, even if the price to be paid in unemployment was a high one. But neither she nor the Chancellor of the Exchequer believed that the effect of deflationary policies on the unemployment figures would be more than temporary. Cutting public expenditure, it seemed to them, would result, in a relatively short space of time, in a healthier and more competitive British industry that would, in its turn, take up the unemployment slack.

The trouble was that this did not happen and she attracted, therefore, two different kinds of criticism. On the one hand there were those who, like Prior and Patrick Jenkin — the Secretary of State for Social Services — believed that the social and political cost of substantial spending cuts was unacceptable. Such critics — and others, notably Sir Ian Gilmour, the Lord Privy Seal and Foreign Office spokesman in the House of Commons, author of a number of studies on the nature and history of Conservatism — blamed the country's difficulties principally on the world recession and rising oil prices and favoured ameliorative spending policies to cushion the people from hardship until times improved. On the other hand, there were those who believed that the government was excessively timid in its approach to the harsh business of bringing down public spending. The most important of the latter was Enoch Powell who, in a memorable speech in the House of Commons in November 1980, savagely assailed the government for its pusillanimity. While in the same debate Edward Heath attacked the Prime Minister from the other side of the argument his criticism, which could be put down to disgruntlement and envy, was less hurtful than Powell's, because Powell had been one of the seminal influences on the thinking of Margaret Thatcher and Keith Joseph. Indeed, though he had left the Conservative Party in 1974, a collection of his speeches, *Freedom and Reality*,[6] was one of her favourite pieces of reading.

In any event, inflation and unemployment alike went on remorselessly rising. In remarkable contrast to Harold Wilson in 1967 and Edward Heath in 1972, the Prime Minister decided that this state of affairs required not a change of policy but an intensification of policy.

This decision brings us to the third reason for the difficulties the government found itself in at the end of 1980. It is, very simply, the controversy and resentment aroused by the way in which the Prime Minister chose to run the government. Yet — and here is the paradox — there was no other way than the one she chose if she was to carry through her policies.

Although the public became gradually aware of the fact

that the full Cabinet was never given the opportunity of considering economic policy as a whole (the first of a series of
such discussions took place in June 1981, and the interval
between the 1979 general election and that date is without
precedent in modern British political history), consciousness
of the controversy she was provoking grew principally
through anecdotes about her manner which was, to put it
mildly, abrasive.

'I simply could not believe,' said one member of her first
Cabinet, 'how rude she could be to Keith. After all, he was her
friend. If she treated him like that what hope was there for the
rest of us?' On another occasion she detected an inconsistency
in a briefing document from the Foreign Office. Lord Carrington, the Foreign Secretary, apologised for the error. 'It's not
just an error,' she replied, 'it's incompetence, and it comes
from the top.' A number of ministers regularly regaled — if
that is the right word — the press with such stories. Her
government came to be known as one of the most leak-prone
of modern times, and if the principal cause of this was the fact
that ministers, baulked in the pursuit of their own objectives,
used journalists as a court of frustrated appeal, another was
surely the very human reaction of individuals who had been
subjected to her particular brand of conversational terrorism.

It should not be forgotten, of course, that Margaret
Thatcher has a remarkable record of gaining, and holding, the
loyalty of those who work for her. Penny Junor — whose biography, together with that by Tricia Murray is as much, or
more, concerned with the Prime Minister as a human being
than as a politician[7] — more than once records[8] her failure to
discover a single former member of Margaret Thatcher's staff
who was not utterly devoted to her. Her legendary concern
for others extends to the private, though not the public, or
political, lives of her colleagues, though even in the latter area
there are exceptions: Norman St John Stevas, for all that he
was later to become embittered by her treatment of him, had

particular reason to remember with gratitude an occasion when, as her junior minister at the Department of Education, he failed to turn up for an important House of Commons debate. Without complaint or reproach, and unbriefed, she stood in for him. Nevertheless, and fiercely though members of her private office insisted on her humanity as the criticism mounted, her behaviour unquestionably exacerbated existing tensions within the ranks of the government.

Her capacity to enrage is something she either denies or ignores, and it is certainly true that she rarely intends to wound. The frequent brusqueness and dismissiveness of her manner is, rather, a function of that bustling desire to get on with the job that is one of her most engaging characteristics. What she has never seemed able to understand is that what one can only call her attacks of motherliness, if they follow a tirade, can be almost as offensive as the tirade itself. William Keegan, discussing the appalling state her relations with Gordon Richardson, the Governor of the Bank of England (and, incidentally, a Heath appointment) had reached by the middle of 1980, reports a Bank official as saying, 'I'm not sure which Gordon found more distasteful: having his word questioned by that woman, or being forced by her to eat a cream bun at the end of one of her attacks.' Although it is a matter for discussion in a later chapter, it is also worth recording here that her treatment of — and her suspicion of — civil servants was even harsher than her treatment of her political colleagues. At all events it should be noted that it is another personal characteristic that she reacts to crisis with heightened energy, and repays criticism with savage volleys of her own, the wounding effect of which she frequently fails to appreciate. Her attitude in the face of mounting economic crisis in 1980 was to deny any possibility of a change of policy. At a CBI dinner in 1980 she quoted approvingly an American general in difficulties towards the end of the First World War: 'Retreat? Hell, no. We just got here.'

But words, even the fiercest, even the most defiant, were not enough to get her her way, or to impose those policies she most fervently believed in. For that cunning and determination were required.

Getting the 1979 budget past the Cabinet was not an especially difficult task. The election victory was so recent, and the urgency of presenting a Finance Bill to Parliament so evident that prolonged scrutiny of what she and Geoffrey Howe proposed to do was impossible. The testing time began immediately afterwards.

Like all Conservative politicians Margaret Thatcher professes an avid admiration of Winston Churchill. Unlike most of them she is thoroughly familiar with his writing. When she told Kenneth Harris in his much-quoted interview with her in the *Observer* in 1979 that she knew she would be given only one chance to lead her party at a general election, and that she would be summarily dismissed in the event of failure, she had been re-reading Churchill's *The Second World War*. At the time she was especially fond, when relaxing over a drink, of quoting from the chapter in the second volume describing the construction of the coalition government of 1940.[9] 'A Constitution,' Churchill quoted Napoleon as saying, 'should be short and obscure', and this maxim he used to justify his own refusal to spell out what powers he was arrogating to himself as Minister of Defence. But she is also particularly fond of a disquisition on leadership. 'At the top,' Churchill wrote,

there are great simplifications. An accepted leader has only to be sure of what it is best to do, or at least to have made up his mind about it. The loyalties which centre upon number one are enormous. If he trips he must be sustained. If he makes mistakes they must be covered. If he sleeps he must not be wantonly disturbed. If he is no good he must be pole-axed. But this last extreme process cannot be carried out every day; and certainly not in the days just after he has been chosen.

Of course, the situation in 1979 was not the same as in 1940, and Margaret Thatcher is not Winston Churchill. But the parallels were sufficient to be sustaining for her: in both cases there was a critical situation, a divided party (it is too readily forgotten by Conservatives today how many of the party's MPs simply refused to applaud Churchill's early speeches as Prime Minister), and a single-minded Prime Minister. And just as Churchill ran his government as an extension of his own personality, so was she determined to do.

Because of the sharpness of her personality, because of her relative lack of experience in high office, and because the intellectual rifts between members of her government were so serious, the extent to which she has behaved dictatorially has been somewhat exaggerated. The example of Churchill has been quoted. But it is generally true that most prime ministers operate, as far as they can, with some kind of inner Cabinet: Lord Wilson of Rievaulx and Edward Heath most certainly did so. Moreover, Heath was an abrupt and abrasive Cabinet chairman, cutting short discussion on frequent occasions, and behaving to his colleagues in a manner often seen as domineering. Loquacity, however, was not one of the features of his conduct, as it is of hers. Her loquacity, indeed, is one of the things about her that most irritates: 'An interview with her always turns into a speech by her,' one colleague says, 'and the speech is invariably a catalogue without cerebral content. I don't mean to say she's not clever. She is. And what is more, her capacity to take a decision and stick to it is admirable. But she very rarely pauses for reflection. All her so-called philosophising consists of the reiteration of conclusions she came to years ago.' The fact of the matter is that the quirks of her temperament were combined with a necessity to avoid rather than confront her Cabinet critics and this led to a very clear extension of the power of the Prime Minister's office. Certainly, she built on some things Wilson and Heath had prepared; but she went much further down the road to a centralisation of policy decision-making.

The most notable overall change, as already remarked, was the refusal to hold general economic discussions at meetings of the full Cabinet. There is no specific obligation laid on the prime minister of the day to provide time for such discussions, but they had hitherto been an occasional, and important, feature of government business. And in 1977, for example, when the International Monetary Fund made it clear to the then Labour government that further credit would not be advanced without the introduction of a package of domestic austerity measures, the issue was taken to the whole Cabinet, and the matter thrashed out there. From the outset of her first term Margaret Thatcher determined that no such exchanges — involving, as they clearly did, the possibility of the spending ministers lining up against herself and her Treasury team — would take place. This is not to say, of course, that specific decisions to spend or to cut did not come before the Cabinet, and from time to time these exploded into general argument about the fundamental direction of economic policy. Even when that happened, however, the Prime Minister's technique kept the potential rebels from forming ranks: it was her practice, instead of allowing ministers to speak as the spirit — or their worries — moved them, to invite opinions one by one, and herself to conduct, often fiercely, individual arguments with each one. Here the force of her personality was a decisive weapon, for she bore down opposition by her vehemence, even where she could not convince by her logic.

The decline of the Cabinet as a forum for the discussion of economic policy necessarily led to the elevation of Committee 'E', the principal economic committee of the Cabinet chaired by the Prime Minister and consisting, at least in theory, of the

Chancellor and the main economic ministers. It became clear, however, that even here she could not be sure of getting her way, and early in 1981 the press learned, not that 'E' had ceased to exist but that it no longer met, as it always had, on Tuesday of each week and, indeed, that it had not, at the time of the reports, met for five weeks. The official reason given for the planned and deepening desuetude of this once-powerful body was the need for security: there were, it was said, too many leaks, and government policy quite simply had to be discussed in confidence. On the other hand, it was learned, a new committee — dubbed by its critics the 'Star Chamber' — had come into existence, consisting of Howe, Biffen, the Deputy Prime Minister and Home Secretary William Whitelaw and Christopher (Lord) Soames, the leader of the House of Lords and last Governor of Rhodesia. The words 'wet'[10] and 'dry' to describe the Prime Minister's critics and supporters respectively were by now in fashion, and it was pointed out that the committee was perfectly balanced as between the two factions. This justification was spurious for, while Howe had a massively detailed grasp of his brief, and Biffen was a distinguished economic thinker, neither Whitelaw nor Soames made the slightest pretence to expertise on the matters under discussion. The method of operation of the committee, moreover, ensured that the balance of debate went almost invariably in favour of the Chancellor and the Chief Secretary, for the system was for individual spending ministers to appear before the quartet and submit to quizzing on their departmental budgets. Of course ministers defeated in the 'Star Chamber' could appeal to the Cabinet, and some — notably Francis Pym, who in November 1980 resisted the imposition of cuts in the defence budget through the threat of resignation — succeeded. But it was a haphazard and toilsome business. Suffice it to say that while the Prime Minister often did not get her way in detail, she did get her way in general.

Still, by the end of 1979 it was clear not merely that there was no light on the horizon but that the Chancellor was unlikely to achieve his targets. The process of cutting into public expenditure would have to continue; indeed, it might become a permanent feature of government.

It was necessary, therefore, for the Treasury team not merely to impose cuts, but to devise a system of surveillance and control of economic activity which would operate almost automatically. Since economic policy as seen by the Prime Minister and the Chancellor had as its most important element the control of the amount of money in the economy (which control, they believed, would reduce and eventually eliminate inflation), a satisfactory method of calculating the money supply was required. Over and above all this it was clear that the principal target for thrift was the Public Sector Borrowing Requirement (PSBR).

It is necessary, here, to define some of the problems and terms more technically than hitherto, so that what follows can be clearly understood. Put simply, PSBR is the amount the government needs to borrow each year to make up the difference between its revenue from taxation and its spending. Under the dictates of the doctrines of John Maynard Keynes, post-war governments have in general believed that PSBR should go up during a recession, both to make up for lower tax receipts and to provide for increased social security outlays (due to unemployment) and forward investment. The monetarists who influenced Margaret Thatcher and Geoffrey Howe, on the other hand, believe that excessive government spending and borrowing lead to inflation. Hence the attack on the PSBR.

Measuring the amount of money in the economy is an extremely complicated business. However, given the fundamental belief of the first Thatcher government that control of the supply of money was a crucial weapon in the battle against inflation it was, obviously, necessary to find a satisfactory method of measurement. Alas, there were many such methods on offer, from the relatively simple definition of money as the amount in circulation to ever more complicated and esoteric formulae. By the end of 1980 the Chancellor had decided to settle for a formula known to economists as M3, which comprises both the notes and coins in circulation, and the total sum of bank deposits and building society deposits (known together as PSL2, or Private Sector Liquidity category 2). The reason, of course, for including monies on deposit is that they form the security on which banks and building societies can advance credit or undertake investment and are thus a part of what makes the wheels of the economy go round by creating or satisfying demand. From 1980 onwards, but particularly from the March budget of 1980, Geoffrey Howe used M3 as the basis on which to make all of his calculations about expenditure and taxation. Unfortunately, it was to prove a dangerously inadequate formula, and M3 figures never gave anything other than contradictory indications about the future activity of the economy.

As time went on it became clear that it was highly desirable — indeed, that it might well be absolutely necessary — to bring some order into the chaos of debilitating individual guerrilla actions on departmental budgets. The new Chief Economic Adviser to the Treasury, Dr Terry Burns, a monetarist sympathetic to the objectives and tactics of the Prime Minister, favoured the adoption of a medium-term plan under which clear goals would be set for several years ahead. His ideas were supported enthusiastically by the Financial Secretary, Nigel Lawson, who used his considerable force of intellect and personality to press the plan on politicians unwilling to risk a repetition of such a fiasco as Labour's National Plan of the mid-1960s, a grandiose scheme which collapsed in humiliating futility (though, as William Keegan bitterly observes, the National Plan was a scheme for expansion, while Burns and Lawson were planning contraction).[11]

The debate eventually produced the Medium-Term Financial Strategy which was the heart and soul of the 1980 budget. While Lawson and Burns had initially wanted to set extremely tight and specific targets for monetary growth for each of the next four years, however, they eventually agreed to the targets being set within certain percentage ranges. Thus, the money supply would be allowed to grow by between seven and eleven per cent in 1980–81 but would have declined to between four and eight per cent in the financial year 1983–84. These targets would be achieved by the steady contraction of PSBR and once achieved would make room for tax cuts (coyly entitled 'fiscal adjustments') just before a general election in 1983 or 1984.

There were two difficulties about all this. The first was M3's unreliability as a guide, and since the Medium-Term Financial Strategy (MTFS) was locked in with a deep faith in M3, its targets simply could not be met. The second difficulty was that in devising MTFS the government fell victim to the ancient error of willing the end but not the means. The targets of the strategy were just that and no more: no independent mechanism would be provided to ensure that those targets were met, nor that those who did not strive their best to meet them would be punished, for such kinds of regulations were reminiscent of the prices and incomes policies which the government had abolished. My view (and, I think, the view of the present Chancellor, Nigel Lawson, the political father of MTFS) is that too much hope was vested in the whole idea, and too much was claimed for it at the outset. The Keynesians — and Mr Keegan is among their number — think that the futile chasing after MTFS targets led the government astray in a number of areas over the following years. But in truth it was not at all a bad, and might even be considered a good, thing for the government to have some fairly clearly-set-out idea about where it wanted to go. But it was foolish to believe that the mere statement of aims which its unveiling constituted would mean that those aims would be achieved.

After the 1980 budget matters went on much as before, and as it became clear that MTFS targets were not being met the Chancellor came under increasing pressure. It was then that colleagues, critics and the public alike began to realise that in Geoffrey Howe they had a politician whose willpower matched that of the Prime Minister herself. His self-effacing manner, his invariably lowered voice, and his slightly bumbling manner of speech, together with the owlish expression on the plump face suggesting a rather earnest schoolboy, gave an impression of the ineffectual. In the course of 1980 he needed every ounce of determination he could muster; and it became clear that he had a great deal.

It had been apparent for some time that there was something awry with the exchange rates, the pound being so strong in currency markets as to damage British exports. Further the monetary figures grew worse rather than better as envisaged in the MTFS. Relations between the Prime Minister and the Governor of the Bank of England deteriorated at speed, and when in September 1980 it was announced that over two months the rate of M3 growth was eight per cent whereas the strategy required only a growth of nine per cent in a full year, the Prime Minister laid all the blame at the Bank's door. Finally, amid the catalogue of doom was the fact that British industry was begging for interest rates to come down; expensive money, they believed, was strangling the economy.

The government, even the Prime Minister, were adrift. When in the autumn ICI, the company regarded as the flagship of the British economy, announced a loss, it seemed that the Thatcher experiment was crumbling to disaster. What made matters worse was the fact that almost everybody on whom she called for advice — everybody, that is, within the monetarist school — offered her different reasons for what was happening, and different solutions to her problems. Outside the circle, of course, the critics were baying for a loosening of the monetary squeeze — for, in a word, reflation.

At about this time the Prime Minister took three important decisions. One, on 14 November, was to sanction a cut in interest rates; another was to prepare for a new round of public expenditure cuts; and the third, and perhaps ultimately the most important, was to appoint a personal economic adviser. This was Professor Alan Walters.

Walters, a tall, gangling genius with a bluff, no-nonsense Yorkshire manner, had been one of Britain's early monetarists. He has a capacity, moreover, for boiling down the most complicated and arcane economic arguments to simple formulae without doing violence to their meaning. Some years previously, despairing of ever seeing created in Britain the free-enterprise society of his dreams, he, with his second wife, had emigrated to the United States, where he was professor of economics at Johns Hopkins University in Baltimore and an adviser to the International Monetary Fund. He had, however, collaborated with Keith Joseph in the setting up of the Centre for Policy Studies and was a personal friend of its director, Alfred Sherman. On a visit to London in September 1980 he was recruited to serve as the Prime Minister's non-political right-hand man on economic policy.

The state of the debate within the government — and within the Prime Minister's own circle — was at this time at a highly interesting stage. Most outsiders — and the better part of the media — were convinced that a change of policy was required and that either Mrs Thatcher would be forced to provide it or, if not, that someone else would be found to do the job. John Hoskyns was in charge of the Policy Unit at No. 10 Downing Street and believed that the problem was that the government was not being tough enough. There were those who agreed with him, and feared any slackening of monetary controls, including, though in a qualified way, Samuel Brittan, the economic commentator of the *Financial Times* who had long had the Prime Minister's ear.

At this stage Alfred Sherman suggested that matters might be helped if a complete outsider was called in, as it were, to check the books. Walters nominated Professor Jurg Niehans, from the University of Berne. When Walters took up his appointment in January 1981 Niehans had completed his own work and written up his findings. Two treasured shibboleths of current thinking were exploded. In the first instance Niehans did not believe that the strength of the pound was a function of the fact that Britain was now an oil-exporting country. In the second he believed that M3 was an inadequate instrument for measuring the growth in the money supply.

It was of very great political significance that Niehans' detailed findings corresponded to Walters' fundamental instinct on his earlier visit to London in September. He had been proved right, and he had the political clout to carry the argument to the Prime Minister. Meanwhile, continuing high interest and exchange rates made it increasingly difficult for British companies to raise capital at home and to sell goods abroad; and ministers were girding their loins to face Treasury demands for yet another round of spending cuts. Alan Walters and John Hoskyns came to the conclusion that monetary policy must be relaxed, but it was a corollary of this view that public expenditure should come down further. Many in their circle expressed the view — particularly at a seminar taken by Professor Niehans just after he finished his report — that fiscal policy should be tightened. And here another word of technical explanation is required.

Monetary policy is a response by government to the fact that because it spends so much and borrows so much it is a major — *the* major — force in the market. How it uses the power that fact creates is, obviously, of consequence to everybody. Pre-Thatcherite economists, however, in general believed that the use of this power in monetary policy — principally by varying interest rates — was only one of many ways available to a finance minister in running the economy. The distinguishing characteristic of the monetarist doctrine, however, is that monetary policy is the main, or even the only, way in which governments can and should act on the structure of a national economy, by controlling the supply of money.

Fiscal policy is concerned with the non-monetarist method of economic management. It deals with such matters as taxes, social security and spending on public works. The economists who followed John Maynard Keynes believed that lower taxes and higher public spending increased demand and relieved unemployment. It also brought on the danger of inflation but, provided inflation was kept within limits, the Keynesians believed, it was a worthwhile price to pay for full, or nearly full, employment. It follows from this that such economists are particularly in favour of fiscal action in times of recession, for these are the times when there is much suffering and when, on this argument, government can do most to increase economic activity and hasten a return to prosperity, at which moment it might be necessary to raise taxes and cut public spending to prevent economic overheating. The fiscalist argument, therefore, involves much more detailed control of the economy than does the monetarist. 'The extraordinary contribution,' William Keegan writes in angry horror, 'of the Thatcher government was to reverse the normal Keynesian procedure, and to cut public spending and raise the tax burden when the economy was already in recession.'[12]

While these expert discussions continued (and there was an alternative plan put forward in the Treasury by Terry Burns and Peter Middleton, a senior Treasury civil servant) the purely political dogfight had been continuing. In October 1980 the Prime Minister told the Conservative Party Conference, 'Turn if you like. The lady's not for turning,' but her rapturous reception that year masked a growing sense of unease about the future of her government. Geoffrey Howe announced to stunned colleagues that he would be seeking public spending cuts of £2,000 million in a mini-budget he hoped shortly to present to Parliament. While hitherto the most frequently argued opposition to his policies had been on the ground of their political unacceptability (that is the assumption that they were electorally dangerous), Howe on this occasion turned the tables. If the cuts were not made, he stated, taxes would have to go up and that, too, was politically unacceptable. The most dramatic response to this dramatic *démarche* was that of Francis Pym: he would not, the Secretary of State for Defence declared, accept the suggested cuts of £500 million in his departmental budget. Rather, he would resign.[13] In the end he accepted a reduction of £175 million.

The mini-budget at the end of November provided for £1,000 million by way of increased taxes on North Sea oil, £1,000 million by way of increased National Insurance charges, and £1,000 million by way of cuts in public expenditure. It was in the nature of things, given the debate boiling up in the Treasury and in No. 10 Downing Street about the shape of the 1981 budget, that controversy would now become even more intense.

It behoved the Prime Minister to reduce the political opposition within the ranks of the government. The long war of attrition in Cabinet and by way of formal as well as informal Cabinet committees could not continue. Discussing the options — short of a reversal of policy, which she never contemplated — available to her with Walters and Hoskyns, observing the mounting tide of public criticism (as expressed particularly in unfavourable public opinion polls) and nerving herself to yet another series of hard decisions, she came to the conclusion that the moment had arrived to exercise her authority in the way a Prime Minister most effectively can: by means of a Cabinet and government reshuffle.

It was not a major reshuffle, and did not compare, for example, to that of July 1981 which was to remove or render ineffective all of her major critics. 'It was simply,' as one of her advisers said, 'a crack of the whip over their heads.' The major victim was Norman St John Stevas, Leader of the House of Commons, brilliant in many respects and also a sort of licensed intellectual jester; but a critic of her policies with very little Cabinet or backbench support. Out, too, went Angus Maude, an old ally but one now seeking retirement, and Reg Prentice, a Minister of State in her government, but a former Labour Cabinet minister who had crossed the floor. He had been found a Conservative seat and given Conservative office in the hope of encouraging other Labour moderates to follow him, though that hope was not realised. He was unwell, and he had served his purpose. But the principal move of the reshuffle was the shifting of Pym from Defence to lead the House of Commons. His November rebellion had been so marked that it could not be forgotten: he now had no departmental budget to defend. Finally, at the same time she added Leon Brittan — brother of Samuel of the *Financial Times* and with similar economic views — to the Treasury team, while Norman Fowler, a loyalist, came into the Cabinet with the Transport brief. John Nott was moved to the Ministry of Defence to impose the financial discipline that Francis Pym had refused to accept.

In the middle of January 1981 the Prime Minister held a review meeting at Chequers and the grim news was conveyed to her that all the monetary indicators were getting out of control while continuing high interest rates were squeezing business. A little later Walters, Hoskyns and David Wolfson, her Political Secretary, presented a memorandum encouraging her to consider 'an unthinkably low PSBR'. The Treasury was uneasy, not least because its function of advising governments on economic policy seemed to be undergoing a process of usurpation. There was, however, less difference between

Terry Burns and Alan Walters than the press were, at the time, inclined to suppose. And all debate was, after all, dominated by Margaret Thatcher herself who said, 'I know that we are right. The only question is the mechanics of *getting* it right.'

What was vitally important from the tactical point of view, of course, was that the Cabinet should not learn too much about what was happening. It is true, of course, that Cabinet members are never told budgetary details until the morning of the day when the budget is to be presented. They generally have had in the past, however, a fairly good idea of the drift of things, not least from those wide-ranging discussions of economic policy which were once a feature of British government. It would not by March 1981, moreover, have been unreasonable to expect some retraction of policy, even from Margaret Thatcher. After all, practically the whole of outside opinion was demanding it. The view, in another area, of Walters and Hoskyns that public-sector wage rises in the coming round should be limited to six per cent, having been twenty per cent the previous year, was regarded as laughable to the point of insanity and, indeed, led to a long series of public-sector strikes. Events, thought the critics, would force even the Prime Minister to relent.

It came as a considerable shock, therefore, when on the morning of 10 March 1981 the Chancellor laid before the Cabinet a budget which envisaged taking £4,300 million out of the economy and reducing the PSBR from £13.5 billion to £10.5 billion. This was an action which flew in the face of all previous governmental economic practice. The taxes on oil, drink, cigarettes, petrol and motor cars were all increased. Even then, the Chancellor grimly informed his colleagues, he was by no means certain that he should not have gone for an increase in income tax as well. 'It is not too much to say,' one dissenting minister later reminisced, 'that we were all reduced to a state of catatonic shock.'

If Geoffrey Howe's message was grim that of the Prime

Minister was grimmer. The dissenters — notably Peter Walker, James Prior and Sir Ian Gilmour, but including Francis Pym and Christopher Soames — had a clear choice: they could support the budget or resign, and their decision, of course, would have to be made in a matter of hours. She was prepared to concede that in future there would be better opportunities for all ministers to engage in Cabinet discussions on economic policy, but for now the die was cast.

There is a certain amount of evidence that at least one of those who decided to stay believed that the budget would provoke such an economic crisis that the Prime Minister herself would be forced to resign. For whatever reasons — unwillingness to provoke a governmental crisis of unimaginable magnitude, lack of courage, reaction to the sheer dominance of the Prime Minister, or simple division within their ranks which she had so patiently engineered since the beginning of the government's life — all the critics decided to stay. It did not increase her respect for them and later in the year she began to pick them off more ruthlessly than she had done in the first 1981 reshuffle.

What the Chancellor and the Prime Minister achieved on 10 March amounted almost to a coup. The budget, naturally, provoked savage opposition criticism and in general had a bad press (which led her only to recall Iain Macleod's maxim that the ultimate judgement of a budget is the reverse of the instant reaction to it). Through the spring and summer months she was constantly out and about defending what she and Howe had done. And then the rate of inflation began to fall.

The 1981 budget was the crucial event of the first Thatcher term, and that judgement stands whether one is a supporter or a critic of the Prime Minister. Its crucial character was, moreover, bound up with her own personality.

It is a commonly held belief in Britain — particularly in the Civil Service — that office blunts the appetite of radical politicians. It was therefore — and on the basis of past experience not unreasonably — assumed that Margaret Thatcher would give her monetarist notions a run in government and that when they failed to work she would change them. It is a common belief, further, that the early life of a government carries the seed of its fate: if it fails then it never recovers.

This dictum has applied with depressing frequency. Shortly after the 1959 general election, which was a triumph, Harold Macmillan's administration ran into the sand. It is true, of course, that the Conservative Party had been in power since 1951, and might reasonably have been tired. But Macmillan had just had his first (and, as it turned out only) general election victory and he should have been still full of running. If we take the 1964 and 1966 general elections together (since there was never much doubt that Wilson would seek a stronger mandate at a very early date after his narrow victory of 1964) we can see that 1966 and 1967 were watershed years. The devaluation of sterling, after so many assurances that it was something the government would never contemplate, was a defeat that issued in the larger defeat of the 1970 general election. Edward Heath, having assumed the reins of power, attempted policies not at all dissimilar to those later adopted by Margaret Thatcher. By 1972 they seemed not to be working, and Heath changed course, only to go down to defeat in 1974. Similarly, in 1977 the Callaghan government accepted the fiat of the International Monetary Fund, survived in office only with the aid of a motley collection of minority parties, and duly went down at the polls in 1979.

I would not say that the moral of this summary is that changes of policy are necessarily preludes to disaster. But there does seem to be at least *prima facie* evidence first, that there are tremendous, almost irresistible, pressures to change radical policies and, second, that the change unhinges the rhythm of continuing belief in purpose of a government. Margaret Thatcher endured more intense pressure to change than has any modern prime minister, and her faith in the essence of what she was doing never wavered. By her enemies this is considered proof of an exceptional and unthinking stubbornness; by her friends it is thought to show a courage and determination unmatched in modern (post-war) political history. The consequence of sticking to her guns in March 1981 conditioned everything that happened in the domestic political field for the rest of her first term.

· CHAPTER FIVE ·

Work in Progress

It is a common observation, that mankind were originally equal. They have indeed by nature equal rights to their preservation, and to the use of their talents; but they are fitted for different stations; and when they are classed by a rule taken from this circumstance, they suffer no injustice on the side of their natural rights. It is obvious, that some mode of subordination is as necessary to men as society itself; and this, not only to attain the ends of government, but to comply with an order established by nature.

— Adam Ferguson, *History of Civil Society* (London, 1823)

In October 1982 John Hoskyns, who had left No. 10 Downing Street a few months previously, made a speech to the Institute of Fiscal Studies. Like most of his recent writing and speeches this one made clear that he had departed the service of the Prime Minister because he had failed to gain sufficiently wide and powerful support for his views on the absolute necessity of drastic reform in the structure of the Civil Service. Without such reform, Hoskyns believes, the achievements of any reforming government will be evanescent. The Prime Minister and he continue to like and respect one another: they parted company largely because, while she takes very little interest in the machinery of government, he is preoccupied with that subject to the point of obsession. This is not to say that she is not attentive to the importance of bending the Civil Service to her will. As the next chapter will show, her time in office had been marked by a spectacular, and spectacularly successful, assault on the assumptions and personnel of Whitehall. But, unlike her quondam adviser, she is sceptical about the necessity of changing the institutions themselves.

Hoskyns made his fortune through his foundation of a company specialising in the use of computers and in efficiency analysis in business. It was after he had sold this company that he first offered his services to Margaret Thatcher, while she was still Leader of the Opposition. On the basis of the bare details of his record, therefore, it would be easy to think of him as a bloodless, though perhaps fanatical, systems analyst. Yet the tone of his speech to the Institute contradicts — as do others of his writings — that image. It was with raw patriotic fervour that he told his audience, after suggesting that the first necessity in Whitehall was to fire every civil servant over fifty and begin again, that 'The first thing to realise about civil servants is that few, if any, believe that the country can be saved.' Here is the authentic note, the passion being as important as the words, of Margaret Thatcher and those who support her. This is not to say, of course, that other politicians (including those in other parties) are unpatriotic, or less patriotic than Margaret Thatcher. It is simply that the concept is more palpable to her than to perhaps any other major British politician with the exception of Enoch Powell. I choose John Hoskyns to illustrate the extension of the feeling to her entourage principally because such open emotionalism is rarely associated with men of his kind of professional expertise.

I have already illustrated the kind of misunderstanding about her intentions that can arise when an observer or reader of one of her speeches fails to understand that her concept of things is not always the same as that of other politicians — that, often, she is speaking in what amounts to a different language from them, and from the basis of different values.[1]

The patriotism is the apex of a whole series of moral values, on the origins of which in her youth at Grantham all of her biographers have dwelt at length. The values are all simple ones — of thrift, work, application and individualism — and they are most famously etched in those comparisons between household and national economics which have earned her such repeated derision. The important point is that they are deeply embedded in her character, and if recognition of that fact has often led to complaints that she has had no new general thoughts since she was a girl, the fact that that is the case shows that they are a singular source of strength to her. Over the years she has, certainly, drifted away from the Methodism of her youth (her children were baptised in the Church of England) and she went through at least one period of her life, just after her election to Parliament, of dislike for her native Grantham.[2] But the fundamentals have never changed. And it was because of them that, after becoming Leader of her party in the way that she did, she approached the task of preparing for government with a missionary zeal.

More patrician Conservatives, notably Francis Pym and Ian Gilmour,[3] dislike and distrust zealotry, and regard it as alien to the Conservative tradition, though there have, of course, been highly innovative Tory governments in the past. The context in which one should see the reaction of Conservative critics — such as Gilmour in particular — not only to the substance of Margaret Thatcher's policies, but to her style and manner of carrying them out, is the post-war consensus commonly knows as Butskellism, in which the two main parties agreed on the broad aims of economic and social policy and differed only on the means of achieving them and, elsewhere, only on the margins of public policy.

But — and this cannot too often be emphasised — the first Conservative attempt to break with this consensus was made not by Margaret Thatcher, but by Edward Heath between

1965 (when he became Leader of the party) and 1972, when he reversed a number of the most important policies on which he had been elected in 1970. The contrast between the two prime ministers in their reaction to adversity is an instructive one.

In his time as Leader of the Opposition he demonstrated that he, no less than she later, had a vision for the future of Britain which would involve a reversal of the nation's comparative decline over the years. In his determination to lead the country into the European Economic Community, for example, he displayed a will equal to her own on economic policy in 1980–81. There were, however, two great weaknesses.

The first lay in his attitude to the EEC. It was clear that he saw no future for the country outside the European grouping, and it was later made clear, in the referendum on membership held by the Wilson government, that the electorate agreed with him. But he embraced that conviction with enthusiasm while the people embraced it reluctantly. Insensibly, his European advocacy drew him away from identification with the electorate in their prejudices and whims as well as in their beliefs. Such drawing away from the roots would be impossible for Margaret Thatcher, so completely does she identify herself with the people. It may well be, of course, that this identification is based on a somewhat idealised picture of the average citizen; but even her worst enemies do not deny that she seems able to touch a popular chord in a way no other leading politician can. As Andrew Gamble has written '... unless Labour can recapture the "popular" from Thatcherism, it will remain on the defensive, ideologically and politically, and threatened by decline into a permanent minority position.'[4]

The second weakness lay in Heath's addiction to a managerialist philosophy. During his years as Leader he consulted every conceivable strand of opinion in the nation for advice on what a Conservative government should do in power: his attention flattered experts, and he was remarkably open in his attitude to their recommendations. Some regarded this as laudable; others had their doubts. 'It's all very well,' observed the psychiatrist Dr Anthony Clare, after hearing Heath give the closing address at a conference on mental health to which he had himself spoken, 'but what's Conservative about it?' This marked failure to nourish the roots of Toryism stood Heath in poor stead during and after the elections of 1974. Before that, in 1972, he was assailed by the conviction that the policies espoused in 1970 had failed, so he adopted a new set. There was a heavy blow, in doing this, to his *amour propre*, but he could not see in reality that he had done anything wrong, or damaging.

The mechanistic view of policy-making is utterly alien to Margaret Thatcher. It is fair to say, of course, as her Tory critics do say, that she has by her words and actions sought to establish a strand of Conservatism as the whole of that tradition. But at least it *is* a strand, and an important one, and her remarkable success in gaining and holding the urgent fidelity of the party in the country, while at the same time gaining sufficient purchase on the non-Tory electorate to acquire and hold office, entitles her to act with great authority in redefining what the Conservative tradition is. Again, as Andrew Gamble says ' . . . the New Right has won the battle to shape the new consensus on how to respond to the recession. The new agenda of public policy will reflect their priorities, and the opposition parties will be pulled along in their wake.'[5]

The truth of Gamble's remarks I will discuss later. For the moment it is important to define and emphasise the sources of inner strength which sustained the Prime Minister in her attempt to change the assumptions of the British political system by, in essence, injecting her own set of moral and cultural values into that system. Just after her election victory in 1983 she told an American television interviewer:

> When the ratings were very bad it was an acutely difficult time for us, and nevertheless I knew that we had to do certain things economically in order to get things right in the longer run. There are certain right ways to go, and you have to stick to it long enough to get the results. We were doing that: then along came the Falklands, one applied just exactly the same principles.

There is expressed the fundamental principle of her political activity: all problems, all challenges, are to be met with exactly the same blend of resolution and defiance. This is because all problems are susceptible to attack by a politician possessing the right convictions in sufficient strength. This is not to say that she is never defeated, or that she never gives way, though the giving way often consists of a purely tactical withdrawal. In 1981, for example, when a coal strike threatened, she over-rode her Secretary of State for Energy and yielded to the National Union of Mineworkers.[6] But she promptly began the build-up of coal stocks which placed her in so powerful a position in 1984. In matters of perhaps lesser consequence her rhetorical habit of dissociating herself from the government of which she is head when she has failed to win an argument is a facet of her singularly self-contained approach to all matters of business.

Once the 1981 budget was through that character — that resoluteness — was put yet again under particular strain. In some respects the task she faced then was the hardest she ever faced, for it required her to wait to see the effect of that budget. Even she, moreover, knew that something had to give. She had conceded to her opponents in the Cabinet the principle of general economic discussion, and the first such debate was to take place in June. The public opinion polls were set steadily against her: for the first eighteen months after the 1979 election they showed both James Callaghan well ahead of her personally, and the Labour Party comfortably ahead of the Conservatives. Towards the end of 1981, indeed, Gallup carried out an elaborate poll which suggested that forty-eight per cent of the electorate believed she would be remembered as the worst Prime Minister ever. Against such figures as these it was little consolation to officials in Conservative Central Office to be able to note that listeners to BBC Radio (where her frequent appearances on the 'Jimmy Young Show' were designed to develop her supposed rapport with housewives) had voted her Personality of the Year, or that there was a generally high opinion of her conduct of foreign affairs.[7]

The blunt fact of the matter was that she knew there would be no chance for a further budget like that of March 1981 unless there were favourable changes in her circumstances. At the June Cabinet review of the economy her known critics — Prior, Gilmour and Pym — were joined in greater or lesser measure by the Lord Chancellor, Lord Hailsham, and the Secretary of State for the Environment, Michael Heseltine, while even John Biffen and John Nott expressed doubts and fears about the future.

Nor was Britain outside the Cabinet room looking any friendlier to a beleaguered Prime Minister. It had always been a fear of her critics that her economic policies, while bringing no success, would provoke social disorder. The rush into anarchy seemed to begin with a series of riots in major cities in the summer. The press noted, and jeered at, the fact that the government was prepared, through the medium of its most famous monetarist, Sir Keith Joseph, to sanction large drafts of cash both for British Steel and for British Leyland, and the defence that these were justified as investment preparatory to selling off both industries to private owners was greeted with scepticism. And when the Prime Minister herself intervened in the dispute with the National Union of Mineworkers to sanction the withdrawal of a plan to close twenty pits, to boost government investment in the industry and to reduce imports, the Secretary of State, David Howell, hitherto one of her strongest supporters, told her that he had great misgivings. She replied. 'It'll be forgotten in a week. And it gives us time to get ready.' Her thinking here was purely political: she had seen how action by the miners had brought down the Heath government in 1974, and she did not believe that the time for a confrontation, which she thought would come, was the middle of 1981. 'You see,' she said to a friend who supported Howell in his willingness to make a stand, 'I don't at all mind having enemies. But not too many at the same time, please.'

The year also saw a prolonged and bitter confrontation with the Civil Service unions, issuing in a series of strikes, as a direct result of her acceptance of the advice proffered by Walters and Hoskyns to the effect that their pay increase for the year should be no more than six per cent. Attitudes to these disputes deeply soured relations between the Prime Minister and Christopher Soames, the minister responsible, who was not allowed, for months, to relax the Hoskyns–Walters target by as much as half a per cent. In the end, however, he got his way, though she excluded twenty civil servants from the New Year's Honours List as a direct result of their opposition to her policies. Only she herself, and the Chancellor, dared make much of the fact that, in May 1981 inflation was recorded at 11.7 per cent, 10 per cent down on the figure of a year earlier.

In the maelstrom of events and arguments men and women were moved by all sorts of considerations, some being principled, and some practical. When Ian Gilmour exclaimed, at the Cabinet meeting of 21 July 1981 — the second of those promised by the Prime Minister with a view to allowing a general discussion of economic policy — 'This is the end of the Tory Party', he was being both. He had just heard the

Chancellor of the Exchequer say, in that unemphatic and almost sleepy way of his, that the Treasury would require a further £5 billion in public expenditure cuts. This was a moment of the highest possible risk for the Prime Minister, for she knew in her heart that the kind of outright budgetary victory she had enjoyed earlier in the year was unlikely to be won a second time around.

The motives of her opponents were mixed. There is no reason to doubt that men like Gilmour and Hailsham, Pym and Walker, were appalled by the events of the summer, by the riots in Southall and Brixton, Liverpool and Manchester. They were appalled by the rapidly rising figures of unemployment. They could not see that the policies in hand would work outside an academic theoretician's study. And even if they could work in laboratory conditions, the government had no time to make them work. For the first time in serious tones the possibility of a replacement for Margaret Thatcher began to be discussed. It was to continue until, and even through, the Party Conference that October particularly when, by a tactless error she, by applauding a speaker who had just launched an attack on the law and order policies of the Home Office, gave great offence to her deputy, William Whitelaw. She afterwards apologised to Whitelaw, and well she might, for in bad times and good he had, since his defeat by her in the leadership election, supported her with a determined and impeccable loyalty which she had done little to deserve, even though he disagreed with her instinctively on almost every aspect of her economic policy.

The critics were also, of course, and quite properly, concerned with the electoral prospects of the Conservative Party if what appeared to them to be an utterly disastrous policy, leading to an utterly disastrous sequence of events, continued. The Conservative Party's managers, less susceptible to considerations of principle than the politicians, were running scared. There had, in spite of the party's poor showing in the polls and in by-elections, been one or two unexpected bonuses. In November 1980, sickened by factional bickering within the ranks of the party he led, James Callaghan had resigned. He was replaced by Michael Foot, generally considered to be an amiable figure in his way, but not of the stuff of which prime ministers are made. His election, and the advance of the left wing in the Labour Party, led to a breakaway from its ranks by twenty-four members of Parliament. These formed the Social Democratic Party, in which the dominant figures were the former Chancellor of the Exchequer, Roy Jenkins, the former Education Secretary, Shirley Williams (neither of whom held parliamentary seats at the time), David Owen, the former Foreign Secretary, and William Rodgers, the former Transport Secretary. At first, although the new group formed an alliance with the Liberal Party, the Tories were overjoyed. Any break-away from Labour's ranks took attention away from their own troubles.

But then the new Alliance began to win seats at by-elections. Jenkins fought a gallant, and only narrowly losing, campaign at Warrington and, quite improbably, won a seat at Glasgow Hillhead, while Shirley Williams overturned a massive Conservative majority at Crosby. It was not readily to be seen at the time that these spectacular gains (and there were to be others, notably that of the Liberal candidate in Croydon) would, as Enoch Powell put it, fade like snow in the sunshine in the course of a general election campaign. The Conservatives were worried and when, in November 1981, Gallup recorded forty-five per cent of the voters as supporting the SDP/Liberal Alliance, while only twenty-five per cent supported the Tories, something very nearly like panic set in.

Ministers assembled for the 21 July Cabinet certainly felt the touch of that near panic. In the previous twelve months unemployment had risen to two million seven hundred thousand. Asked if he thought that was the ceiling, the Chancellor said no. Several of those present had been members of Edward Heath's front bench in the period before the 1970 election, and could readily recall Heath taunting Harold Wilson with the prospect, once considered impossible, of an unemployment level of a million under a Labour government. They had seen that, and worse, come to pass. The Chancellor was asked whether the figure could possibly pass three million and he replied, 'I'm afraid so.' None the less, supported only by the Prime Minister, Keith Joseph and Leon Brittan (the new Chief Secretary to the Treasury, who had moved there when John Biffen had become Secretary of State for Trade in the January reshuffle), Howe adamantly refused to countenance an adoption of the Keynesian idea that a period of recession and rising unemployment dictated, of necessity, higher, not lower, public spending. He still wanted £5 billion more taken out of the economy, and that requirement would dictate all negotiations between the spending departments and the Treasury during the period running up to the budget of 1982. By most accounts the Chancellor did not give a distinguished performance on this occasion, but judgements to that effect are, I think, less comments on his technical and histrionic abilities than reflections of the fact that his listeners simply could not believe that he, in his quiet way, had the impertinence to offer them no definite hope.

At this moment the Prime Minister had fears of a Cabinet revolt. 'Why did Mrs Thatcher win?' asks Peter Riddell.[8] 'The main reason was that the "wets" were never clear about what they wanted to do, nor did they have the will to press their case. Their objection to the existing strategy was instinctive rather than ideological.' And he adds, having observed the fact that, beyond Prior, Walker and Gilmour,[9] it was never very clear who the 'wets' were, 'The networks were too loose to be effective. At times it seemed as if Ministers did not talk to each other, and the "wets" were successful only when allied with other members of the Cabinet.' Riddell makes another point of real importance:[10]

> Similarly, the 'wets' were ineffective on the backbenches. There were perhaps fifty or sixty of them, but there was little coordinated action. Some dined together, cracked jokes and sniped at Mrs Thatcher and her circle, but they generally held back from open rebellion. Their forte was heavily masked criticism in witty articles and speeches. The prevailing ethos of the Conservative Party was against them; loyalty counted more than doubt. They knew that Mrs Thatcher had gauged the mood of the Conservative activists correctly and that there would be little support for any challenge.

There was, however, one exception in the general picture of ineffectiveness offered by the government's backbench critics: a series of cogent and powerful speeches on and after the 1981 budget by the member for Horncastle, Peter Tapsell, a stockbroker and once, briefly, a member of the opposition front bench Treasury team under Howe. What was particularly remarkable about these speeches was the accuracy of some of Tapsell's predictions, notably of the effect of the government's policies on unemployment, the consequences of the use of M3 as an indicator, and the necessity of developing a strategy for financing industry, which last the government undertook in the course of 1982. But Tapsell is a loner, and sought always to influence the government from a basic assumption of loyalty: he, too, was no conspirator.

I believe Riddell is correct in his conclusion that there was nothing remotely in the nature of a conspiracy forming against the Prime Minister in the summer and autumn of 1981. On the other hand, so hostile were the remarks made in private against her, so cruel the jokes, and so vehement the criticism, that it was readily understandable that her private staff began to believe that a conspiracy was being hatched.

Francis Pym, who was, in addition to his work as Leader of the House of Commons, responsible for government communications, made a speech in Northumberland which predicted gloomy days ahead. The prediction was not necessarily out of line with policy on the presentation of the government's views: the Prime Minister herself had frequently warned of hard times ahead. But Pym contrived by his manner to dissociate himself from what was going on. And when, a little later, the Chairman of the party, Lord Thorneycroft — a hero of Margaret Thatcher since her Oxford days, the man who resigned as Chancellor of the Exchequer when the Macmillan government refused to cut public spending by £50 million,[11] the man recalled to politics by her in 1975 — made a speech in similar vein, it became clear that she was surrounded by danger, within as well as without. She decided to take a holiday in Cornwall. She needed a rest in advance of a Party Conference that might well prove to be stormy.

I have remarked before that she is most formidable in adversity. With the single exception of the inflation figures, which did not enjoy, in the midst of all the problems besetting the nation, the prominence she had accorded to them earlier or managed to accord to them later, there was nothing good visible on the horizon. And she faced yet another series of Cabinet battles on the 1982 budget; battles which, quite apart from the general economic situation, would be made more difficult by her agreement to occasional Cabinet discussions on the economy.

In September, therefore, she dismissed Thorneycroft (who, because of his age — he was seventy-two — was not unwilling to step down), Ian Gilmour, Mark Carlisle and Christopher Soames. Prior was told he was being sent to Northern Ireland. He refused to go. She told him that no other post was on offer, but gave him the sop of remaining on the 'E' Committee, and the opportunity of taking a day to think over his response. She knew, as he did himself, that the job of Secretary of State for

Northern Ireland would preclude his attendance at almost all 'E' Committee meetings, and it would certainly be too onerous to allow him time to brief himself properly on economic policy. Prior hesitated, and did himself great damage thereby. At first he told his friends that he would refuse the Northern Ireland Office. Then, upon the suggestion being made that this might appear unpatriotic, he accepted her offer. He gained neither respect for resolution nor admiration for public spirit, though the first could have been his if he resigned, and the second if he had accepted without demur. 'The "wets" are wet indeed,' said one of her staff.

For the rest, she promoted Norman Tebbit to the Department of Employment. He was one of the toughest of House of Commons debaters, and one of the hardest of politicians. She had become impatient with Prior's tendency to go slow on trade union reform[12] and felt she could rely on Tebbit to speed things up. Keith Joseph took over education, a demotion more apparent than real, which has become obvious over the years since, as he has settled to the job of reconstructing the principles of the British educational system with a relish he never displayed in any earlier Cabinet post. Cecil Parkinson, a junior Minister of Trade, became Chairman of the Party, with a seat in the Cabinet, and the monetarist hawk, Nigel Lawson, was brought out of his junior role at the Treasury to be Secretary of State for Energy. David Howell was demoted to the Ministry of Transport, while its incumbent, Norman Fowler, went to the Department of Health and Social Security, whose chief, Partrick Jenkin, was shifted to the Department of Industry.

In one swift series of moves the balance of the Cabinet was altered completely.

The potential rebels scattered, the Party Conference in October, despite a good deal of disgruntled muttering behind the scenes, was adjudged a success, the Prime Minister continuing in the same defiant tone of the previous year. 'You never,' she said, 'throw in the towel when you are within an ace of success.' As inflation continued to fall, the argument that the beginning of the end of recession and contraction had come became her constant theme in speeches that winter. There was evidence, now, of a shift in tactics. With her new Cabinet she needed to spend less time on internal argument. Her speech at the Lord Mayor's banquet in November, her New Year message to the nation, and a major speech in February 1982 all contained a hint of electoral evangelism. And she had certain grounds for hope: productivity in 1981 had been the best for any year since the war — though, of course, from a smaller industrial base. None the less, the screws were still being tightened: on 2 December 1981 the Chancellor announced increases in prescription charges and National Insurance contributions designed to provide him with half of the £5 billion he had regarded as necessary the previous July. He found the rest in the budget itself.

The reaction to Howe's fourth budget was an interesting one. It seemed as though its very predictability, its similarity to all that had gone before, had an anaesthetising effect on press, Parliament and public. There was little in the way of furore, such as had greeted its predecessor. It was now clear that, although the monetary targets were loosened somewhat, no power on earth was going to deflect the Prime Minister and the Chancellor from their chosen course. The situation, indeed, was somewhat analogous to the later one, following the 1983 general election, when the opposition were stunned into apathy by the size of the Conservative majority, and the impossibility of significantly deflecting the government from its aims.

In any event, the war in the Falklands switched public and political attention from the economy — from the moment of the Argentinian invasion of the islands on 2 April 1982 to 14 June, when Port Stanley was surrendered to British forces. I will discuss the war later: for the moment it is sufficient to say that for two and a half months it preoccupied the nation to the exclusion of almost everything else.

But the steady march of economic decision-making continued. It emerged in the course of the summer, as yet another rebuke to those who believe that governments can forecast in any detail and with any accuracy the consequences of their actions, that the PSBR for 1981–82 had, after all, been, at £9 billion, £1.5 billion *less* than had been allowed for in the 1981 budget. There was room, therefore, for slack to be taken up without offence being given to the principles of the favoured economic strategy. Whether this slack *should* be taken up was, however, a matter for quite heated debate. The government's critics, naturally, repeated and emphasised their earlier derision of the tightness of its monetary policy, and they pointed with scorn to the now-proven inaccuracy of M3 figures as a guide to the performance of the money supply. Indeed, with the 1982 budget, M3 was virtually abandoned as an instrument of policy and with its abandonment the death of monetarism was proclaimed in many quarters.

Monetarism was not, however, dead simply because one of its instruments was proved faulty: indeed, in his first budget speech as Chancellor (in 1984) Nigel Lawson, who now wore the mantle of Sir Geoffrey Howe — though with infinitely greater panache — announced both his continued belief in the usefulness of a revised form of the Medium-Term Financial Strategy and his conviction that methods of measuring money supply could be devised. The monetarists were still around, and still powerful, in the summer of 1982, and the discovery of under-spending to the tune of £1.5 billion led to controversy among them.

In strictly monetarist terms that discovery demonstrated a triumph. After the battering received from the critics in 1981 when it appeared that quite apart from failing to achieve non-inflationary prosperity the application of monetarist techniques could not even ensure accuracy in the prediction of economic behaviour, it now appeared that an important gain had been made. For the first time the PSBR had come in under target: the squeeze had worked. The question was, what to do next?

The purists believed that matters should be left as they stood; these included Alfred Sherman and Nigel Lawson. The more politically-minded among the monetarists, however — and their ranks included the Prime Minister — argued in quite a different way. Their argument can be put quite simply. If a target of £10.5 billion was satisfactory for the financial year 1981–82 and it had been more than achieved, and if, in the 1982 budget, a further contraction in the money supply had taken place, so that the gradual squeeze required by the four-year MTFS was actually happening, then some relaxation of economic conditions for industry could be allowed. The political pressures to provide some relief, some evidence of recovery, were enormous as time unravelled towards the budget for 1983: a general election had to take place at the latest by 1984, and it was generally thought unwise to wait until the last possible moment. For practical purposes an election some time in 1983 had to be considered likely, whether June or October was the chosen month.

None of this meant that the Prime Minister would yield to the idea that the election would be preceded by what is usually described as a give-away budget. Her commitment to the restructuring of the British economy through a monetarist strategy went far too deep for that. But it did mean that the most should be made politically of what few items of good news there were — most importantly the evident conquest of inflation, down to between four and five per cent at the beginning of 1983 and, at that level, several percentage points below the average rise in real earnings. It also meant that a more positive attitude could be taken towards the increasingly plaintive demands of industry.

Things were done in two specific areas. One concerned the

treatment of nationalised industries, and the other concerned the consumer. In July 1982 all hire-purchase controls were abolished. Given that this action was taken at a time when real incomes were rising faster than inflation, it obviously indicated the possibility of a consumer-led boom; and it indicated, further, that the Treasury smiled on such a possibility. Strictly speaking, the decision to abolish hire-purchase controls was against monetarist dogma, for it led, of course, to an expansion of credit, that is to say, an effective increase in the money supply.

But the benefit to the consumer was equalled by the benefit to industry. True, as it turned out, British manufacturers tended to meet the new wave of demand from stock and, thus, there was no very marked increase in production, and no diminution in unemployment, of the kind which attends a genuine economic revival. None the less, it may be said that the monetarist philosophy lives in as broad a church as the Keynesian. There is a part of it which argues for de-regulation, and there could be no more obvious — and readily-felt, throughout the population — act of de-regulation than the abolition of hire-purchase controls. After all, if a private firm chose to advance credit to its customers that was its business; if it was repaid it made profits; if it was not repaid it went bankrupt. The decision, in a free-market economy, should be made by the firm, not the government.

This thesis was — and is — not without plausibility. A difficulty arises, none the less, when it comes to be applied to a nationalised industry — one owned by the government. Throughout Margaret Thatcher's first term as Prime Minister all the principal nationalised industries which were in deficit received huge government subsidies. Coal, steel and motor cars gained particularly. Yet British Leyland, the consumer of billions in government — or taxpayers' — money, was likely to derive great advantage from the absence of restrictions on hire purchase. So incidentally, were the nationalised gas and electricity industries. It is in the nature of things that a nationalised industry can almost never be allowed to go bankrupt, since the government owns it, and that sort of thing does not happen to governments. None the less, there was a certain element of robbing Peter to pay Paul in the circular activity of allowing the consumer to buy goods from companies owned by government, the losses of which companies, if incurred, would be met by the government itself. More of expediency than of principle was suggested here.

There was, however, a defence of sorts.

Installed as managers both of British Steel and of British Leyland were men — Ian MacGregor and Michael Edwardes respectively — whom the government trusted ultimately to discharge their briefs of ending disruptive trade union activity, eliminating uneconomic practices, restoring profitability, and paving the way for a return to private ownership. MacGregor faced a destructive fourteen-week strike, ended, finally, by the exhaustion of the steel union consequent upon their realisation of the fact that the world market for steel was growing even smaller, and by the injection of another substantial *tranche* of government money. Edwardes faced what seemed at times an almost infinite number of strikes, often localised, but invariably highly disruptive, but by reiterated appeals to workers over the heads of their union leaders he seemed to be winning what was an exceptionally long-drawn-out battle. While there were many among the Prime Minister's closest supporters who, at one moment or another, favoured abandoning one or the other of these two industries to chaos and bankruptcy, the counsel that prevailed was one which accepted the advice of MacGregor (who had been recruited by Keith Joseph personally) to the effect that time was needed to sort out things. And since time cost money, government subvention was needed. The consolation for ministers was that whereas their Labour predecessors seemed prepared to bail out British Steel and British Leyland indefinitely, their own commitment merely was to give the Mac-Gregor and Edwardes experiments time to prove themselves. It should be said, further, that the huge sums required to implement a policy supportive of both managers in these two industries (and similar commitments in the coal industry, which was a separate case) were not at the expense of the overall budgetary plan: the money was found through cuts elsewhere and, as we have already seen, the PSBR in the middle of 1982 was substantially less than that allowed for in the 1981 budget.

'But whether we think this particular instance of State interference wise or foolish,' wrote Lord Hugh Cecil in 1912, 'it is for our present purpose more important to emphasise that a policy of State interference is not, as such, alien to Conservatism.'[13] Various of Lord Hugh's objurgations were on the lips of Sir Keith Joseph during the difficult years when, while the overall national budget was being squeezed in the interests of a policy theoretically devoted to withdrawing the state from the economic life of the nation, large sums were being made available to inefficient state-owned industries. But there is no doubt that Joseph, as long as he was Secretary of State for Industry, went through terrible agonies of conscience over the apparent contrasts between his principles and his actions, which contrasts made him the butt of many an unkind joke.

The seeming contradictions became more glaring during 1982. It was all very well to proffer the necessity of supporting Ian MacGregor and Michael Edwardes for a limited period as an excuse for public expenditure but it seemed, at times, as though both the managers and the government considered the purse of the state to be bottomless. It was perfectly reasonable to argue that, if the money was going to be spent anyway, it should be spent on schemes of public expenditure which would bring relief more quickly to the unemployed. And, in general, it was argued by Ian Gilmour in 1983,[14] the government was inconsistently doctrinaire: it was in principle against public expenditure and a large PSBR, yet it spent enormous sums of public money in the wrong places.

Was it then, after all, this debate that had generated such agony of mind from the intellectually inclined among politicians, and such hardship in so many sections of the community, only about tactics, where the money should be spent, rather than whether it should be spent?

This is most certainly not how the Prime Minister saw it at any moment of her stewardship. She had been free, immediately before and immediately after the general election of 1979, with remarks to the effect that she would need two terms to accomplish her purpose of a revolution in British ways of thinking about politics, society and the economy. Most of these remarks were put down as examples of the common coinage of pseudo-confidence in politicians, designed to scare their enemies, of which perhaps the most famous — and now the most readily traduced — is that by Lord Wilson to the effect that Labour had become the natural governing party.[15] Nobody I have discussed the matter with, who met her between 1979 and 1983, and who had any sort of general discussion with her, reports failing to hear the repetition of the belief that she needed two terms, the first to get the main lines of economic policy straight, the second to see through the structural reforms of British economic society with which any successor government, of whatever party affiliation, would have to live. It is yet another paradox in her character and record that, whereas she is quite uninterested in the way in which individual institutions — the Civil Service, the Cabinet Office, a given company — work, she is intensely interested in the structure of the nation as a whole. I once put the paradox to her and she replied, 'When we get the big things right the small ones will fall into place.'

As 1982 approached its close the preparation for the 1983 budget began. Whatever the Prime Minister had to fear from the opposition or the electorate, it was by now clear that she had nothing to fear from enemies within her own party. The apparent inconsistencies between the monetarist strategic policies of the Chancellor, his continually tight fiscal policies (those concerned with taxation, social security and public works) and the lavish industrial provisions made by the government, were of little relevance except as matters for discussion over dinner tables. For those who still maintained their adamant — if now, in the main, private — opposition to her philosophy it became the fashion to attribute her growing standing in the country, and the growing likelihood that she would be victorious in a general election contest to two factors, subsumed together in the phrase of one of those most hostile to her as 'the bitch's luck'. The first was the almost comical disarray of the Labour Party, the second was the war concluded in June in the Falklands, her conduct of which had clearly won her the unstinting praise of the public.

Because the idea persists that it was success in war that won Margaret Thatcher a second term of office, and because that notion is, on the evidence available, a ludicrous one, it ought to be scotched. Politicians (and writers, too) are, of course, inclined to quote opinion polls when these modern forms of divination support their case, and not, when they do not. None the less the polls, rough though they are as guides, and inaccurate though they have sometimes been (in the general election campaigns of 1970 and February 1974 in particular) do provide a certain amount of raw evidence for judgement. The evidence is that the Falklands war made very little, if any, difference to the Prime Minister's prospects for re-election.

As already mentioned at the end of 1981 the poll of polls conducted by the Gallup Organisation found Margaret Thatcher to be, in the judgement of those polled, likely to be remembered as the worst Prime Minister in memory. By the middle of March 1982 — two weeks before the Argentinian invasion of the Falkland Islands, she enjoyed a substantial lead over Michael Foot as the people's choice for Prime Minister, and her party enjoyed an equally substantial lead over the Labour Party. The Liberal/SDP Alliance, enjoying a forty-five per cent level of support in the polls in November 1981, had fallen into third place. It was a substantial third in percentage terms — the polls varied quite noticeably, but a fair average for the Alliance would be about twenty per cent — but, given the nature of the British electoral system, one unlikely to bring them much joy in the way of seats. In the polls taken immediately after the defeat of the Argentinians in June her, and her party's, predominance in the polls was roughly the same, given the invariable provision by the pollsters of the possibility of a margin of error of three per cent either way. Any proposition, therefore, that there was a Falklands factor in her massive 1983 general election victory has to rest solely on individual instinct and guesswork. I repeat: all the evidence that is available suggests that she had won a general election, if that were to be held in 1983, weeks before she sent the Task Force to the South Atlantic.

This is an unpalatable proposition for her critics to grasp. Nobody doubted the fact that her conduct of the war was greatly admired by the ordinary people of the country, whatever reservations the *cognoscenti* might have about it. Most commentators judged it unwise of Neil Kinnock to attack that conduct during the 1983 campaign, especially since he got his facts wrong. Enoch Powell, even, urged her to go to the country immediately the war was over, so as to ensure, in the glow of victory, the perpetuation of her economic policies: this blandishment she resisted. The fact of the matter, it seemed to her, was that while it was not improper to celebrate the triumph of British arms, nor unfair to take her proper place in that celebration, it would be thought gross deliberately to exploit the victory. She even at first resisted advice to ask for a dissolution of Parliament as early as June 1983, for fear that she might be accused of making political capital out of the war. She yielded, in the end, to the arguments of Geoffrey Howe, that June was the right time.

The success of the war was an argumentative excuse for the critics of Margaret Thatcher. It was — and understandably — difficult for them to grasp that after all their forebodings — however carefully expressed in public — the early months of 1983 had seen a massive swing of support to her in the country: her message had got through. She was, undoubtedly, lucky in the fact that the Labour Party was in disarray and that its Leader, Michael Foot, was increasingly seen as a shambling incompetent. According to Peter Riddell the 1983 election was '... a rare case of a campaign being lost by an Opposition...'[16] This is pitching the matter too high: every prime minister requires a certain amount of luck. The inescapable fact is that, through perseverance and commitment, whatever illogicalities may have marked the industrial policy of the government she led, however many mistakes her economic advisers have made, Margaret Thatcher had won through by the time of the 1983 budget.

That budget was not quite the mixture as before, but it was not an electioneering budget either. Howe announced that — again — PSBR was under target: £7.5 billion had been spent instead of the permitted £9 billion. This was good housekeeping with a vengeance, although, it has to be said, the pre-election months saw ministers arguing that spending departments should actually start spending again. The imminence of an election has its effect on even the most principled of politicians.

For the rest Howe felt he could allow a certain amount of loosening of the monetary strait-jacket. He felt he could permit a twelve per cent increase in tax allowances, while holding the PSBR to £8 billion in the financial year 1983–84. Mortgage relief was increased by £5,000 and there were various other of those delights referred to by politicians and journalists as 'election sweeteners'. It was promised, however, that the government, still feeling the necessity to reorganise the structure of the national economy, would in the future press on hard and fast with its proposals for reform of the law governing the activities of trade unions. Delight of delights, the Chancellor reported that inflation had fallen to just over four per cent. The goal of goals that the government had set itself — inflation at nil per cent — was in sight.

The remarkable thing about the government's discharge of its duties over the four years in which it had held office was not its variations from the line that it had laid down in opposition, but the consistency with which it had held to its objects. Alongside that had to be laid another consideration. Even in his fourth — and last — budget, Howe had made no significant concession to the now three million plus unemployed (the majority of whom who voted in 1983, again remarkably, voted Conservative). This was to offend against one of the cardinal assumptions of British politics in the post-war era, which assumption stated that the number of people out of work and what could be done to bring them back into work was the essential bone of contention between parties. The Chancellor not merely offended against it: he ignored it. It is in the fact that he did so, and did so with electoral impunity, that we can find the strongest evidence that Margaret Thatcher's first term had changed the whole nature of the way British people looked at politics and at their politicians. It was the constant complaint of leading Labour politicians during the general election campaign of 1983 that although the polls showed that the electorate considered the problem of unemployment the most important facing the nation, they did not blame the government for the unprecedently high figures. This was a conundrum that nobody could penetrate. And it was a conundrum that unmanned the leaders of the Labour Party, whose whole stance was based on the belief that the voters would react favourably to their indictment of the heartlessness of Thatcherism.

But, of course, Margaret Thatcher did not come to office merely to perpetrate conundra. The fact that her will and her cunning had kept in being an economic policy very generally denounced (the implementation of which seemed for three years to produce very little in the way of results, while even the predictions of its creators went constantly awry), though it might provide material for a study of a very odd and untypical episode in British political history, did not justify the extravagant claims she had made at the outset of her party leadership — and, more importantly — at the outset of her first term of office, that she would be the one to save the nation.

The question remained at the conclusion of her triumph in June 1983: had she simply conducted an economic experiment which ended as a monetary and fiscal holding operation? Or had she, while fighting endless battles of the budget, still managed to find time for the laying of the foundations for a restructuring of British political society? In 1977, when I was preparing my earlier book on her, she told me, 'I've changed everything', which was a statement in its essence hyperbolic unless she went on to become Prime Minister, and to effect the changes she had in mind. We must now examine what she did in the way of lasting change.

· CHAPTER SIX ·

Reforming the Nation

Very few citizens of London to-day, depending for their
wealth, their sustenance and their mental atmosphere on
what the State does and has done, are better or so good as
St John the Baptist who lived in the wilderness and fed on
locusts and wild honey . . . When, therefore, we are judging
as we are bound to do, political action by a moral standard,
the State has to conform to the individual's code.
— Lord Hugh Cecil, *Conservatism* (London, 1912)

The Labour Party manifesto in 1900 covered about half a
sheet of paper and laid down twelve fairly specific points of
policy, including the immediate nationalisation of land and
railways. The sheet concluded:

> The object of these measures is to enable the people
> ultimately to obtain the socialisation of the means of
> production, distribution and exchange, to be controlled by
> a democratic state in the interests of the entire community,
> and the complete emancipation of labour from the
> domination of capitalism and landlordism . . .

Ultimately these aspirations were enshrined in Clause Four of
the Labour Party's constitution, and when Hugh Gaitskell, as
Leader, tried to have Clause Four expunged, on the grounds,
first that no further nationalisation was required and, second,
that the continued presence of a commitment to nationalise

was damaging to the party in the eyes of the electorate, he was defeated. One way or another, both within and between the two major parties the issue of nationalisation has been present in British politics for the whole of this century. Sometimes it has been a fringe issue, but sometimes, as in recent years, it has been at the very heart of controversy. The only new developments in the controversy are the intensity with which the two parties now hold to their points of view and the fact that the Conservatives now call denationalisation 'privatisation'.

It is instructive to recall that when Gaitskell was calling for the erasure of Clause Four from the Labour Party's constitution some of his followers argued that he should leave well alone.[1] The issue, they thought, was moribund. Nobody really believed that a Gaitskell government would nationalise anything. The presence of Clause Four was a now antique symbol of past Labour yearnings. It was part of the folklore, and like other parts of folklore attempts to get shot of it would merely raise the ire of political conservationists. The great post-war settlement — the Butskellite settlement — between the parties now determined the ideological character of the British political system. Gaitskell, a stubborn man, went ahead, and failed.

It was the decision by the Conservatives, in opposition between 1945 and 1951, to accept most of what had been done by the Labour government of 1945 that laid the foundations of Butskellism. It was not until the election of Edward Heath as Leader of the Conservative Party in 1965 that any serious intellectual challenge was made to the set of assumptions of which it was constituted. Even then, Heath was prepared, in office, to accept some of the innovations of Harold Wilson. The most important of these was nationalised steel. Attlee had nationalised steel, and the Conservatives had denationalised it. Wilson nationalised it again, and nationalised it remains to this day.

To the Tories of the New Right, gathered enthusiastically behind Margaret Thatcher from 1975 onwards, their party had been too ready by far in the past to accept things Labour governments had done: the consensus had shifted too far to the left. And although not much was said about privatisation in the 1979 manifesto (not much, as I have already observed, was said about anything in the 1979 manifesto) the question of the nationalised industries and their future was in the forefront of many minds, notably that of the Leader. She and her allies were only too conscious of the fact that the Heath government, too, had come to power with a commitment, albeit also a general one, to denationalise, but in the end its most important move had been to *nationalise* Rolls-Royce. Speaking in 1984 of the present government's privatisation programmes, one of Margaret Thatcher's senior ministers — one of the many who think that the privatisation programme is the government's greatest achievement — said to me, 'Ted told us he would denationalise. But what did he denationalise? A couple of pubs and a travel agency. Compare that to what we've done.'

The scathing reference was to the privatisation of the Carlisle breweries, some public houses attached to them, and of Thomas Cook Ltd. These achievements were meritorious enough — what, after all, is a government doing owning saloons and travel agencies? — but they were minuscule compared to the sheer size of the state sector in industry. They were as nothing compared to the opposite decision to nationalise Rolls-Royce when the aerospace division of that company looked like bankrupting itself through its over-hasty investment in carbon fibres. The argument of the day was that there were certain companies (called 'blue-chip' companies) which were either so important as suppliers to the armed forces or whose existence was so bound up with national prestige that they simply could not be allowed to go to the wall. The experience and the memory of it, however, serve as a useful reminder of the fact that, though in general opposed to nationalisation in theory, and though usually opposed to specific acts of nationalisation, the Conservative Party has never been completely dogmatic on the subject. It was, after all, a Conservative government that first nationalised coal mines, and this was something constantly brought out in argument by Conservative opponents of Margaret Thatcher's privatisation programme. However, her commitment to privatisation ran deeply and strongly: it is impossible to imagine her, whatever the circumstances, acting as Heath did over Rolls-Royce. There has now developed, under her guidance and with her support, a determination on the part of ministers to denationalise wherever possible. The tone as well as the substance of the commitment was sufficiently displayed in a speech made by Nigel Lawson (then Secretary of State for Energy) on 23 September 1982:

> Long and hard experience has demonstrated that no Government can eradicate the inherent defects of nationalisation. The time has come to liberate ourselves from this burden — and then to liberate the industries themselves from this condition.

Privatisation is not, as several of the government's experiences have demonstrated, an easy business. The policy none the less rests on a very important principle of the Prime Minister's thinking, a principle which is best described as minimalist. Government should only do — this seems the best way to put it — what only government can do. Everything else should be left to the individual. Quite apart, of course, from the fact that the conditions of modern life are such that no government can be as standoffish as were, say, governments in the nineteenth century, the long reign of Butskellism left the incoming government in 1979 with an exceptionally complex series of unscrambling jobs to do before its wishes could be fulfilled and it found, too, that chairmen of national-ised industries often had a great deal of power to resist mini-sterial wishes, as Sir Denis Rooke, Chairman of British Gas, resisted even so determined a minister as Nigel Lawson between 1981 and 1983 by putting all sorts of obstacles in the way of disposing of the oil assets of British Gas.

Disposal of state-owned assets was — and is — difficult for two main reasons. The first is that so many of them — British Leyland and British Airways were the most dramatic examples — were making huge losses, and were thus worth only scrap value in the market place. It was necessary, there-fore, through subsidisation and more efficient management to make them attractive to the private investor. Here arose the second difficulty, and the opposition. If, in large part because of the injection of the taxpayers' money, an industry became profitable how was it right to sell it off to the private sector when the revenue from the sale could do very little indeed to compensate for the huge sums previously made by way of investment and loan and which would have to be written off?

There was a fundamental difference of principle and approach here between the Labour and Conservative parties. The Labour Party considered the assets up for sale to be the property of the community. They skipped quickly over the disagreeable fact that state-owned industries, whether manu-facturing or service, can never in any real sense belong to the community as a whole since they are, in effect, managed and owned by the bureaucracy of the state. The Conservative Party, by contrast, regarded the whole apparatus of the nationalised sector of the economy as one huge encumbrance. The government determined to rid itself of as much of that encumbrance as was humanly (and politically) possible. On the way, however, they ran into further problems, which the opposition was quick to exploit. Essentially, these revolved around the problem of what price to set on an industry that was to be offered to the market, and on what terms the offer should be made. The government was sensitive to the accusation that it was its intention to use taxpayers' money to refurbish industries in trouble and then sell them to its City friends at knockdown prices. It was therefore decided, in 1980, to try to spread the ownership of shares in newly privatised companies as widely as possible and this, of course, necessarily involved the government in regulating the terms of sale. There was also a tendency on the part of those who bought small numbers of shares at the moment of issue to sell almost immediately. It was discovered, for example, that the number of shareholders in British Aerospace fell from 157,800 to 27,200 within a year, and the number of shareholders owning less than a hundred shares fell from 40,000 to 3,200 in the same period.[2]

Yet another problem arose in the matter of how the shares were to be issued. If they were sold at a fixed price, with or without conditions as to the number of shares to be sold to any one purchaser, then the small shareholders tended to sell quickly to make a profit. On the other hand, if the shares were put out to tender, which involved underwriters, they tended to be undersubscribed; the underwriters were left with large holdings and a loss — this was the case with Britoil — making other potential underwriters less keen to take up the next issue. The government's concern both to get a reasonable price for the assets it was selling off and to spread the ownership widely led it into contradictions, and there were a number of messy sales provoking highly unfavourable publicity.

The desire both to sell and to sell not simply at the rate the market would bear but to particular kinds of purchasers thus involved the relevant ministers in a wide range of difficulties. Even the government itself, however, accepted that not everything could be sold off, and that there were unavoidable delays while some industries were being prepared for sale. So, at the same time as the privatisation programme gathered speed — with the Prime Minister constantly urging more and more speed — a programme of liberalisation was embarked on. This had two prongs: it was designed to make existing and remaining state-owned industries and services more competitive and more attuned to the consumer, but also to ensure that the privatised companies did not manage to gain for themselves a monopoly position in the market. Before, however, we examine privatisation and liberalisation at the point where they interlock, it would perhaps be useful to examine the one area in which the sale of what the Labour Party would call a national or community asset went almost exactly as the government planned, politically as well as financially, in spite of stubborn rearguard actions by local authorities where Labour was in power. This was the programme for the sale of council houses.

The whole issue of publicly provided housing, how much of it there ought to be and what to do with it over its life, is another that has been present in British politics for many years. Just like Labour governments Conservatives have, in the annual discussions on the Rate Support Grant (the amount central government gives annually to aid income from the rates) been prepared to discuss how much should be spent on the building of new houses by councils for rent.

Labour, however, has had a more toughly principled understanding of what a council house is than have the Tories. To the Labour Party (at least until very recently) the pool of publicly owned housing was a community asset. If a tenant, let us say, moved to another area, or perhaps bought his own house elsewhere on the private market, then his old home remained in the pool available for another tenant. In no circumstances could the idea of actually selling off property to existing tenants be countenanced. The Conservatives, on the other hand, from time to time contemplated the adoption of a policy of sale, perhaps on a very large scale, perhaps even with quite lavish inducements. (One policy group even suggested, in 1978, *giving* the houses away to sitting tenants.) The advantages, even allowing for the possibility of losses on sales, were obvious. They included considerable savings on administration and the provision of an impetus to the movement of labour: one of the great obstacles to labour mobility among council tenants was the frequently experienced difficulty of finding rented accommodation in a new place of work. The idea appealed to Edward Heath, and proposals to sell council property were included in the 1970 manifesto. During the life of the government some sales were, indeed, made, but the programme was never pushed with vigour, and Labour councils were able to put many obstacles in the path of ministers. The view therefore gained currency in the higher echelons of the Conservative Party that council tenants quite simply did not, in the main, *want* to buy their homes; there seemed little mileage in the idea.

The idea of selling off council houses is one that might have been invented solely for Margaret Thatcher, and the urgency with which she approached it is demonstrated by the fact that the relevant Act of Parliament, making it possible for council tenants to buy their homes at discounts of up to fifty per cent of their market value, was pushed through both Houses by 1980.

The Prime Minister has developed and applied to policy with religious enthusiasm the truism that most people like to own their own home. She thus brings a moral zest to the business of selling off council property which no previous Conservative minister charged with handling the issue has mustered. During the period of opposition between 1975 and 1979 she constantly returned to the subject, constantly demanded to know how plans were getting on for implementing the policy and overcoming the opposition of recalcitrant local authorities. Her evangelism on the subject was such as to provoke more than the occasional sneer from Conservatives who simply did not share her enthusiasm for the subject, and preferred to leave things simply as they were. Her determination in the matter fed the view, as put by one critic, that she was 'a terribly commonplace, suburban woman, always going on about council houses and bloody council tenants. They'll never vote Tory.'

There were economic arguments for the sale of the council houses, and there were political arguments too — if the new owners voted Conservative in substantial numbers. But it was neither of these considerations that moved her to push and push again, in opposition and in power, for the policy to be pressed to its utmost limits. Rather, she simply found it hard to imagine anybody who did not want to own their own house, or who was incapable or unwilling to make the purchase on such favourable terms as she proposed: the moral — or, if you are a critic, moralistic — and the practical combined, in just that way which, when it happens, makes her a virtually irresistible force.

She was proved triumphantly right in every part of the argument. Polls taken in 1979 showed that a majority of those who voted Labour preferred Conservative policy on council housing. Between 1979 and 1983 there was an increase of one million in the number of owner-occupied houses and flats, fully half of which were council properties newly acquired by their former tenants. More: a BBC/Gallup survey in June 1983 showed that fifty-six per cent of those who had bought their council houses intended to vote Tory; only eighteen per cent still favoured the Labour Party. Worse for Labour: fifty-nine per cent of those who had voted Labour in 1979 and had subsequently bought their homes intended to vote for the Conservatives or for the Alliance. The obstacles placed in the way of purchase by Labour councils very likely helped this switch in allegiance. The suggestion on the left of the party that it should become policy to repossess all properties sold in the event of a Labour general election victory undoubtedly scared off some voters. No wonder then that, since the 1983 general election, Neil Kinnock has been trying to nudge his party towards accepting the principle of council house sales. Moreover, the change that she has wrought has been visible. Council estates, claimed John Stanley, the Housing Minister, in February 1983, 'as they become areas of mixed rather than single tenure, are changing before our eyes — and for the better. They are becoming more varied, more individualistic...' All this, of course, is precisely what the Prime Minister had wanted and predicted.

The sale of council houses is not normally thought of as part of the privatisation programme, because it is not concerned with industry. The principle involved, however, is exactly the same for housing as for industry, the devolution of work and capital away from the state (or local authorities) to private-sector companies and to individuals. Moreover, and especially given the disappointing response of the small (and perhaps often the first-time) shareholder to the industrial privatisation programme — signified by quick disposal of shares for a profit, rather than their retention for income — the freedom to purchase one's previously rented home represented an important step on the road to the creation of a capital-owning democracy. The favourable terms on which the sales were and are being made offer many citizens a once in a lifetime opportunity to acquire a substantial capital asset: the Prime Minister's faith in the propensity of the great majority of those who take that opportunity to continue to improve the asset is unshakable.

Further, the selling of council houses, considered as a part of privatisation, is a policy that immediately and deeply touches the lives of the ordinary citizen, in a way that the sale of large companies and corporations, however desirable in itself, does not. And this is an important consideration when set against the difficulty of persuading people to become share owners.

'Anything she wants done,' said one of her advisers, 'she

wants done yesterday.' It has been a matter of intense frustration to the Prime Minister that she could not instantly proceed with the sale of everything in the nationalised shop window. Therefore, while sanctioning (albeit reluctantly) the expenditure required to make some of the industries destined for privatisation efficient and potentially profitable, she was impatient for movement in any conceivable direction that would reduce regulation and stimulate competition. This programme of liberalising the economy has been patchy in its effect, but it was probably Norman Fowler's decision at the Department of Transport to remove the licencing system for long-distance express road services, resulting as it did in lower fares through intensified competition, that ensured his promotion to the Cabinet in the 1981 reshuffle.

The very fervour brought to the task of creating a thriving free-enterprise economy has, inevitably, resulted in the impression of frenetic over-activity, even though there is a Cabinet committee (MISC 14, the Ministerial Steering Group on Government Strategy) which is charged with overseeing and making coherent what often seems to be the hyper-activity of ministers. As mentioned above[3] the first — and important — steps to a liberal end were taken in the 1979 budget. But since then a large number of controls — particularly planning controls — have been relaxed. Enterprise zones (designed to attract business to declining areas with the bait of reduced taxation and relaxed restrictions, especially on development) have been created though they have had, so far, a doubtful effect. Business taxation and employers' contributions to National Insurance have both been reduced. Assistance has been proffered in the way of loans and grants to small companies, and there has been a substantial thrust (headed by the then Minister of Information Technology, Kenneth Baker) of investment into the new world of high technology. The Thatcher government is thus not averse to state spending, provided it is limited in duration and has the clear purpose of creating a new or reviving an old company and enabling it to stand on its own feet. Some critics have argued,[4] however, that economic liberalisation has in fact been far less thoroughly carried through than the Prime Minister's rhetoric suggests, and they cite in particular the continuing will to protectionism which often seems to dominate the government's attitude towards the international market — for instance, in taking steps to limit the Japanese presence in British markets and, in one famous case in July 1983, the decision of the Ministry of Defence to buy a British anti-radar missile rather than a cheaper, and quite possibly more efficient — American model. But this is to miss the point about Margaret Thatcher's whole attitude to politics. There is no sense now, and there never has been any sense, in which she is a *laissez-faire* liberal of the old school (such as favoured international Free Trade as opposed to Imperial Preference in the destructive intra-party conflicts of the late nineteenth and early twentieth centuries). She is first and foremost a nationalist. An important part of her nationalism in regard to domestic affairs requires the creation of a free-enterprise economy and a society concerned more with the individual than the mass. She has no compunction whatsoever in resorting to stratagems antipathetic to the liberal ideology if it gains a British company or a British industry an advantage over a foreign competitor, though she recognises that there are limits, ordained by treaties, agreements and practical international politics, to protectionist actions or measures. 'She will fight his corner,' said one of her ministers, 'for any British businessman in competition with a foreigner. But she reserves the right to blast him if he's not running his factory efficiently at home.'

By the general election of 1983 the privatisation and liberalisation programmes were under way, but the will of the government in proceeding with them was as yet uncertain of assessment. Once the general election was over, however, she resumed the attack with zest, and it is quite remarkable to note how far the government has gone, in actual and projected action, at the time of writing. Shares have been sold in Associated British Ports, Britoil, Amersham, British Petroleum, British Aerospace, Cable and Wireless, British Sugar, Jaguar, and in a whole series of companies originally under the sponsorship of the National Enterprise Board. Proposals are in hand for the sale of British Gas's Wytch oilfield and the gas showrooms, of British Airways, Cable Broadcasting, the Royal Ordnance factories, British Shipbuilders and Rolls-Royce. Various state-owned enterprises have been compelled to sell off ancillary activities — British Rail its laundries, hovercraft interests and hotels, British Leyland its interests in the refrigeration industry, agricultural motor manufacturing and Jaguar. The National Freight Corporation has been sold in its entirety (with great success) to its own employees. And, finally, in electricity, airports, telecommunications, postal services, the steel industry and the Property Services Agency, steps have been taken either to provide for the injection of private capital or to allow private companies to enter into competition with what has hitherto been a monopoly.

The array of activity is bewildering to survey and, therefore, difficult to assess. In every area, however — indeed, in relation to almost every decision — it is possible to spot flaws and hiccups. When a state-owned enterprise — particularly one of the giants, like British Telecom — is sold off *en bloc* to the highest bidder, then the danger of its remaining a monopoly, private rather than state owned, is obviously considerable, and it can readily be argued that a monopoly in private hands is more dangerous to the interests of the community than one in state hands. But if an attempt is made to disperse shares widely, and these later congregate in a few hands, the danger remains. The tension between the struggle to prevent monopoly and that to widen competition remained unsolved as Margaret Thatcher entered her second term. But what may be said without reservation, and before trying to pass overall judgement on the effect of all these changes, is that nothing on such a scale could conceivably have come to pass under any other recent prime minister.

When other changes are considered — the ending of the monopoly by solicitors on conveyancing, for example, or the monopoly hitherto enjoyed by licensed opticians (though both of these started as Private Members' Bills in the House of Lords) — the overall thrust of the government is clear. The Prime Minister and her increasingly like-minded Cabinet are evidently determind to create vast, even seismic, changes in the whole structure of the British economy and British political society. And it is only when one stands back and looks at the decisions and their overall effect together, that one appreciates that they constitute less a stream than a tidal wave.

A flavour of the style of the Prime Minister in going about the business of reducing the power and size of the state machine, and the personal attention she gives to so many of the necessary operations, is to be found in her handling of the Quango question. A Quango is a Quasi-Autonomous National Government Organisation, invariably a collection of individuals paid to oversee and regulate aspects of industry and enterprise. A number of Conservative members of Parliament, but particularly Philip Holland,[5] had argued for the abolition of most, if not all, Quangos, on the grounds that they were bureaucratic excrescences and inhibiting to enterprise. Sir Leo Pliatzky, a just-retired civil servant of some distinction, was invited to investigate what could be done. On his first meeting with the Prime Minister he began to discuss the amount of time he would require to investigate the situation and make his report. She told him she knew exactly what she wanted to do, passed him a copy of Holland's pamphlet and told him he would find all the information he needed in it. It was perfectly clear that she merely wanted, for purposes of window-dressing, Pliatzky's imprimatur on a decision to carry out a Quango massacre. She did not get it, and the extent of government activity against Quangos has been, for the more radical of her supporters, disappointing. None the less, on past form, she seems likely to return to the subject on a later occasion, when circumstances are more propitious for the kind of decisive action she favours. Even with her will and her energy, it is impossible to fight all the battles at the same time, particularly when one is trying to overturn the habits, and the consequences of the practice, of a generation.

The fact that she is not always — indeed, far from always — inclined to headlong action is confirmed by her attitude to and action on the reform of the trade unions. Following the disputes in the mining industry in 1973 and 1974 which brought down the Heath government, the Conservative Party was sharply divided in its views about what could, and should, be done about the trade unions. There was a fairly widespread acceptance of the proposition that the size and power of the trade union movement — particularly given the extra immunities and privileges it enjoyed following legislation (under the aegis of Michael Foot) by the Labour governments of 1974–79 — were severely inhibiting to the growth of British industry and, particularly, the development of free enterprise.

One section of the party — and James Prior, first the Shadow and then the real Secretary of State for Employment, was among their number — took the view that the unions considered as a whole (with the TUC as their governing body, though with varying influence if a powerful union was involved in a dispute) now constituted a separate estate of the realm. It was no use, the judgement ran, deploring the fact: it was one that had to be lived with. All of the so-called 'wets' were, in 1979, to be found on this side of the argument. They feared that increasing unemployment, and the monetary and fiscal squeezes which in part at least caused it, would provoke ever more strident union militancy. In consequence the need to deal with and, if necessary, placate, the trade unions was an important part of their argument at various points during the first term for at least some measure of reflation.

The opposing section of the party was bitterly disappointed at Prior's appointment in 1979. This section had two wings. The first consisted of those intellectual Thatcherites who believed that the unions, considered collectively, constituted a labour monopoly which had to be broken if an economic breakthrough was to be achieved. There was a division within a division here, between the pure monetarists who reckoned that trade unions were no more than a nuisance (and that strict monetary policy would foreclose on any power they had to create inflation through excessive wage rises) and those who believed, with Hayek, that a free-enterprise economy could not be created unless the trade union movement was severely weakened. The less intellectual element on the right wing of the Conservative Party simply thirsted for revenge on the trade unions for the humiliations of 1974. Both sections came together in a revolt in the House of Commons on 22 April 1980. Forty-five Conservative members voted in favour of an amendment to industrial relations legislation then before Parliament. The Bill had not provided, the amendment would provide, for secret ballots in elections to trade union office. The amendment did not succeed, but there was ample evidence in its being tabled that substantial elements in the party were impatient with what they believed to be pussy-footing on the part of the government in the matter of the reform of trade union law. The Prime Minister made it fairly clear that her heart was with them.

None the less, throughout the first term the whole approach of the government was gradualist. While the press abounded with rumours of the Prime Minister's dissatisfaction with Prior's go-slow approach on union legislation, and though it was widely believed that Norman Tebbit was drafted into the job in 1981 to speed things up, all the evidence is that she was quite content with the pace of things, even if she was also quite content to have Prior blamed for that pace. The truth of the matter is that the legal ratchet has been slowly tightened on the trade unions, and with the implementation of the 1984 Trade Union Act providing for secret ballots, the rebels of 1980 will see their desires at last satisfied.

The reasoning behind the decision to go slowly on trade union reform is simple. On arrival in office Edward Heath had passed into law a massive Trade Union Act, implementing reforms considered at great length in opposition. The legislation (the parliamentary passage of which was masterminded by Geoffrey Howe, the then Attorney General) provided an instant focus for massive trade union rebellion. As the government retreated, industrial disputes — and most notably those instigated by the National Union of Mineworkers — became more prevalent, and it became clear that the provisions of the Act were quite insufficient to cajole or coerce the unions into what the government considered to be reasonable behaviour. In 1979 the Prime Minister was determined not to allow the trade union movement so large a target.

For all but the impatient radicals of the right, the cumulative effect of the government's legislation is impressive, even if some of the legislation is not always invoked in disputes: for example, at the time of writing, the National Coal Board has not sought legal redress against the picketing activities of the National Union of Mineworkers, even though such activities are clearly in breach of the law. (It should be mentioned here that much of the recent legislation can be triggered only by an employer, not by the government itself.)

The Thatcher government has legislated on average once every two years on the trade unions. The various changes have restricted the definition of lawful picketing, relieved to some extent those workers who refuse to join a union in a firm where a closed-shop agreement has been reached between employers and employees (by way of financial compensation), made it more difficult to create new closed shops, restricted trade union immunity in the matter of secondary picketing, removed those parts of Michael Foot's Employment Protection Act which affected small businesses, made it unlawful, in provisions which applied particularly to local authorities, to exclude non-union firms from tender offers, made it more possible for civil actions to be taken against trade unions, and restricted the definition of what constitutes a lawful dispute.

'A revolution it ain't,' said one minister, 'but we're well on the way.' It cannot be argued that the legislation had much effect either on the incidence or the conduct of industrial disputes during the first term. The weapon of the government in weakening the trade union movement over that period — and it was obvious, by 1983, how weak the movement was by comparison with 1974 — was the recession and the tight monetary policy which went along with it. In the case of disputes in both the private and public sectors, moreover, it was willpower on the part of management (in the public-sector case the willpower of government) that achieved such triumphs as there were. At British Leyland Sir Michael Edwardes managed successfully to appeal to his workers over the heads of their shop stewards. In 1980 the steel workers and in 1982 the railwaymen, unions hitherto regarded as virtually all-powerful, were mauled in bitter disputes with the government. The Civil Service strikes of 1981 and the National Health Service dispute in 1982 likewise ended in government victories and demoralised unions. All attempts to organise united trade union action on a broad front failed, notably the Day of Action on 9 March 1980. It is extremely doubtful that the government and the various managements involved in all these battles could have been successful had it not been for the background of high and rising unemployment figures.

The one possible exception to this picture of retreat from union militancy remained, at the end of the term, the National Union of Mineworkers. In 1981, as we have seen, the Prime Minister retreated from a confrontation with that union. This retreat did not encourage the union members to greater militancy and, indeed, both in January and October 1982 the miners, against the wishes of their leaders, voted to accept wage offers from the Coal Board. None the less, there were those who believed that even the combination of gradualist legislation and the recession would not, in the end, be sufficient finally to establish as one of the Prime Minister's advisers put it, 'the right of government to govern and the right of management to manage'. It was believed, therefore, that at some stage there would have to be a conflict on a major scale between the government and a union, or even several unions. The Prime Minister noted, in reply to a memorandum she received in 1981 on this gloomy possibility, that she would neither seek nor avoid such a confrontation. In 1984 the confrontation began with, as was generally expected, the National Union of Mineworkers, under the militant presidency of Arthur Scargill.

In dealing with nationalised industries the Prime Minister has always been reasonably content with managers she felt she could trust, notably Ian MacGregor, Sir John King, and Sir Michael Edwardes, though Edwardes recalls that the course of their relationship was not always a smooth one.[6] Their differences were exactly as might have been expected: Edwardes, while recognising that the object of the operation was to return British Leyland to profitability in order to sell it off, saw his job as simply the return to profitability. He would not hurry it along however impatient the Prime Minister became. For most of the others she had little time, as little as she had for the organisations they managed. Various steps were taken to improve the efficiency of the relationship between Whitehall and the nationalised industries, particularly with a view to restricting their budgets, but also with the intention of streamlining their relations with central government. There was a serious contradiction here. On the one hand the government wanted to free the industries from the stultifying hand of state bureaucracy. On the other hand they wanted to be sure that nationalised industry spending would not get out of hand, and that required careful monitoring from Whitehall. Although a number of improvements were effected the Prime Minister's frustrations mounted.

She was already, when she came into office, profoundly suspicious of the Civil Service. 'Do you,' a friend asked her in 1980, 'hate all institutions?' She frowned and replied, 'Not at all. I have great respect for the monarchy and Parliament.' But for the City, the trade unions, the Civil Service and the Church of England she has a dislike that some would call hatred and certainly veers regularly over into contempt. 'How does one get through to these people?' she exclaimed on an occasion when a Treasury report did not produce the answer she wanted. Her suspicion of the Civil Service, fuelled by determination and frustration, led to what one senior civil servant called 'a reign of terror' in Whitehall.[7]

'She caused,' says one minister who sat on several of the most important of her committees, 'a bigger cultural shock in Whitehall than any of her predecessors. She is both unpredictable and inimitable.' At the end of the first term she was on course to her objective of a reduction of over one hundred thousand in the number of civil servants by 1984 (an objective which has since been achieved). According to Peter Hennessy,[8] however, it was her decisions, made again and again, to appoint to the senior jobs in Whitehall men regarded by those senior to them at the moment of their appointment as far too young for those jobs, which made the most important differences in the Whitehall structure. What above all maddened her Whitehall opponents — and especially those who had felt the lash of her tongue — was what they regarded as her unreasoning approach to their beloved Civil Service. Her decision to cut their numbers by one hundred thousand was arrived at, they believed, arbitrarily and intuitively, and she was quite unprepared to allow it to be examined at length by scrutiny committees with an almost infinite amount of time at their disposal.

This ferocious attitude to the Civil Service, which she rarely bothers to justify in terms of greater efficiency or savings made, is one she has held for a long time. I recall an occasion in 1977 when I was helping her to prepare a speech in which there were to be a number of references to Churchill. I told her that when I had been working on a book on Churchill some years previously I had interviewed General Sir Ian Jacob, in 1940 a Deputy Military Secretary to the War Cabinet. I knew from the papers I had read that Sir Ian had been highly critical of Churchill before he became Prime Minister, and highly supportive afterwards. I asked him if there was any particular time when he had changed his mind. 'Yes,' he replied after a moment's reflection. 'It was on the thirteenth of May 1940. I saw a Permanent Undersecretary in a corridor in Whitehall in his shirtsleeves, *running*. Then I knew that Churchill could shake up the machine.' The anecdote gave her enormous pleasure.

If, as the minister quoted earlier believes, she delivered a tremendous culture shock to Whitehall, it was not done in any schematic way. She has simply applied a highly generalised instinct to whatever she has found in front of her, and not all of the results have been of the kind she wanted. In one of Peter Hennessy's fascinating *Times* articles,[9] for example, the thesis is put forward that the apparently unending series of leaks from which this government has suffered is a direct result of the low morale created by the dismissive attitude of ministers in general, and the Prime Minister in particular, to their work. He quotes a senior official as saying:

> ... to be told by politicians that they don't want
> whingeing, analysis or integrity — that we must do as we
> are told and that they have several friends in the private
> sector who could do the job in a morning with one hand
> tied behind their back — is a bit much. It seems to be
> injudicious to attack the people upon whom you rely.

That official gave Hennessy a very fair picture of the Prime
Minister's attitude to the Civil Service in general: for individual civil servants — like Sir Douglas Wass, formerly Permanent Undersecretary at the Treasury, of whom she
entertained initial suspicions, and Clive Whitmore, her own
Principal Private Secretary, whom she promoted to be Permanent Under Secretary at the Ministry of Defence over several
alternative candidates — she can develop a high regard. It is
understandable, of course, that her initial blitz on morale and
numbers has had adverse effects, but it may be that her own
belief is correct, and that by establishing in the highest post
men of a new generation, skipping several layers in between,
she will be seen in the end as a successful reformer.

And yet, as mentioned before, she has always declined
seriously to consider any major structural reform of the
machinery of government. When he was her Shadow Leader
of the House, John Peyton (now Lord Peyton of Yeovil) constantly urged her to examine the matter, on the ground that a
radical policy would best be implemented through a re-
designed system of government. You cannot — this was
Peyton's message — put new wine in old bottles. John
Hoskyns joined the staff at No. 10 almost solely with the
objective of replanning the machine. In June 1982 Alfred
Sherman sent her a closely argued paper proposing the
creation of a Prime Ministerial Department.[10] None of their
schemes or proposals found favour, and at one time her Policy

Unit at No. 10, reporting directly to herself, consisted solely of John Hoskyns, Norman Strauss and one civil servant or, as one of her previous advisers disgustedly put it, 'two men and a mangy dog'. Hoskyns was replaced, on his resignation, by Ferdinand Mount, at that time political editor of the *Spectator*, and the staff fluctuated somewhat in numbers. Occasional *ad hoc* appointments are made, such as that of Sir Anthony Parsons as adviser on foreign policy after the Falklands war, but nothing has been done to develop the kind of substantial department responsible to the Prime Minister alone such as heads of government in most countries enjoy. 'There's no need for it,' said one sympathetic minister to whom I put the comparison, 'there's a total exclusion zone around Margaret, and she defends it herself.'

This innate conservatism applied in other areas. When Sir Derek (now Lord) Rayner was asked to return to Whitehall in 1979 to do for her the sort of job he had sought to do for Edward Heath during the 1970 government — the sort of cost-cutting, quality-control exercise he has performed so successfully for his firm, Marks and Spencer, over the years — there was a hope that he might be encouraged to think in strategic terms about the functioning of the Whitehall machine. He was not. And although the usefulness of his examinations between 1979 and 1982 (when he returned to his company) are not in doubt (135 examinations produced annual savings of £300 million a year) there was a great deal of disappointment that so formidable a man had not been given a job more commensurate with his abilities.

The rule, then, was that there would be no structural changes in the administration of government. There were, to be sure, three important ministerial committees, two of which — the so-called Star Chamber and the Ministerial Steering Group of government strategy — have already been discussed. The third was the Family Policy Group. One of the reasons for Ferdinand Mount's appointment to the Policy

Unit was the fact that he had written a philosophical book on the family[11] which attracted a great deal of attention, and it was clear that the Prime Minister wanted ideas and plans for strengthening the position of the family in relation to children, for giving parents more power in schools and, in general, for reducing the role of the state and of local authorities in the upbringing of children.

Again, this was to fly in the face of the established practice of the Welfare State, if not absolutely of its theory. Over the years, particularly through child allowances, school meals and other forms of subsidy, the state had accepted greater and greater responsibility for the sustenance of families. The very name of one of the most important pressure groups working in this field, the Child Poverty Action Group, demonstrated how much the emphasis in such movement was on children, particularly those in poor and deprived homes. But, again over the years — or so it seemed to the Prime Minister — there had been a significant (and to her undesirable) extension of public at the expense of family (or parental) authority. Teachers in schools and local education authorities, the army of social workers created by reforms first recommended by Lord Seebohm in the late 1960s — recommendations accepted by both major political parties — and the administrators of the supplementary benefit system created by the Labour government in 1976, all seemed to her to be encroaching upon the domain of the family. The philosophical purpose of the Family Group is to find ways of counteracting this tendency, and the early months of the second term saw the production by Keith Joseph of highly detailed plans for, in particular, increasing considerably the influence and the authority of parents within schools.

Beadier eyes than those of the Family Policy Group were, however, fixed on the Welfare State and its gigantic apparatus. The fact that any Treasury official charged with seeking ways of balancing the national budget has to face is the high cost of the Welfare State. The largest single charge on government resources in the financial year 1982–83 was social security, at £32,473 million, the next was defence, at £14,411 million, the third was health, at £13,879 million, and the fourth was education and science, at £12,628 million. These represented respective differences over the period since 1979 of plus 19.9 per cent, plus 16.7 per cent, plus 13.4 per cent and minus 1.1 per cent.[12] Wherever the famed slashing of public expenditure had come it did not seem to be in these fields.

It was the contention of the radical thinkers who found themselves sympathetic to Margaret Thatcher that the welfare figures simply had to be reduced if the ultimate goal of a free-enterprise economy was to be reached. The defence figures were another matter: it was universally accepted within the Conservative Party that the government of the day must spend whatever was necessary to defend the realm, though argument could and did take place about whether the most effective use was being made of existing resources. The proposed defence cuts of 1980, therefore — over which Francis Pym threatened to resign — caused a great deal of agony within the party.

Welfare and health spending was another matter altogether. A stream of papers from the Institute of Economic Affairs[13] argued first that the public in general were sympathetic to the idea of widespread changes within the welfare system, if these could be shown to make that system more efficient and, second, that reorganisation of the National Health Service, together with a system of personal health insurance (of the kind that obtains on the continent and in Australia) would lift a great burden from the public purse and thus dramatically improve the prospects for the creation of a low-taxation high-productivity economy. In September 1982 the Central Policy Review Staff (generally known as the Think Tank) produced a paper (which was leaked to the press and created an enormous furore) suggesting savings in public expenditure which included the introduction of compulsory insurance and other charges into the NHS (a saving of between £3 billion and £4 billion a year), in education the end of all automatic state funding for higher education, and in social security the end of the system whereby benefits rose in line with prices. The response of the Prime Minister was to rule out all the proposed changes and, just after the 1983 election, to abolish the CPRS.

Certainly, all radical proposals for the Welfare State face political difficulties, not least among which is the continuing popularity of the National Health Service with the electorate. But there are three other general difficulties. The first is that the NHS is a service free at the point of use: this means that demands on it are theoretically unlimited. The fact is that no service of its kind that is free can possibly meet efficiently all the demands made upon it, hence the frequent outcries about long waiting lists for operations and care of various kinds. The second difficulty, faced by the social security system, is that the very high unemployment figures dictate a vastly increased disbursement of unemployment relief. The third difficulty also faced by the social security system, is that improved health care means that people live longer. The 1983 Public Expenditure White Paper predicted a rise of two hundred thousand in the number of retirement pensioners between 1982–83 and 1985–86. It would probably be impossible for any government to keep pace with the increasing pressures on the creaking machinery of the Welfare State. It is certainly impossible for a government with the monetary and fiscal policies of the present one to do so. Indeed, although global figures on welfare spending have risen substantially during the first term (except in education) there has been a certain amount of squeezing as well. Child benefit was initially frozen, and thereafter rearranged: over the term as a whole the benefit lagged behind prices. Earnings-related supplementary benefit was abolished and the rate of unemployment and sickness benefit was fixed at a level lower than prices. The indexing of long-term benefit to either earnings or prices was likewise done away with. And in 1981 certain benefits which had been paid because the 1980 prediction of the inflation rate was too high were clawed back.

All of this was tinkering, however much outcry was raised against it, particularly by the opposition. Even with increased budgetary drafts there seems little doubt that the quality of social provision will decline. From the beginning of the term the government had embarked on a series of review exercises — one of which led to the abolition of the middle tier of management in the National Health Service, itself instituted by a Conservative government — designed to cut waste and improve efficiency. The idea that it is possible to make substantial savings through good housekeeping, admirable in itself though such saving may be, carries greater conviction with the Prime Minister than it does with hard-pressed Treasury ministers.

At the end of the first term, therefore, there was undoubtedly an important change in the political climate. The people had come to accept that there were strict limitations on the ability of government to achieve things — this was the most significant educative effect the Prime Minister herself had on the electorate — and so, though they deplored unemployment, they did not blame the government for its level. If the conquest of inflation had not been completed there was a fairly general consensus that the battle was nearly over. The Labour Party was in a state of disarray that many commentators deemed terminal, and the SDP/Liberal Alliance was a very long way from a breakthrough in electoral terms. In policy generally, however, and in monetary and fiscal policy in particular, there had been no deep-seated change: anything the government had done could be reversed by a successor government. The welfare juggernaut continued on its course, battered here and there and perhaps seedier here and there, but still consuming a vast quantity of the national treasure. Only in the field of privatisation had radical steps been taken which, if continued with determination, might in the end fundamentally alter the nature of the British economy, and prove irreversible by a successor government of a different cast of mind. The Thatcher government had been true to its word in its tactical conduct of policy, and its wishes for the strategic and long-term conduct of the future were perfectly clear. Whatever Margaret Thatcher's rhetoric had been in opposition, there had, between 1975 and 1979, been severe doubts about her will or her ability to hold to the monetary undertakings she had given once she was in office. By 1983 all such doubts had been dispelled: what she made up her mind was right to do, she would do. But it is a precariously balanced government that depends on one individual, however remarkable, for its success and, more important, for its legacy.

The principal problem a reforming government faces is how to ensure that what it does will endure. The trade union legislation of the Heath government, for example, was judged by many independent commentators to be admirably fair and reasonable. It was certainly comprehensive. But one general election defeat sufficed not merely to see it overthrown, but to see it replaced by legislation dictating a movement in entirely the opposite direction. A thoroughgoing privatisation plan, on the other hand, would prove far more difficult to reverse, and the early moves on privatisation in the second term showed that the Prime Minister was determined to proceed in the future at a speed that even its most enthusiastic proponents doubted could be kept up.

On the other hand the Prime Minister's refusal to consider any major alteration in the Welfare State left her open to accusations that her radicalism was nothing like as profound as her rhetoric suggested. By the end of the term, however, it was beginning to dawn on most ministers that the welfare burden had to be reconsidered and, somehow, reduced. A massive review of social security payments is currently being conducted, under the personal chairmanship of the Secretary of State for Social Services, Norman Fowler. A similar review of the whole curricular system of education in the United Kingdom is being carried on by Sir Keith Joseph. The main thrust of the government in the second term is therefore broadly similar to that in the first, with the important differences that the prolonged battles, made more bitter because of a sequence of errors in calculation, over budgetary and economic policy, need no longer take the time and drain the energy of ministers: the kind of economic policy the nation is to see under Margaret Thatcher is now immutably fixed for as long as she is Prime Minister. And although the second term began with a number of embarrassing hiccups — notably the row over the banning of trade unions at General Communications Headquarters (GCHQ) and the total confusion that attended a debate in the House of Commons on capital punishment — none of these affected more than the margins of public policy: the central purpose of reform was still being pursued. Industrial relations, and particularly those with the miners, presented a far greater threat to the authority of the government, but again it seemed clear that the Prime Minister was standing by her guns. She had always said she would need two terms to change the historical direction of the ship of state. In the first term she charted a course, and she has been given a second to reach her destination.

CHAPTER SEVEN

The Prime Minister Goes to War

But it is not on our fleets and armies, however necessary they may be for the maintenance of our imperial strength, that I alone or mainly depend in that enterprise on which this country is about to enter. It is on what I most highly value — the consciousness that in the Eastern nations there is confidence in this country, and that, while they know we can enforce our policy, at the same time they know that our Empire is an Empire of liberty, of truth, and of justice.
— Benjamin Disraeli, Earl of Beaconsfield, in the House of Lords, on the subject of the Berlin Treaty of 1878

The two greatest — certainly the two most dramatic — events of the first term in foreign policy came just after the beginning and just over a year before the end. They were the resolution of the imbroglio in Rhodesia (discussed in Chapter Three) and the war in the Falklands, discussed later in this chapter. In between there were continually acrimonious exchanges with the EEC, fairly serene relations with America (ripening into friendship after the election of the like-minded President Reagan in 1980), and a continuingly glacial state of diplomacy between the United Kingdom and the Soviet Union. The Prime Minister's activity in bringing about the settlement in Rhodesia was atypical of her diplomacy during the first term, in that she opted for conciliation rather than conflict. From the beginning of the war in the South Atlantic she was to exhibit the unrelenting side of her nature, to even more decisive effect.

It is right to emphasise the lack of experience in high politics of Margaret Thatcher when she became Prime Minister. Even the few months she had enjoyed as a Treasury spokesman in opposition were spent as number two to Robert Carr. She had never been a figure of significance either in the councils of government nor, even, in the councils of her party. True, she had laboured assiduously between 1975 and 1979 to make up by study what she lacked in experience; but the lack was nevertheless there. In her early handling of the machine of government, and particularly in the preparation of the 1979 budget, her inexperience was painfully apparent.

In opposition she had read deeply in foreign policy. But she had not read widely. Her principal interest — as was witnessed by the series of speeches which earned her the soubriquet 'Iron Lady' — lay in relations (or the state of conflict) between the Western Alliance and the Soviet Union. Through this reading she came to a view about the relationship between nations which matched her instinct about politics generally: all was a state of conflict. Given this perception on her part, and the way in which it corresponded to her nature, the many writers who have compared her to General de Gaulle are correct. Like him, she is a nationalist, first and foremost. Like him, she believes that will is the foremost attribute in negotiations, whether in domestic or foreign policy. And, like him, she distrusts compromise although, again like him, she is prepared to accept compromise when it is necessary or useful. In international relations, however, her attitude for her country is very different from his attitude for his. While de Gaulle sought to place France — with or without the EEC — in a position of balance between East and West, Margaret Thatcher looks steadfastly across the Atlantic. For the purposes of foreign policy generally, but even more for reasons of defence and security, she looks eternally westward.

It was not so much her attitude on policy, however, as her negotiating style, which brought her at an early date into conflict with the Foreign Office, which Department of State she came to dislike and distrust more than any other. It would not be going too far to say that her hostility to the Foreign Office was in proportion to its pretensions.

The Foreign Office regards itself — and is regarded by other departments of state —as a world apart. From the time of Sir Val Duncan's report in 1969, which recommended the integration of the Home and Foreign Civil Services, the Office has been conscious of fighting a rearguard action and they have, indeed, successfully resisted integration: transfers of individuals between the home departments and the Foreign Office are so rare as to be virtually unknown. Considering itself to be the only unchanging and permanent guardian of the national identity and the national interest the Foreign Office believes itself to be above governments, and to be wiser than the government of the day in the formulation of policy.[1] In 1979 the Foreign Office was determinedly Euro-centric: its denizens disliked the idea of a Prime Minister whose trans-Atlantic sympathies were worn on her sleeve, whose naked hostility to the Soviet Union offended against all their canons of diplomatic conduct, and whose enthusiasm for the European connection was less than obvious. Later in the first term diplomats who had been conducting for years what they considered to be a planned and sensible withdrawal from a group of barren islands in the South Atlantic, a withdrawal hindered only and postponed only by occasional outbursts of anger in the House of Commons, were appalled and dismayed to feel the full fury of her rage at what she considered to be their utter failure to protect vital national interests. They did not see it that way.

The clash between the Prime Minister and the Foreign Office is full of interest not merely because of differences over the direction of policy. Its underlying nature may be explained simply. Over the years of Britain's declining power and retreat from empire the Office has invested more and more of its time, energy and intelligence in the technicalities of diplomacy. As a body, it has certain distinct views on policy: it is, as I have already observed, Euro-centric rather than Atlanticist. In the Middle East it favours Arab interests over those of Israel. It was happy during the period of *détente* between East and West introduced by President Carter and Chancellor Brandt, not least because *détente* offered opportunities for the practice of the diplomatic arts, whereas the kind of confrontation apparently favoured by Mrs Thatcher (and by President Reagan) offered little opportunity for the practice of those arts. In sum, and over the years, the Foreign Office has come to equate the practice of diplomacy with the purpose of policy, and to treat these two very different entities as of equal value save where diplomacy was considered more important than policy. Gone, indeed, are the days when Lord Curzon, one of the greatest of British foreign secretaries, decreed that there were only two rules in diplomacy: 'The first is to know your own mind and the second is to make sure that the other fellow knows it.' The difficulty into which this equation led British diplomats was a serious one. If diplomacy, as an art, was as worthy as policy, then policy could be split for a diplomatic end. That is to say, just as a trade union and an employer may often split the difference over a wage claim so, in international negotiations, a split of the difference in favour of a resolution that can be proclaimed as a success serves the ends of diplomacy, even if it does not serve the ends of policy. When a prime minister is as clear cut about policy as Margaret Thatcher evidently is, it is difficult to assert the technical primacy of diplomacy, and difficult to avoid breakdowns in negotiations. The Foreign Office, in a word, is suspicious of policies too clearly defined, for these are less susceptible to negotiation.

The Prime Minister made clear, early on, that her view of

the Foreign Office was close to that of Norman Tebbit who observed, 'The Ministry of Agriculture is there to look after farmers, and the Foreign Office is there to look after foreigners.' From the beginning to the end of her first term, and on into her second, she took Tebbit's view of the Foreign Office rather than the view even of her first Foreign Secretary, Peter Carrington, whom she liked, and even, from time to time, admired.

The idea that foreign policy was, somehow, different from the domestic variety was, from the beginning, anathema to the Prime Minister. She brought to its conduct, however, certain clearly defined views, of which her attachment to the Atlantic Alliance was the most important. She has never been able to muster a similar enthusiasm for the European Economic Community for all that from time to time she makes the correct responses in a formal way. During the 1975 referendum on the continuance of British membership of the Community she took as small a part in proceedings as was consonant with her leadership of a party which had brought the United Kingdom into the EEC in the first place, and many of whose most senior members were enthusiastic proponents of the fellowship of Western European nations. Instead, she left the bulk of the campaigning to Heath, on the ground that he had negotiated the treaty of membership. After one speech on the subject she asked Neave how he thought it had gone. 'I wish,' he replied 'you didn't gabble it so much.'

I have already described negotiations with Britain's partners in the EEC during the first year of her first term.[2] The deal she had, by the end of that year, negotiated was satisfactory in its own limited terms: the United Kingdom ended up by paying far less into Community coffers than it would otherwise have done. But her announced determination, throughout 1980, to seek a complete reorganisation of Community finances, for all that it had the support (tepid but real) both of the Netherlands and of the Federal Republic of

Germany (themselves net contributors to the EEC budget) fell on deaf continental ears.

From 1980 to 1982, and largely as a result of the Prime Minister's determination, Britain recouped £1,800 million of her payments: the net outflow of British funds to the Community in 1980 and 1981 was thus under £200 million for each year. However, no permanent settlement of payments in and out had been reached and in 1982 there was a further storm, this time over agricultural payments. Britain, in the person of Peter Walker, vetoed a farm price package agreed by the other powers and was promptly overridden by their majority vote, although that action was contrary to the provisions of the Treaty of Rome. The matter was resolved, after further bruising negotiations, by an agreement to increase refunds to Britain. This agreement was, in turn, rendered inoperative for a time by a vote in the European Assembly.[3] The same process of agreement and disagreement was followed in 1983 and 1984.

For three years the budgetary battle ebbed and flowed, and in the second term it has continued. What started, on the British side, as a simple refusal to pay into central funds the sums predicated by earlier agreements between the member states of the Community developed into a debilitating series of political battles. At all times the Prime Minister refused to sell British oil on preferential terms to the European allies, and the Chancellor refused to join the pound to other currencies in the European Monetary System. The government, however, did not rest on the defensive: gradually it developed its demand for two changes of great significance to the structure of the Community. The first was for a ceiling to be placed on agricultural spending, although the Common Agricultural Policy — the price exacted by France in return for her signature to the Treaty of Rome — was a cornerstone of the whole organisation. The second was for a complete reform of the whole system of EEC financing. By the middle of 1983 it appeared that, for all that both sides — the United Kingdom on the one hand, and all her European partners on the other — had made some concessions to each other, the major problems were no nearer solution.

The essence of the matter lies in entirely different visions of what the EEC is, and what it should become. All of the continental powers, but especially Germany, have at some time made sacrifices for the common good of the EEC as a whole. Even France, recalcitrant as she has so often been in her own interests, regards the Community as something essential to her national being. All major continental politicians of recent years have paid rather more than lip service to the ideal of a united Europe and, of course, the essential fact that the Franco-German rapprochement which is at the heart of the organisation seems to them to guarantee future peace in Western Europe means that they invest emotion as well as substance in the continuance and the development of the EEC. Even before the United Kingdom joined, crises in relations were not unknown and that in 1966, when for a time France absented herself from Community deliberations, was of a profoundly serious character. None the less there continued — and continues — to be a sense of common identity between the continental powers which is not shared by the Thatcher government.

Her view of the EEC is that it is a necessary rather than a desirable grouping. She is perfectly prepared to join with other European governments where matters of common interest are concerned — as, for example, in presenting a united front to the rest of the world on textiles, or steel. But the prospect of closer European unity or, for that matter, the development of a Community identity which is separate from, and perhaps in some sense above, the individual identities of the states, does not cause her heart to beat any faster. It is interesting to note from reports that whereas she is tetchy and impatient at the summit gatherings of the heads of government of the EEC countries, she is recorded as being, while hard-headed, constructive and clear-sighted at the summit meetings of Western nations, from Tokyo in 1979 to Williamsburg in 1983. At the Ottawa summit in July 1981 even the then Prime Minister of Canada, Pierre Trudeau, who had no personal rapport with her, and who disliked her seemingly intransigent stance on relations with the USSR, went out of his way to praise her contribution to the meeting. The simple truth of the matter is that she is more at home at the larger summits of Western nations, where the individual identity of each country is not in doubt, than at the smaller — the more local — EEC gatherings where, apart from the ten nations assembled, there is an eleventh and impalpable presence, that of the Community itself. The point is emphasised by the extreme suspicion with which the Prime Minister has regarded any proposal to provide the Community with further 'own resources' — that is, essentially money that can be spent collectively by the EEC without unending recourse to the separate national governments. To some extent, of course, the 'own resources' issue is a bargaining point with her: the one per cent rise in VAT and the related proposed agricultural tax (to be levied according to a complex formula based on agricultural output and Gross Domestic Product) which would be required to provide these resources could be traded off against a satisfactory agreement on the contribution Britain makes to the communal budget. But if that is done it will be done reluctantly, even grudgingly. And it is the sour (or admirably principled, depending on your point of view) stance of the British government in these negotiations that from time to time arouses particular ire on the continent.

A minister who discussed these matters with her during one of the particularly fraught periods of Anglo-European relations suggested that relations might be made easier if she made even a gesture — perhaps by way of rhetoric — towards the European ideal. It was not necessary, he argued, to believe in the creation of a United States of Europe (the dream of the founding fathers of the Community, and notably of the Frenchman, Jean Monnet, who did more than anybody else to bring about its creation) but it was highly desirable at least to doff one's hat in the direction of that ideal, to, so to speak, pay one's respects to it. She listened, he records, and then impatiently waved her hand. 'But I've done all that,' she said. He tried to explain to her that what she had done had been done without apparent conviction, and that it might be expedient to put a little more spirit into her formal expressions of pro-European sentiment. 'At this point,' he says, 'I felt I'd lost her. She started looking around the room and when I stopped talking she said, "Why?"'

It can be argued, of course, that this kind of cutting out of argument demonstrates how narrow her mind is, and how blinkered her vision. 'Blinkered?' she once asked while reading an article in which the writer deployed that adjective in its usual pejorative sense. 'Does he know what blinkers are *for*? They are to make the horse better able to see straight ahead.' If one happens to share her view on any particular issue, naturally, one regards as a strength what others consider to be a limitation. Few politicians waste as little time on the common cant of political discourse and on the rare occasions on which she feels it necessary to pay obeisance to some political shibboleth she sounds singularly unconvincing.

The Prime Minister reacts decisively to challenge, but is not always decisive in approaching a problem. This fissure in her attitude to public affairs can be illustrated very well through a consideration of her record on Ulster. Strictly and constitutionally speaking, of course, Ulster is a domestic problem, the six counties of Northern Ireland being a part of the United Kingdom. But because of the involvement of the Republic of Ireland, and because of widespread interest in the past, present and future of the province in the United States, domestic concerns spill over from time to time into the realm of international relations.

Almost everything the Thatcher government has attempted to do in Northern Ireland politics has failed, just as the efforts of previous governments have failed. Within the narrower spectrum of security it may be said that, from the entry into office of the Labour Party's last Secretary of State for Northern Ireland, Roy Mason, matters have somewhat improved. In spite, even, of the massive breakout from the Maze Prison which marred James Prior's record in office, the killings and maimings which have characterised the Ulster conflict in its present phase since 1969 have been reducing steadily in number, though this is not always apparent from media reaction to the frequent incidents of exceptional violence which do occur. At the end of his time at the Ulster Office (in 1984) Prior ruefully confessed that the Ulster Assembly (designed as a first stage in the return of government devolved from Westminster to Belfast) had failed; and he advised his successors to disregard the notion — hitherto entertained by every secretary of state since the post was created by Edward Heath — that political initiatives of any conceivable kind would bring peace. And, indeed, the Prime Minister has been clear throughout her first term that Northern Ireland was probably not susceptible to political system-building: the fact that Prior was allowed to get on with his scheme for an Assembly (boycotted, incidentally, by the mainly Catholic Social Democratic and Labour Party)was merely a consequence of the fact that she allowed him a relatively free hand in his new posting, partly as a consolation for his exclusion for all practical purposes from economic policy-making in Whitehall.

Her attitude to Britain's most troublesome province has, therefore, been one of *laissez faire* in political terms. On the other hand successive Irish prime ministers — the two men who alternated in that office during her first term, Charles

Haughey and Garret Fitzgerald — have found to their cost that her seemingly pliable and certainly friendly attitude in negotiations with them conceals a steady refusal to make any significant concessions towards their point of view, that point of view being that, even if the united Ireland of their dreams is for the foreseeable future unattainable, the Republic should be involved much more than she at present is in designing a future for Ulster. She has taken the same attitude towards American politicians, mainly those with Irish racial connections, or with substantial Irish-American elements in their constituencies, such as Senators Edward Kennedy and Daniel Moynihan and Congressman 'Tip' O'Neill, the Speaker of the American House of Representatives. Over the years of her first term, moreover, there were substantial electoral advances recorded by Sinn Fein (the political wing of the Irish Republican Army) at the expense of the moderate SDLP. It was urged upon her that some concession towards, or even gesture in the direction of, John Hume, the SDLP leader, would help to turn this tide. No concession or gesture was made. Her recommendation of Gerry Fitt, the founder of the SDLP who lost his seat in West Belfast in 1983, for a peerage was a recognition of his sterling personal qualities (he had been much admired by Airey Neave) rather than a gesture to a party from whose ranks he had by that time departed. Indeed, offence was taken in Catholic circles in Ulster at Fitt's ennoblement: the SDLP regarded him as a renegade, and had even put up a candidate against him in his constituency.

On matters of security the Prime Minister's actions and gestures have been much more clear cut than in politics. She frequently visits the province, and took particular care to do so in the immediate aftermath of the murder of Lord Mountbatten in August 1979. This trip was, to Irish Catholic eyes, offensive, not because it was made (the murder of Lord Mountbatten had aroused as much horror in the Republic as in the United Kingdom), but because she chose to be photographed during it wearing a flak jacket and the symbolic red beret of the Parachute Regiment. Before the photograph was taken, anxious officials of the Northern Ireland Office tried to persuade her not to wear the beret, fearing the likely Roman Catholic reaction to a politician donning the distinctive symbol of a regiment which had some years earlier opened fire on an unarmed crowd in Londonderry. If anything, this advice made her more determined to dress as the paras wished her to.

That her determination in the face of criticism and opposition was not merely confined to gestures she made apparent in the case of Northern Ireland in 1981. A series of hunger strikes began in the Maze Prison. The first hunger striker, by name Bobby Sands, was, in his absence, elected to Parliament in a by-election. The prison authorities, the Northern Ireland Office, a number of church leaders in Ulster and various concerned parties in Britain were all anxious that some concession — particularly on the major issue in the dispute, the dislike of IRA prisoners for wearing prison clothes — should be made. This was not altogether a matter of sentiment, nor an anxiety to placate the IRA: it was feared — rightly, as it turned out — that the death of Sands, and perhaps of others, would have undesirable political repercussions in Northern Ireland, in the Republic and in the United States. The Prime Minister was adamant, repeating her favourite litany with reference to the acts of violence for which Sands and his companions had been jailed, 'A crime is a crime is a crime.' As far afield as Abu Dhabi in April she repeated the theme, laying the blame for any deaths on 'those who are ordering these young men to commit suicide', namely the leaders of the IRA. After ten deaths the hunger strike was, on 3 October, abandoned.

On the surface at any rate Margaret Thatcher was evidently most resolute when challenged by violence or the threat of violence. A nature instinctively combative in the ordinary business of political exchanges became much more definitely so when the matter at issue was one of defence or military security. The Conservative Party — for all that its defence policy in government throughout the 1950s and 1960s is open to withering criticism[4] — tends to think of itself as the natural custodian of the defence effort of the nation, and the Leader it acquired in 1975 was no exception to that rule of behaviour. In her case, however, there was an added responsibility: her warnings in opposition to the effect that the Soviet threat to the West was a growing and determined one laid upon her a particular obligation to step up the defence effort of the country. It was, therefore, painful for her to consider, let alone attempt to implement, cuts in defence spending amounting to £600 million in 1980. The fact that, because of the principled stand of Francis Pym, these cuts were reduced to a sum of £175 million made no difference either to her personal feeling that something had gone badly wrong or to her decision to grit her teeth and take her medicine: the replacement of Pym by John Nott in September 1981 was a sign that the original intention that the defence budget should suffer nearly as much as any other in deference to the monetary policy of the Treasury and the government would be implemented. A recalcitrant Secretary of State for Defence was replaced by a pliable one; that was all.

The Prime Minister's position in regard to that spending on defence (which was more thoroughly linked with her foreign policy than was the case with any of her post-war predecessors) was curiously similar to her position on the subsidisation of nationalised industries.[5] A theoretical defence could be mounted for her actions in both areas, but whatever its plausibility, to the student possessed of a reflective and objective mind, it invited ridicule. The idea of the Iron Lady embarking on a series of swingeing defence cuts attracted satirical as well as concerned attention, and much abuse.

Yet until the Falklands war broke out the strategic as well as the economic aspect of the defence policy introduced by

John Nott in 1982 had — again, in theory — a number of merits, not least of them that it corresponded to the Prime Minister's own priorities in foreign policy. Essentially the surface Navy was to bear the brunt of the cuts, and this decision led to the resignation of the junior minister responsible for the Royal Navy, himself an officer in the Royal Naval Volunteer Reserve, Keith Speed, who subsequently wrote a cogent and powerful book on the issues involved.[6]

Because of her inherent, and somewhat naive, conviction that a large defence budget was a necessary part of good government, however, it was 'with almost tearful resentment', as one of her ministers put it, that Margaret Thatcher agreed, in the words of a tactful (or would-be tactful) Treasury minute on the subject, that the defence budget would have to be 'trimmed and rearranged'. She was the victim, though not the first by any means, of a way of thinking about defence in the Conservative Party which regards any reduction in defence expenditure as a sign of weakness, whether or not it reflects a sensible policy. As it happens, my own view is that the United Kingdom should spend more on defence, though also that it should be spent in a different way from that visualised in the 1982 White Paper on defence, the outcome of the prolonged review lasting from 1980 through 1981. In principle, however, the litmus-paper test of a defence policy is its effectiveness, not its cost. In global terms the Thatcher government had not done badly by the armed forces. A 32 per cent rise in their pay was announced as early as 11 May 1979, and overall expenditure on defence was to rise by 16.7 per cent during the first term. The vital questions should not be how much? but where? and why?

In 1981 the errors made and the difficulties experienced in the implementation of monetary policy were such as to make the economic issue an overwhelming one. If the Prime

Minister could not get that right, she could get nothing else right. If — and this is the way the balance of the argument seemed to those involved in the 1980 and 1981 public expenditure reviews — departments had to suffer budgetary surgery then the Ministry of Defence could not be exempt. The economic strategy was the vital one, and everybody had not only to suffer but be seen to suffer, even those whose job it would be, in any ultimate crisis, to defend the very existence of the nation.

'She saw a need,' says one former Secretary of State for Defence, 'which had nothing to do with defence, and she rationalised it.' While her judgement may have been (and, I think, was) mistaken, I find this man's view unfair. The defence strategy which issued from the cuts of 1980 and 1981 was perfectly congruent with her foreign policy.

To Margaret Thatcher in the middle of 1979, looking at her first briefs prepared by the Joint Intelligence Committee for the OD — Overseas and Defence — Committee of the Cabinet, it seemed clear that defence policy was essentially concerned with the defence of Western Europe against the USSR. This had been her own perception in opposition, and nothing she saw by way of the information she received in government changed it. Her understanding of the defence matters with which she had immediately to concern herself led to three conclusions.

The first was that the armed forces in general were disillusioned and on the brink of demoralisation: no recent government, they thought, appreciated what they were doing. Their pay structure, careers and prospects all seemed to be inadequate when compared to those individuals of similar capacity in civilian life. This she dealt with through the armed forces pay rise of 1979. Her decision had a direct, and important, effect on morale. But that effect was principally on the Army, and on the Army based in Germany at that. The fear above all fears was of a Soviet attack in the centre of Europe.

The second conclusion, which was based on a Ministry of Defence submission to her in June 1979, was that the principal strategic role of the Royal Navy would be that of fighting the submarines of the Soviet Navy. Surface ships, in this view of affairs, were important only in so far as they could detect and destroy enemy submarines at large in the area of Britain's particular maritime responsibility, the North Sea. Aircraft carriers, for example, like *Invincible* and *Hermes*, were, it seemed, irrelevant to what was necessary. John Nott's Defence White Paper of 1982 faithfully reflected these judgements, to the chagrin of Admiral Sir Henry Leach, the First Sea Lord, and of his staff.

The third conclusion was that the British independent nuclear deterrent should be brought up to date. The principal ingredient in the deterrent force was the submarine-launched Polaris missile. The Wilson and Callaghan governments had undertaken a modernisation of Polaris — called the Chevaline programme. The question that faced the new government in 1979 was whether a modernised Polaris force was sufficient for the nuclear needs of the United Kingdom. 'We must have the best,' the Prime Minister told the Chiefs of Staff. The best appeared to be not a refurbished Polaris, but the projected American missile system — like Polaris, submarine-launched — Trident. The decision was taken to purchase Trident, and the prospects for the defence budget soared: according to the 1983 defence estimates it would amount to £7.5 billion or, by 1990, six per cent of the total defence budget.

At the same time, it has to be remembered, the government had undertaken, in conjunction with the other NATO powers, to increase general defence expenditure at the rate of three per cent (in real terms) each year. Unlike the other European NATO powers, Britain has more than kept that promise: over the period of the first term there was an annual increase of just over four per cent. Indeed British defence spending is higher, considered as a proportion of Gross Domestic Product, than that of any other European member of the NATO alliance. When the whole issue came to be considered in 1980 it was clear that something had to give.

What should give, it was decided, was the Royal Navy. The projected number of destroyers was cut, in 1981, from fifty-nine to fifty. Whereas the existing plans called for three aircraft carriers (of the *Invincible* class: *Hermes* was already regarded as outmoded) the government reckoned on getting by with two, and even their construction was in doubt. On the other hand, the commitment to keep more than fifty thousand soldiers in Germany was maintained, and four submarines were to be built to carry Trident. Indeed, the number of nuclear-powered submarines was to go up from twelve to seventeen.

All British prime ministers since the signing, in 1949, of the treaty which established the NATO alliance had accepted that the USSR was the major threat to the security of the United Kingdom. In the 1950s and 1960s, however, Britain remained willing — indeed, was eager — to shoulder what were called 'out of theatre' responsibilities. That is to say British governments considered that their country had roles to play in geographical areas which were not part of the area covered by NATO. To some extent this was obviously true: in Hong Kong, for example, in Belize in Central America, and in the Falkland Islands in the South Atlantic Britain still had colonies, and possession entailed responsibility. Reluctantly, and even grudgingly, Harold Wilson's government in the 1960s came to accept that the range of oceanic responsibilities constituted too great an economic burden: the withdrawal from positions east of Suez — and most notably from Malaysia and Singapore — became a matter of policy. The end, in 1979, to the war in Rhodesia was, in its post-imperial context, the drawing of a line by Margaret Thatcher under the conclusion arrived at by Denis Healey as Secretary of State for

Defence in the first two Wilson governments, a conclusion to the effect that Britain could no longer consider herself to be an oceanic power.[7] Her security requirements dictated a preponderant, perhaps even a sole, concentration on the European theatre. The trouble with this relatively tidy idea was that some of the overseas possessions remained.

Their retention was not, however, considered to involve outrageous expense. Hong Kong was for the most part held on lease from China. It was accepted by all British governments, of whatever party, that the leased (generally called the 'new') territories would be restored to whatever government rules in Peking in 1997; and that the islands (supposedly held by the United Kingdom in perpetuity) could not be defended, and would not in any case be economically viable on their own once the lease ran out: the only question was a diplomatic one — what terms could be made for the inhabitants of the Crown Colony once their time as a colony was up? In Belize a battalion of British soldiers (some six hundred men) and a few aircraft were deemed sufficient to deter any likely move against the colony by any of the successive overweening dictators of Guatemala. Even though Belize was being moved gently towards independence throughout the 1960s it was accepted that the battalion should stay on station even after the colony became a state. Likewise, in Brunei in the Far East (though only after protracted and often difficult negotiations) it was accepted that the Gurkha regiment would remain as military guarantors of the territorial integrity of the sultanate, the Sultan meeting all of their bills. In the Middle East, and particularly in Oman, elements of the Special Air Services Regiment supported the Ruler's forces against incursions from the Republic of South Yemen, a satrapy of the USSR. And, of course, British officers on secondment served in most of the armies of the states in the Arabian Gulf, and in Africa. None of these presences involved excessive expenditure or commitment.

The Prime Minister's three major speeches — and their theme was repeated in many interviews on radio and television and in newspapers — while she was Leader of the Opposition on the Soviet threat dictated the emphasis of her defence policy when she came to power. Although those speeches showed a deeper understanding of the character of Soviet convictions and ambitions than was possessed by any of her colleagues or rivals in the political world, they were made without reference to, or understanding of, the totality of British strategic requirements. The very intensity of her focus on the political nature of the Soviet Union, accurate though most of her supporters thought it to be, precluded thinking about the flexible use of British power around the world. Worse: it excluded thinking about appropriate responses below the nuclear level in the European theatre itself. The decision to opt for purchase of the Trident missile was a decision in favour of a particular defence strategy which assumed an all-out Soviet onslaught on Western Europe which could be met only by the possession of — and independent control over — the most powerful weapon on Western drawing boards.

As, during 1980 and 1981, the debate about defence priorities proceeded, the naval staff were forced continually on the defensive. Their desire to retain a powerful surface fleet (and it is worth remembering that, at that time, the Royal Navy was the third most powerful in the world, after the fleets of the United States and the Soviet Union) was ascribed to their supposed nostalgia for the days in which they had ruled the oceans of the world. In vain did Rear Admiral (now Admiral of the Fleet) Sir Henry Leach point to the growing power of the Russian Navy, its ability to interdict the flow of Western trade, and its capacity, even, from its base in Murmansk to dominate the North Sea and close the Western Approaches (north of Scotland) and the English Channel. The Navy's thesis was that a powerful surface fleet was required for NATO duties even within the European theatre itself.[8] The difficulty they saw in the choice of Trident related — and to this day relates — to the inflexibility imposed on policy by the possession of a nuclear weapon strategic in character. The First Sea Lord wanted to be able to deal with, say, a Russian naval probe, without recourse to the awesome power of Polaris; and he wanted his successor sea lords to be able to respond to such a probe in the future without recourse to Trident.

In 1981 and early 1982, however, the facts that prevailed were not the ones on which Sir Henry Leach chose to place emphasis. In real terms the defence budget was destined to rise, in accordance with Britain's commitment to NATO and the Prime Minister's disposition. It could not, however, rise as fast as she would have liked because of the nation's parlous economic condition. She was about to commit her government to the acquisition of a vastly expensive strategic nuclear weapon, so savings had to be made. She, and her country, were deeply — and, as matters were seen by the Cabinet, irrevocably — committed to the maintenance of large land and air forces in the central plain of Europe: the most undesirable political repercussions imaginable could be expected if there was any reduction in British forces in Western Germany. The fleet, for all that Leach had to say, was the designated sacrificial victim.

Trident became a symbol of political will in another context. In April 1979 the NATO Nuclear Planning Group (effectively the defence ministers of the member countries of the alliance) met to consider the build-up of Soviet strategic missiles in Eastern Europe, particularly missiles in the SS class — intermediate-range rockets with multiple warheads,[9] which posed a deadly threat to the nations of Western Europe, though not to the United States itself, against which country the principal Soviet threat was the ICBM (Intercontinental Ballistic Missile) system. It is a fundamental tenet of the 1949 founding treaty of NATO that a threat against one member is to be considered as a threat against all. The Americans therefore proposed — and Britain, Italy, the Federal Republic of Germany, Belgium and Holland all accepted — that the newest generation of American nuclear weapons, cruise and Pershing 2, should be deployed in Europe.[10]

Before this deployment, however, the United States began, in Geneva, talks with the Soviet Union on the restriction on both sides of Intermediate-range Nuclear Forces (INF). President Reagan proposed what came to be known as the zero option: neither cruise nor Pershing would be delivered to their designated sites in Europe if the USSR dismantled those of her intermediate-range missiles which were already in place. The United Kingdom and France — the two Western European nuclear powers — declined to have their independent nuclear forces included in any agreement made between the Americans and the Russians. The Reagan administration made it perfectly clear that, unless agreement was reached on the dismantling of the SS series of missiles, cruise and Pershing would be brought to Europe. In spite of mounting protests by those opposed to the possession of nuclear weapons by any nation, that deployment began, because the Russian negotiators refused to countenance any reduction in their nuclear power in Europe. The Russians broke off the INF talks in May 1983.

Strictly speaking, unless one was of the faction that opposed all nationally owned and controlled nuclear weapons, Trident on the one hand, and cruise and Pershing on the other, were parts of separate arguments. But they were fused together in the political as well as the public mind. Opposition to cruise and Pershing became associated with opposition to Trident — to, in a word, any proposal that the nuclear power of the United Kingdom might become greater than it was. The Prime Minister came to the conclusion that the propaganda war — led by a revivified Campaign for

Nuclear Disarmament — was dangerous to all nuclear dispositions. Therefore, in January 1983 she transferred the populistically inclined Michael Heseltine to the Ministry of Defence, to replace John Nott, who retired from politics at that time, to lead a — successful — public relations campaign in favour of the retention and development of Britain's nuclear defence. Of course, between the 1979 NATO decision and the Heseltine appointment Britain had fought a war in the South Atlantic. In the interim, however, it was clear to those closest to Margaret Thatcher that the acquisition of Trident had become insensibly bound up with the European placing of cruise and Pershing. 'She thought,' says one of her ministers, 'that, in the words of the old song, you can't have one without the other.'

The genesis and development of the war for the Falkland Islands must be considered against this background of intense debate about the future defence policy of the United Kingdom. From the beginning of the term the Prime Minister's emotions, especially in the discussion of defence, were at war with her reasoning. I use neither word, here, with any normative content, for I think that her emotions — her instincts if you like — were often better guides to the conduct of public policy than were her frequent and detailed reasonings; and the converse often applied. Nevertheless, it has to be said that the conflict between emotion and reason led her first to neglect burgeoning difficulties in the South Atlantic, and then to be the leader most capable of resolving them by any force that was required.

'The Falklands Islands' misfortune,' wrote Max Hastings and Simon Jenkins in the arresting opening sentence of their splendid book, about the war which dominated British politics from 2 April 1982 to at least the end of that year, 'has always been to be wanted more than they are loved.'[11] From the late seventeenth century onwards various powers had engaged in desultory conflict about sovereignty over them, and for fifteen years before Margaret Thatcher became Prime Minister the British Foreign Office and the Argentinian Ministry of Foreign Affairs had been engaged in lazy and courtly dispute about who they properly belonged to.

By 1981, however, the discussions between the two countries were becoming anxious rather than lazy. For reasons of domestic politics the ruling Argentinian *junta* needed an achievement to its credit. Britain was thought by them to be indifferent, except in the matter of saving face, to any change in the government of the islands. Argentinian diplomats, indeed, had had, over the years, sufficient assurance from their British opposite numbers that the fate of the islands was a matter of little concern in London. True, on almost every occasion on which the issue had been discussed in the House of Commons a formidable array of backbench opinion had demonstrated, to Labour and Conservative ministers alike, that the House would not tolerate any settlement of the Falklands dispute which did not entirely satisfy the wishes about their future of the islanders. True, again, when Nicholas Ridley, the Foreign Office minister responsible for the Falklands, proposed in late 1979 an arrangement whereby the United Kingdom would recognise Argentinian sovereignty over the Falklands, but would lease the territory back from the government in Buenos Aires, the Prime Minister's response was described as 'thermonuclear' by Peter Carrington, the Foreign Secretary, who with Ridley put forward the idea. True, finally, when on 2 December 1980 Ridley presented to the House of Commons his options for policy on the Falklands — which included the lease-back proposals — he was savaged by members on all sides of the House; it was clear to anybody who understood British politics that Parliament would not stand for any deal that might be represented as a sell-out of the interests of the islanders.

Still, nothing was done to convey to the Argentinians the

potential anger of Britain in the face of any attempt on their part to exercise *force majeure*. The Foreign Office continued to assume that Argentinian intentions were honourable, and that the stately minuet of diplomacy would continue. Margaret Thatcher, after her explosion of temper in 1979, seemed content to let the matter rest, and paid unfortunately little attention to suggestions that matters were moving towards a crisis.

If the Prime Minister was culpably inattentive to developments in the South Atlantic, however, the Argentinian government was excessively attentive, but to the wrong signals. They saw that the British Treasury showed no interest in the economic development of the islands, in spite of a report by Lord Shackleton to the effect that there was much profit to be garnered from those inhospitable waters. Their contacts with British diplomats gave them confidence that there was an enthusiasm in governing circles in London to be shot of the Falklands Dependency. The British Antarctic Survey had announced its decision to close its research station on South Georgia for lack of funds. And, finally and most important symbolically, the Ministry of Defence had proclaimed its decision to withdraw the armed ship HMS *Endurance* from service within the year. All these developments suggested to the *junta* that the Malvinas Islands (as they called the Falklands) could be taken with great domestic political benefit, and at little ultimate cost in terms of relations with the United Kingdom.

Signs that an Argentinian invasion of the islands might be in contemplation were given by the landing, without the requisite official sanction, of Argentinian scrap dealers on South Georgia in March. *Endurance*, still on station, was instructed to move to Gritvyken to ensure the peaceful departure of the Argentinians. By this time alarm bells were ringing almost everywhere except in the Foreign Office, where officials remained convinced that everything done by the Argentinians was show and bluster. Henry Leach, however, saw things in a different way from the diplomats. His immediate boss, the Chief of the Defence Staff, Admiral of the Fleet Sir Terence Lewin, was in New Zealand. Leach, fully two weeks before the Argentinian landings at Port Stanley, instructed his staff to prepare plans, not for defending the islands, but for re-capturing them. 'Oh God,' said a member of the Civil Service staff at No. 10 Downing Street on hearing of this exercise, 'Henry's trying to save the Navy again.' In so far as anybody concerned themselves with the First Sea Lord's plans they assumed them to be irrelevant. However, the plans made by the Naval Staff assumed the launching towards the South Atlantic not just of a token force, but of the full resources of the Royal Navy. If the politicians decided that it should come to the crunch, virtually the entire naval strength of the United Kingdom, and a substantial part of her air and land power, would be sent into action in the South Atlantic. While John Nott dithered about the possibility, let alone the desirability, of such a deployment, Henry Leach had a plan. For a week before the Argentinian landings at Port Stanley the Cabinet was aware that there might be trouble in the wind. Three nuclear-powered submarines were ordered to take station off the islands. Two were defective and had to sail late. *Conqueror*, the subject of continuing controversy after she sank the Argentinian cruiser *Belgrano* on 2 May, was later on station than her fellow *Spartan*, which arrived in the South Atlantic on 12 April. These responses were, however, partial: Leach's proposals were full-blooded.

On 2 April a hastily convened Cabinet meeting assembled. The Prime Minister was at her most formal ('even stately', said one of the ministers present). Her first words were pellucid. There were six of them. 'Gentlemen,' she said, 'we shall have to fight.' She was by that stage familiar with Leach's appraisal of the possibility of retaking the Falklands, and with his estimate of the enormous cost of the operation.

She did not flinch. However careless she had been in the months leading up to the Argentinian landing she was ready now to see, and face, the consequences. Hastings and Jenkins believe[12] that, had James Callaghan been Prime Minister, a war might have been fought for the recovery of the islands. The general opinion in Westminster at the time, however, was that no conceivable alternative prime minister would have taken up the cudgels on behalf of two thousand people living on islands eight thousand miles away from Britain. Yet, she did so without a second thought, because it was in her nature so to do.

This is not a history of the war for the Falkland Islands, but it is perfectly fair, as most writers on the subject have seen, to regard the conduct of that war, its genesis as well as its conduct, as dramatically representative of Margaret Thatcher's style of government. Acceptance of the idea that Argentina might take military action against the islands and, on Friday 2 April, appreciation of the fact that she was in the process of doing so were quite simply impossible for a government machine in a state — as Hastings and Jenkins put it — 'of paralysing shock'.[13] On that Friday, indeed, the Lord Privy Seal, Humphrey Atkins, the senior Foreign Office spokesman in the House of Commons, assured angry questioners that there was as yet no evidence that the Argentinians were invading, although there was. In the emergency debate on Saturday — the first of its kind since the beginning of the Suez operation in 1956 — the Prime Minister made a poor, and the Defence Secretary a disastrous, speech. Over the weekend three Foreign Office ministers — Carrington, Atkins and Richard Luce, the junior minister into whose area of responsibility the Falkland Islands fell — all decided to resign, and did so on Monday. It was only with the greatest difficulty that the Prime Minister dissuaded John Nott from joining them in their rush for the door. It was some, but small, consolation for her that on the Friday afternoon her most senior predecessor, Harold Macmillan, approaching ninety as he was, called on her unannounced to offer succour and advice, to the effect that she had to prepare for war. By Monday, for all that the Task Force — the composition of which had been so meticulously and far-sightedly prepared by Sir Henry Leach — was starting to sail, the Thatcher government was on the ropes, and there were those in the Labour Party, not all of them by any means opposed to fighting Argentina if necessary, who believed that the fall of the Prime Minister, if not of the government itself, was imminent. Moreover, on Sunday 4 April a more accurate appreciation of her likely reaction to events was available.

On that day Brigadier Julian Thompson of the Royal Marines held a briefing session of his 3 Commando Brigade (and ancillary elements). More or less polite scepticism was manifested by the military men in the face of plans to send a mighty force across eight thousand miles of water. Like most politicians they found it hard to believe that, even if the worst came to the worst, any British government would have the requisite will to send them into action. A face-saving solution through the United Nations, restraint exercised by the United States (already professing her friendship for both countries), the temporary freezing of Argentinian assets in Britain — all these things seemed possible. What seemed most unlikely, even then, was war. It is, indeed, right to add that, according to the testimony of reporters accompanying the Task Force, scepticism continued to be the prevailing mood among the men at sea until operations were begun against South Georgia on 21 April. In spite of all this, however, Thompson's words to his officers on 4 April were to prove prophetic. He had no doubts about the Prime Minister's will. 'I was quite sure,' he said later of his briefing meeting, 'that with our Prime Minister, if the Argentinians didn't fold, we would fight them.' The Argentinians did not fold.

During the opening weeks she had little to worry about in

the matter of military preparations. The assembly and dispatch of the Task Force was put in hand with astonishing speed and — given that some error and some confusion were inevitable in the course of an operation at once so large and so unprecedented — remarkable efficiency. The political complications she faced were more onerous than the military.

The departure of Carrington had advantages and disadvantages. The self-sacrifice of so senior and highly regarded a minister at least lanced a boil: the Foreign Office could be, and was, blamed for everything that had gone wrong, and although criticism of the Prime Minister continued to make itself heard she was, from the Monday, to a very large extent detached from responsibility for the blunders that had encouraged the invasion. On the other hand a new foreign secretary had to be found, and there was nobody available with remotely as much experience of the chancelleries of the world as Carrington. Moreover, it was vital that there should be no major ministerial reshuffle: the government could not be seen in any more confusion than it was. The solution was to hand. The Leader of the House, Francis Pym, who had served for some time as Shadow Foreign Secretary, and who had cherished hopes of being given the substantive post in 1979, was drafted for — as was subsequently to transpire — a brief sojourn. She did not like this solution, for she distrusted Pym, and was beginning to regard him as one of her more formidable critics. On the advice of Harold Macmillan, she decided, in addition, to run the war through a small subcommittee (subsequently, but inaccurately, referred to as the War Cabinet) of the Overseas and Defence Committee of the Cabinet: this body was designated ODSA, or Overseas and Defence South Atlantic. Of necessity Pym and Nott were members, and so was her deputy, William Whitelaw. Surprise and consternation were expressed at her adding to their number Cecil Parkinson, the Chairman of the Conservative Party.

Here, however, there was wise calculation. Parkinson could be relied upon to support whatever decisions she took. Nott, as the minister in direct political charge of the Task Force — once he was over his initial doubts about the operation, and dismissed from his mind the accusation that had his 1982 White Paper been fully implemented, the United Kingdom would not have had the naval forces needed for sending the Task Force — could be expected fully to support the soldiers, sailors and airmen. 'Francis has got Willie,' Nott was reported to have said, 'so I needed Cecil.' The presumption here was that Pym and Whitelaw would be voices of caution, and sympathetic to such diplomatic initiatives to resolve the quarrel as were even then being mounted, particularly by the Secretary General of the United Nations, Señor Perez de Cuellar, and the American Secretary of State, General Alexander Haig. If they opposed any decisive action proposed by Nott and supported by Parkinson, the Prime Minister would exercise the crucial casting vote. In the event, matters did not turn out that way: in the opening weeks Pym was a peripatetic Foreign Secretary, travelling the world to assure other nations that his country's honour was unblemished. Whitelaw, instead of accepting his supposed role as a dove, proved staunch in his support of his Leader. Indeed, when on 4 May Britain lost her first Sea Harrier to enemy action and the Type 42 destroyer *Sheffield* was sunk with considerable loss of life, Whitelaw proved invaluable in sustaining her morale. He has himself since confessed that throughout the war he was haunted by memories of Suez, and the fear of a military catastrophe. But he had commanded soldiers in war (and had won the Military Cross) and thus had a gut understanding of the price of conflict which, in the nature of things, she could not have. She has herself since put on record the invaluable contribution to her own steadfastness of men such as Macmillan, Whitelaw and Enoch Powell (chosen by the Ulster Unionists as their representative in confidential briefings on the course of the war), all of whom had seen fighting and knew what a clash of arms entailed.

It is unnecessary to recapitulate the course of the war. All diplomatic moves foundered upon the rock of Argentinian intransigence and the Prime Minister's insistence that no resolution was acceptable other than the return of the islands to solely British administration. Controversy continues[14] on the order of the British government to HMS *Conqueror* on 2 May to sink the Argentinian battle cruiser *Belgrano*, an action taken on 4 May, which had the direct result of forcing the withdrawal of all Argentinian warships to their home ports for the duration. But the robust view both of the politicians assembled in ODSA and the service chiefs — to the effect that whatever course *Belgrano* was on when she was attacked, her very presence at sea constituted a threat to the Task Force, and that it was right, therefore, to sink her — seems to me to be a correct one. It was certainly seen as such by the British public.

As we have already seen, the Prime Minister was no less guilty than any of her Foreign Office ministers in failing to appreciate the development of an Argentinian threat to the Falklands. She was no more perceptive than they were in understanding that various moves made by Britain in the months before the invasion — most notably the announcement of the impending withdrawal of *Endurance* and the decision, under the 1981 Nationality Act, not to accord a right of abode in Britain to some eight hundred Falklanders who did not have a grandparent born in this country — encouraged the government in Buenos Aires to believe that there would be no more than symbolic opposition to their occupation of islands. But once the war began the Prime Minister identified herself with it in the public mind. Hastings and Jenkins are not alone in their belief that, had James Callaghan been Prime Minister he, too, would have fought for the islands. But few students of the affair would be willing to state with any certainty that any *conceivable* alternative prime minister would have responded in the way that she did. The understanding that there was that in her character which made her a natural war leader, whatever emotional sufferings she had to endure as British losses mounted and the outcome of the air and land battles seemed uncertain (particularly when *Coventry* and *Atlantic Conveyor* were sunk on 25 May) was widespread. The period before the war showed most of her weaknesses. There was, for example, her complete failure to spell out to the Foreign Office, and to give British diplomats the necessary supporting instructions for, her decision, as an act of policy, to refuse all concessions to the Argentinians which did not have the full support of the islanders. Associated with this was her dismissal of the agonised pleas of the Foreign Office to the effect that *Endurance* should be kept on station if, indeed, refusal to concede to Argentina was public policy. Most of this was, of course, the consequence of her obsession with economic policy: *Endurance*'s withdrawal was a saving, and the refusal to send a token naval force south at an early stage was, in part at least, a consequence of the realisation of how high the fuel bill would be.

It has become fashionable, in the aftermath of the war, to criticise the Fortress Falklands policy which has followed it, and the utter rejection of any contemplated settlement with Argentina which might seem to suggest that the battles of the Falklands had been fought to no purpose. There are, however, substantial defence and economic arguments for a continuing sovereign British presence in the South Atlantic.[15] What form the arguments for and against that presence will take in the future remains uncertain. What is undoubtedly historically true, however, is that the period between 2 April and 14 June 1982 showed the Prime Minister at her most typically daring and resolute. The more dramatic events in the life of a government are not always the most important, but the war in the South Atlantic will undoubtedly be seen in the future, as it was at the time, as bearing witness to Margaret Thatcher as most truly herself.

· CHAPTER EIGHT ·

The End of the Beginning

Now, this is not the end. It is not even the beginning of the
end. But it is, perhaps, the end of the beginning.
— Winston S. Churchill, after the battle of Alamein in 1942

Margaret Thatcher's second general election victory in
1983 raised in an acute form the question of whether there
was, or was not, a new political movement — or doctrine —
that could be called Thatcherism.[1] Her rise to and continuance in power coincided, of course, with (from their point of
view) an alarming decline in the electoral pulling power of the
Labour Party, and to that extent she was, perhaps excessively,
lucky. David Butler and Denis Kavanagh[2] carried an analysis
of the stark figures (by Michael Steed and John Curtice) in
their Nuffield study of the 1979 general election: the South —
East and West — and the Midlands — also East and West —
saw swings of over six per cent to the Conservative Party. The
Labour Party, to the horror of its planners, won only fifty per
cent of the trade union and forty-five per cent of the working-
class vote. But what Labour leaders found intolerable as well
as incomprehensible was that the Tories under Thatcher had
done so well in areas of economic decline and high unemployment: their reactions were to be even stronger after her
triumph in 1983. True, the Conservatives came to power in
1979 with a smaller share of the national vote than any
government of their party had received since the victory of
Andrew Bonar Law in 1922. That fact, however, while it en-

couraged the Social Democrats and the Liberal Party (who argued that the number of votes they garnered called for a change in the electoral system) was small consolation to a Labour Opposition faced in 1979 with a substantial, and in 1983 with an overwhelming, Conservative majority in Parliament.

There is, in my view, a phenomenon rightly called Thatcherism which, although it fits more comfortably than its critics would suppose within the main historical traditions of the Conservative Party, is set apart by the views of its adherents from those traditions as laid down by leaders of the party throughout this century. In attitude Thatcherism contrives to be liberal — that is to say, predisposed towards an economy in which the values of the market place are considered to be more important and of greater moral worth than decisions made on behalf of the community by the government of the day — in domestic policy, and nationalistic in foreign (including foreign economic) policy. This combination has been unknown in British politics since the middle of the nineteenth century and the devotion with which it is supported — for all that there have been errors and stumbles on the road to its full implementation — by the most single-minded major politician of our time gives it its right, I believe, to be called a movement. In the face of criticism to the effect that Margaret Thatcher and the governments she has headed have broken with the old consensus — the Butskellite consensus already referred to — her most intellectually aggressive minister, Nigel Lawson, has been defiant. 'The result of the election [1979] which swept the present Conservative government into power,' he wrote in 1980,[3] 'should surely have put paid to that charge [the charge that the draconian economic policies favoured by the Prime Minister would frighten off the electorate] at any rate. Nor is it surprising that people might actually want to vote for a Party that appears to share their views.'

'The notion,' Lawson goes on, in one of the most significant repudiations of the post-1945 political consensus that has been penned, 'that Conservatism is nothing more than a technique of government is altogether too pallid and bloodless an account of the role of a major political party.' And he concludes:

> All that is new is that the new Conservatism has embarked on the task — it is not an easy one: nothing worthwhile in politics is; but at least it runs with rather than against the grain of human nature — of re-educating the people in some old truths. They are no less true for being old.

The tone of Lawson's conclusion of this lecture to the Bow Group demonstrates a continuing Conservative concern with historical legitimacy such as was explored, though in a narrower perspective, in Chapter One. Whereas Margaret Thatcher's critics within the ranks of her own party have, in general, been inclined to refer to the experience of that party since the advent of Disraeli to its leadership in the nineteenth century, and more specifically to refer to the conduct of the nation's affairs by Conservative governments since 1945, her supporters have taken a far longer view of history. Her allies at the Institute of Economic Affairs find their inspiration in the eighteenth-century works of the Scottish economic thinker Adam Smith, and the clear political inspiration for Lawson when he spoke to the Bow Group on 4 August 1980 was the government of William Pitt the Younger in the opening years of the nineteenth century. 'Pitt was the first Tory,' the Prime Minister is fond of saying, in what is a very clear reference to his combination of a rigorous monetary policy at home, and an aggressive diplomatic policy abroad.[4] She put her views on the nationalistic motive most succinctly just after the war for the Falklands:

When we started out there were the waverers and the faint-hearts, the people who thought we could no longer do the great things we once did, those who believed our decline was irreversible, that we could never again be what we were, that Britain was no longer the nation that had built an empire and ruled a quarter of the world.

And then, in a final sentence that summarises that brisk side of her character which dismisses all opposition:

'Well, they were wrong.'

It is immensely difficult to separate Thatcherism from Margaret Thatcher. The overwhelming personality of the Prime Minister serves to identify every policy her government adopts with her. This is both a strength and a weakness. It is a strength in so far as the force of her personality is felt at most levels of government and thus, in spite of her resistance to altering in a major way any part of the structure of the government machine, her expressed wishes cause executives to scurry. It is a weakness in that it is so identified with one leader that its continuance under another must reasonably be called into question. There is no politician, of any party, to whom I have spoken during the preparation of this book who has not, whether in admiration or opposition, expressed the view that Thatcher is essential to Thatcherism. Indeed, one of her ministers suggested that when she had gone the changes — especially in economic policy — that she had inaugurated would go too. 'There is,' he said, 'the Tom King syndrome.'

Tom King is, at the time of writing, Secretary of State for Employment, having previously been a Minister of State at the Department of the Environment and, before that, in opposition, Shadow Secretary of State for Defence. A man of industry and ability, he has an emollient image. The man to whom I was talking believed that, after a long stretch of leadership by Margaret Thatcher the Conservative Party would want somebody more restful. King was his nominee for the succession. Supposing, however, that there was such a change, from the abrasive Thatcher to somebody softer-spoken, how much of the Thatcher heritage would remain? This is the grand historical question.

It is answered, I think, by Andrew Gamble, to whose Marxist essays I have already had occasion to make reference. In *The Politics of Thatcherism*[5] Gamble attempts a definition of the distinction between her policies and those of Edward Heath. He says:

> Although Heath's policy appeared at the time to mark a break with social democracy, in retrospect it can be seen as a last attempt to operate within its confines. The Heath Government sought to put British capitalism on a new course, to arrest national economic decline, and make British companies competitive within the EEC. Heath's competition policy was an attempt to overcome the specific competitive weaknesses of British capital. The means tried at first were certainly influenced by the new current of social market thinking, but once these failed to produce faster growth because of the scale of unemployment and worker-resistance they created, the Government made significant changes in its policies (the so-called U-turns), and opted instead for statutory wage controls, increased public expenditure and much greater intervention in industry. The basic aim remained the same — achieving a higher rate of growth in the British economy.

Now, Andrew Gamble, I think, understands what the Prime Minister is about better than do any of her Conservative opponents. I quote him at length because he sees so clearly that Margaret Thatcher is engaged on a different exercise from that of any recent Conservative government. Later in his essay Gamble says:

The Thatcher Government in its first two years proceeded cautiously, particularly as regards trade union reform. But although it is more cautious there is also much less chance that it will indulge in the kind of U-turn the Heath Government performed. This is because these kinds of U-turns could only be performed by a government still committed to the social-democratic goals of full employment and growth. The Heath leadership flirted with the doctrines of the social market economy as techniques for improving efficiency and raising growth. Since they were only seen as techniques they could always be changed. For Thatcher and her supporters they were not techniques but principles.

It is interesting that the right wing of the Conservative Party — the Thatcher supporters — take exactly the same view of the evolution of British politics as do the authors of essays in *Marxism Today*. Both, I think, are right about what has been happening.

Like Gamble, William Keegan is unsympathetic: in his meticulous and passionate critique of the economic policy of the 1979 government, however, he errs principally in his assumption that her goals were the same goals as those of her immediate Conservative and Labour predecessors: they were not. The breaking of the post-war political consensus on the aims of government has been her most important undertaking and, for good or ill, she has achieved it.

She has done so partly through the way she sees the issues of the day — through, if you like, the employment of her instinct — and partly through that formidable industry which is a subject of awed discussion among those who have worked with or for her. She is, usually, first seen by her staff at nine o'clock in the morning in her study in the six-room flat on the upper storeys of No. 10 Downing Street which is the home provided by the State for the First Lord of the Treasury (the

Prime Minister's constitutionally most correct title). At that hour they receive from her the boxes of documents consigned to her care the previous evening. Every document, they find day by day, has been read, digested and annotated. While the memoranda consequent upon her reading are being prepared she embarks upon a series of meetings with ministers and civil servants. Assuming there is no requirement to provide hospitality or time for, say, visiting foreign politicians, her meetings go on until between eight and nine o'clock in the evening. At about that hour she has a meal with her husband and by then, of course, the next set of boxes of documents has been delivered to her. All of these she reads and comments on before going to sleep. It is worth adding that, in the interstices of this rampant activity, she cooks her husband's breakfast and dinner: there is no resident cook at No. 10 Downing Street.

Thus she keeps her hand on almost every activity of government. Not for her are Churchill's two-hour afternoon sleeps, or Macmillan's solitary walks in the garden at No. 10. I once asked her when she found time to brood: she replied crisply that all her brooding had been done before she took office. The frenetic pace of her working day reflects, I believe, not simply an extraordinary metabolic capacity for work but a conviction that the time allowed to her is only barely sufficient for doing what she believes she has to do. 'The whole of the day,' says one of her staff, 'is taken up with endless meetings, and she is always clear about what she wants from them. And even in the midst of all this activity she finds time for between half an hour and an hour's briefing for Prime Minister's questions [in the House of Commons] on Tuesday and Thursday.'

The difficulty with a pattern of activity like this is that, providing as it does little opportunity for reflection, there occur errors of judgement and misapplications of emphasis. If every subject is treated with the same instant intensity the difference in importance between subjects is apt to go unappreciated. None the less when, after the 1983 election ministers seemed haplessly unable to avoid mistake after mistake — the most embarrassing of which was the loss of an important vote in the House of Lords on legislation preparing the way for the abolition of the metropolitan local authorities and especially the Greater 'London Council — it was evident that the main thrust of her policy had not weakened. The decision, at that time, of the Chancellor of the Exchequer to announce further cuts in public spending before his ministerial colleagues had agreed to them was taken as evidence that the government was tiring in its endeavours and over-hasty in their execution. But the fact remained that Nigel Lawson's budgetary decisions in 1983 were wholly congruent with the policy she had been following since 1980.

Likewise, while the theme of privatisation was merely — or so it seemed — a gleam in her eye when the 1979 manifesto was being prepared it has, in the second term, become the major preoccupation of the government. And this brings us to a consideration of the way the Prime Minister goes about her work which may seem at odds with the description of her almost frenetic activity in office just given. 'I wasn't aware,' a senior Treasury civil servant said to her in 1982, 'that you were planning to go *quite* that far.' He was referring to the privatisation programme and to his own pique at the fact that, though he had been conscientious in his study of the policy documents issued by the Conservative Party throughout her leadership, he had not grasped how thoroughgoing were the changes she had planned. 'How,' she asked when he had left the room, 'is it that these people simply don't understand what I'm getting at?'

These exclamations — and their number is legion — are a rhetorical device. In sum they constitute a very important part of the Thatcher technique of government. When a minister or a civil servant is suddenly confronted with a prime ministerial decision which he finds unexpected and, perhaps, dismaying, she loves to be able to say, with sublime self-confidence, that it was implicit in her stance all along, and the suggestion conveyed — often with lasting damage to her interlocutor's *amour propre* — is that he was a fool not to have seen it. On 5 May 1982, for example, the day after the sinking of the *Belgrano*, an admiring colleague remarked that he had not thought hitherto that she would have the nerve to act so drastically. 'Why ever not?' was her reply. 'I have always said I would do what was necessary.'

Even after five years of office she retains her capacity to surprise. When the 'E' Committee was told, just after the 1983 election, how far-reaching her privatisation proposals were, even her most supportive colleagues were taken aback. And yet, as she again said, it was all clear from the beginning.

The truth is, of course, that while it may have been clear to her it was not necessarily clear to others. She tests the political air with ideas. If they are not immediately acceptable — or if they are greeted with too-vociferous opposition — she appears to drop them only to return to them with even greater force once she has managed to improve the climate for their reception. In this manner she conducted the lead-up to the budget of 1981 and held firm to the strategy it expressed through a Cabinet reshuffle and two successor budgets which confirmed the pattern of economic policy she had laid down. 'For God's sake,' said one of her dissenting Ministers just before the budget of 1982, 'she's not going to do it again, is she?' But by then, of course, opposition to her within the Cabinet and the party had been pulverised into dull acceptance of the fact that she *was* going to do it again, and again after that, if she judged it necessary.

In so active an individual the ability both to persevere and, when necessary, to bide her time, is exceptional. Between 1975 and 1979 she harped constantly on the theme expounded in her *Observer* interview with Kenneth Harris — that she would have only one opportunity to grasp at the palm of office. If she failed in that first try, she rightly saw, her party would regret their experiment in electing a radical woman to the leadership, and pull her down immediately from her plinth. None the less, her reiteration of her consciousness of the vulnerability of her position was invariably accompanied by an equally emphatic insistence on the fact that she needed two terms in power to carry out her purpose. This combination of an acute awareness of the short term and an accurate appreciation of the long term goes far, I believe, to contradict the sporting metaphor of one of her ministers quoted earlier,[6] to the effect that, while brilliant at the net she is much weaker playing from the base line.

At the Conservative Party Conference in 1981 I asked a somewhat bemused Treasury minister how it was that, although the public opinion polls consistently recorded the view of the electorate that unemployment was the most crucial issue of the day, the people did not blame the government for its evident failure to bring down the figures. 'I just don't know,' he replied. 'She's managed it somehow.'

There are two points in that reply worth consideration and emphasis (and the reply is entirely typical of hundreds I have heard from politicians over the years of her prime ministerial stewardship). The first is the use of the personal pronoun. Everything the government does, whether it is adjudged good or bad, mistaken or wise is, in the end, put down to Margaret Thatcher. If a minister blunders the fault is assumed to lie with her. If a minister implements a brilliant stroke of policy it is assumed that its conception, and the decision to carry it through, were made in her office. This, both as to blame and praise, is the inevitable consequence of having a prime minister who maintains such a high personal profile in relation to the activities of the government which she leads.

The second point in the remark is the suggestion of alchemy about her. 'She's managed it somehow' is a sentence which is

expressive of an invariable kind of judgement on her by political supporters and opponents alike. While it is comforting —
and perhaps necessary — for her left-wing competitors to
believe that she won the general election of 1983 because
Admiral Woodward and General Moore and their men had
triumphed in the Falklands, none of the objective evidence
available bears out this belief. She was on course for her
second electoral victory long before the Argentinian flag was
hauled down in Port Stanley.

And yet the position on policy she had adopted was one
which defied all the accepted wisdom about the operation of
the British political system. In 1955, 1959, 1964, 1966, 1970
and 1974 anxious prime ministers sought the assurance of beleaguered chancellors that something in the way of hope or
happiness could be offered to the people in a general election.
The 1979 election was the first since the war which was an exception to this iron rule, but that was only because the government of the day was forced to call it. James Callaghan did not
go to the country at a time of his choosing: indeed, it is now
clear that he resisted the apparently overwhelming temptation to seek a new mandate in 1978 principally because he
felt he had nothing to offer. His parliamentary tactics were to
sustain himself in office until matters either had improved or,
at least, a plausible case could be made for saying that they
would improve. Now, while there were a few minor concessions to this mode of thinking in Sir Geoffrey Howe's 1983
budget, there was nothing substantial, and all pleas for even
the most modest reflationary package fell upon ears which the
Prime Minister had closed.

There are several explanations of why her (in the terms of
conventional political wisdom) unappealing stance should
have issued in victory in the form of a massive parliamentary
majority. 'She has ground the hope out of British politics,'
said Peter Shore on the morrow of her second triumph.
According to this reasoning the most aggressively positive (in

rhetorical terms) of modern prime ministers has reduced the British electorate to so depressed a state of mind that they will not even bother to turn her out. Another suggestion is that the division of the opposition to the Conservatives between the Labour, Liberal and Social Democratic parties has made the election of an alternative government to that of Margaret Thatcher impossible. There is, in my judgement, a good deal of truth in this. But the brute fact remains: the Social Democratic Party was created because its founding members thought that political life in the Labour Party was intolerable, not because of anything Margaret Thatcher had done or left undone. The fissure on the left was created by the left. It has been to her electoral good fortune, but she can be neither praised nor blamed for it.

Circumstances, therefore, have favoured her. She seemed in her second term to be taking rather uncertain advantage of those circumstances. Thus, in a radio interview immediately after the 1983 victory she expatiated on the durability of the Labour Party. 'She needs them,' said David Owen, 'that's why she praised them.' His remark was a fair one, for it is her belief that the Labour Party is in a condition of terminal division, falling back, election by election, on its remaining strongholds in depressed industrial areas. Even she, however, accepts that the Conservative Party cannot remain in power for ever, though she did suggest, after 1983, that it could not unreasonably look forward to twenty-five years in office, thus establishing a hold on power and office similar to that enjoyed by the socialist parties of the Scandinavian countries. It would seem, therefore, that she would be wiser, in the interests of the beliefs she holds and the permanence of her counter-revolution, to encourage the growth of the SDP, and the replacement of Labour by the Alliance as the main challenger to the Conservatives. The development of SDP policy by David Owen since he became its leader suggests, indeed, the pervasiveness of her influence: as uneasy Liberals at their party conference in 1984 recognised, the SDP has accepted that the terms of political discussion in Britain have been altered, perhaps irrevocably, by Margaret Thatcher. 'All Owen can do,' said one of her more thoughtful ministers, 'and he is wise to do it, is to suggest to the voter that he represents Thatcherism with a human face.' A softer, but an only slightly softer, version of the philosophy she encapsulates seems the only one likely to appeal to the electorate in the future. '

There is another consideration and, again, it is the Marxist writers who have most precisely defined it. Stuart Hall and Martin Jacques[7] refer to an underestimation by the left of

> the novelty of 'Thatcherism' as a political force, the 'radicalism' of its political strategy, the long-term shifts and reversals which it regards as its historic mission, and the degree to which the 'natural' swings and roundabouts of the electoral pendulum, along with many of the other rhythms of post-war politics, have been deeply interrupted.

Their conclusion is that she constitutes 'a novel and exceptional political force'. The inescapable fact therefore is that she has altered all the assumptions of post-war British politics.

The seismic change which these two writers describe has, it is important to remember, been brought about by a politician whose actions have often been less decisive than her words suggest. 'Her rhetoric,' Hugh Stephenson wrote, 'is radical, even reckless. But from the start her deeds have shown a politician's instinctive caution.'[8] For all that her closest advisers would have preferred her to act in a far more dashing fashion after her election in 1979, and for all that they deplore what I, with Keith Joseph, have called 'the lost year', it has been her capacity to play it long that has enabled her to engineer the shifts in public expectation and public policy in the face of which those opposed to her stand aghast.

Nor is there much sign of her losing steam, even in the second term, and in spite of its besetting problems and the distressing tendency of her ministers to seek out banana skins and fall over them. When, in 1983, she repaired to hospital for an operation on her eye it did seem, at last, that the Thatcher machine was beginning to run down. But in a matter of days she was back at her ceaseless business of chivvying ministers, exhorting the public and berating her rivals. The truth, unpalatable as it is for those who disagree with her, is that she is relaxed, and even energised, by power. Its concomitant responsibilities and burdens simply do not depress her for more than very brief periods. It is, therefore, her endurance as much as her radicalism that has enabled her to preside over a government for so long, and with such fundamental effect. By the time her second term comes to an end it will be virtually impossible for any politician to present himself (or herself) to the electorate with any hope of success who does not accept the framework of political discussion as designed by Margaret Thatcher.

I once pointed out to her that if her second term ran its full course she would be the longest serving prime minister of this century. It was a casual remark, but she seized upon it. With the aid of a Conservative Central Office diary (which useful little volume contains a record of prime ministerial service since Walpole in the eighteenth century) I showed her that her only likely rivals for duration in office were Harold Wilson and Herbert Asquith, and Wilson's service was interrupted. 'Really?' she replied. 'Who was the longest before Asquith?' If one allows the nineteenth century to extend to 1903, I told her, the Prime Minister who held office longest in that century was the Third Marquis of Salisbury though, again, his tenure was an interrupted one. 'That's fascinating,' she said thoughtfully, and with that distinctive gleam in her eye, 'and he was a *very* great man.' I wonder how often she thinks of the Salisbury record.

Notes

Preface
1 A full list of all the works referred to can be found in the bibliography.

1. *The Quest for Legitimacy*
1 Before Saatchi and Saatchi undertook to be the Conservative Party's advertising agents they did a market research project of their own. Its conclusions were available in 1978. Their judgement was that I had been more or less correct in defining Mrs Thatcher's particular appeal.
2 See Robert McKenzie, *British Political Parties* (new edn, London, 1963). The late Professor McKenzie's book is the finest, and most objective, analytical study of British politics published this century.
3 Marcia Falkender, *Downing Street in Perspective* (London, 1983), pp. 181, 233. On p. 233 Lady Falkender writes, 'I remember they were all laughing, joking and slapping each other on the shoulders, with remarks to the effect that all was now well. "That's it, we're home and dry," was the general tenor. "No need to worry about the next election. It's a foregone conclusion. Well, how could the Tory Party — the Tory Party — possibly win with a woman at the head?"' Lady Falkender goes on to say that she and Peter Shore disagreed with this general view. She quotes Shore as saying, 'I think it's going to be extremely difficult to beat her.' She adds that '...the women's vote, which is of extreme importance in any election and often a pointer as to the final result, could be brought very powerfully into play by Margaret Thatcher.'
4 Hugh Stephenson, *Mrs Thatcher's First Year* (London, 1980), p. 27.
5 F. A. Hayek, *The Road to Serfdom* (London, 1944). See also, by the same author, *The Constitution of Liberty* (London, 1960).
6 Lord Blake and John Patten (eds), *The Conservative Opportunity* (London, 1976), pp. 2–3.

2. *The Apprenticeship*
1 See Ian Gilmour, *The Body Politic* (London, 1969). This book, Sir Ian's

first, is an attempt at combining constitutional history and contemporary Conservative politics. It had a great vogue in its day. He is said to have believed, however, when the struggles of the 1970s began, that it was deficient in that it failed directly to tackle the technicalities of economic questions.

2   Ian Gilmour, *Inside Right* (London, 1977), and *Britain Can Work* (London, 1982). The first book was in part an examination of the work of certain Conservative thinkers, from Halifax to Hailsham, and in part a study of Conservative philosophy in relation to social and economic questions. It is the virtually definitive statement of the rationale of Conservative opposition to Margaret Thatcher. The second was published after he had been dismissed from the Cabinet. Many of Sir Ian's ideas are expressed in a more pithy and, for that matter, more scholarly form in the work of Chris Patten in *The Tory Case* (London, 1983).

3   The *Red Star* article made as many headlines in the West as did the Thatcher speech (which was described by the late Antony Crosland, then Foreign Secretary, as an invitation to war). Since then it has been generally assumed that the Prime Minister's favourite soubriquet was awarded to her by Soviet military men. It is not so. She was first called, variously, 'Iron Maiden' and 'Iron Lady' by Mrs Marjorie Proops in the *Daily Mirror* in 1973. The coincidence of application of a nickname may — or may not — tell us something about what Russian generals read.

3. The Lost Year

1   Mrs Thatcher has an unfortunate habit which offends against the constitution. She regularly refers to the government in which she is First Lord of the Treasury as hers. The proper style to be used by ministers is Her Majesty's Government. She is not, however, alone in this deplorable habit. Sir Alec Douglas-Home — then Lord Home — when Foreign Secretary in the Macmillan government referred to that administration as 'my government' at the United Nations. He meant, of course, the Queen's government.

2   See *Le Fil de l'Epée* (Paris, 1938). See also by Charles de Gaulle, *L'Armée du Métier* (Paris, 1938).

4. The Battles of the Budget

1   The word 'Thatcherism' does not describe a doctrine, and its use may be criticised on the grounds that its meaning is vague and that it is related only to the personality of one politician. Yet most writers about her and her career have used it at one time or another and Peter Riddell

in *The Thatcher Government* devoted a twenty-page chapter to an attempt to define it. I use it sparingly, but I do find it useful. I provide a more detailed analysis of it in my final chapter.

2   William Keegan, *Mrs Thatcher's Economic Experiment* (London, 1984), p. 131.

3   Ralph Harris and Brendon Sewell, *British Economic Policy 1970–4: two views* (London, 1975).

4   *The Right Approach*, Conservative Central Office, 1978.

5   Ernest Hemingway, *A Moveable Feast* (London, 1964).

6   Enoch Powell, *Freedom and Reality* (London, 1969).

7   Penny Junor, *Margaret Thatcher: wife, mother, politician* (London, 1983). Tricia Murray, *Margaret Thatcher* (London, 1980).

8   See especially p. 120.

9   Winston S. Churchill, *The Second World War* (London, 1949 edn), Vol. II, pp. 14ff.

10   It is almost forgotten today but it is amusing to remember that Mrs Thatcher was not the first politician to categorise opponents as 'wet'. It was Edward Heath's favourite term of abuse for his Conservative critics after the general election of 1970.

11   Keegan, *op. cit.*, pp. 142–3.

12   Keegan, *op. cit.*, p. 218.

13   See Francis Pym, *The Politics of Consent* (London, 1984), especially chapter three.

5.   Work in Progress

1   See above pp. 86–7.

2   Penny Junor, *Margaret Thatcher: Wife, Mother, politician* (London, 1983), p. 44.

3   Francis Pym, *The Politics of Consent* (London, 1984). Of Gilmour's books the most immediately relevant is *Britain Can Work* (Oxford, 1983).

4   'Rise of the Resolute Right', in *New Socialist*, January–February 1983. It is worth remarking that some of the most intelligent and incisive writing, albeit from a hostile point of view, about the Thatcher years, has been by Marxist writers, among whom Andrew Gamble stands out. See, especially, his 'Thatcherism and Conservative Politics', in Stuart Hall and Martin Jacques (eds), *The Politics of Thatcherism* (London, 1983).

5   'Thatcher: the second coming', in *Marxism Today*, July 1983.

6   See below, pp. 168–9.

7   See below, p. 171.

8   Peter Riddell, *The Thatcher Government* (London, 1983), pp. 44–5.

9   Riddell adds the name of Mark Carlisle, the Secretary of State for Education and Science, to this list. But Carlisle, while he did his best in office to defend his department, always made it clear that there were no circumstances in which he would rebel against the Prime Minister. He also wrote her a particularly warm letter of resignation in which he undertook to cause her no trouble from the backbenches. For these reasons I exclude him from any list of potential rebels.

10 Riddell, *op. cit.*, p. 46. See, among 'wet' publications, *Changing Gear: what the Government should do next* (London, 1981), and Chris Patten, *The Tory Case* (London, 1983). For a corrective, see Institute of Economic Affairs, *Could do better* (London, 1982).

11 Peter Thorneycroft, *Spectator*, 4 December 1976.

12 See Chapter Six.

13 Lord Hugh Cecil, *Conservatism* (London, 1912).

14 See Ian Gilmour, *Britain Can Work* (London, 1982) and Chris Patten, *The Tory Case*. Patten, now Conservative Member for Bath and Parliamentary Undersecretary of State for Northern Ireland, could be described as a pupil of Gilmour's. During Edward Heath's time as Prime Minister he was appointed Director of the Conservative Research Department, Gilmour being its Chairman.

15 Lord Wilson's remark has been the butt of many Tory jokes in recent years. But it was not an example of hubris. It was a view shared by many, particularly in academic circles. See, especially, David Butler and Donald Stokes, *Political Change in Britain* (London, 1971 edn).

16 Peter Riddell, *op. cit.*, pp. 4–5.

6. *Reforming the Nation*

1   Philip M. Williams: *Hugh Gaitskell: a biography* (London, 1980) and (ed) *The Diary of Hugh Gaitskell* (London, 1983).

2   *Report of the House of Commons Public Accounts Committee, Session 1981–2*.

3   See above, pp. 97–8.

4   P. D. Henderson, 'Mrs Thatcher's Old-Style Dirigisme', in *Journal of Economic Affairs*, January 1983.

5   Philip Holland and Michael Fallon, *The Quango Explosion* (London, 1978).

6   Michael Edwardes, *Back from the Brink* (London, 1983).

7   Peter Hennessy in *The Times* was the only journalist then writing regularly on the affairs of Whitehall, and his columns are required reading for anybody interested in the machinery of government. See his *States*

of Emergency (written with Keith Jeffery) (London, 1983).

8   *Ibid.*

9   Peter Hennessy, 'Whitehall Briefing', *The Times*, 22 September 1984.

10 The present author contributed papers supporting the argument for the creation of a Prime Ministerial Department between 1975 and 1979.

11 Ferdinand Mount, *The Subversive Family* (London, 1982).

12 See *Public Expenditure White Paper*, February 1983. The figures given are in 1980–81 prices.

13 See Ralph Harris and Arthur Seldon, *Over-ruled on welfare*, and Arthur Seldon (ed.), *The emerging consensus?* both Institute of Economic Affairs (London 1979 and 1981 respectively).

7. The Prime Minister Goes to War

1   See remarks quoted from Peter Jay and Roy Hattersley in Peter Taylor, 'Are the F.O. Critics Right?', *Sunday Telegraph*, 16 January 1983.

2   See above, pp. 83ff.

3   The only institution of the EEC which is directly elected calls itself the European Parliament. However, the United Kingdom statute which provides for elections to it refers to it as the 'European Assembly', and I have chosen to use this formulation. The Prime Minister usually describes it as the European Parliament.

4   See Patrick Cosgrave and George Richey, *NATO's Strategy: A Case of Outdated Priorities?* (London, Institute of European Defence and Strategic Studies, 1985) *passim*.

5   See above, pp. 140ff.

6   Keith Speed, *Sea Change: the battle for the Falklands and the future of Britain's navy* (Bath, Ashgrove Press, 1982).

7   In defence parlance a maritime power is one that possesses a fighting navy, usually one intended for use in the seas contiguous to it. An oceanic naval power is, however, one that can deploy a ship-borne force across an ocean.

8   Cosgrave and Richey, *op. cit.*, Chapter Two.

9   Trident, in contrast to the first generation of nuclear rockets, has a multiple warhead system. That, to put it simply, means that it carries several hydrogen bombs all aimed at different targets. If the enemy fails to destroy the rocket before its subsidiary weapons are fired, then he has the task of tracking down each separate warhead before it reaches its objective. The currently most sophisticated weapon in this class is designated MIRV — Multiple and Independently Targeted Re-entry Vehicles. A rocket in the MIRV class first leaves the earth's

atmosphere and then re-enters, spraying its ancillary rockets on targets individually chosen for them.

10 It has become journalistic practice to spell cruise with a capital C. However, cruise is merely a word that describes the technical pattern of behaviour of different kinds of missile. As the word cruise suggests, these weapons are, in comparison to other rockets, extremely slow. Their operational advantage is that they are, again in defence parlance, ground-hugging: while they would take a relatively long time to reach a target their ability to fly very low and follow the contours of the ground they cover *under* any known radar screen makes them an ideal second-strike weapon. No nation planning to use a nuclear weapon in the early stages of a war would employ a cruise weapon when it had available the speedier SS 20 series (like the USSR), the Poseidon system (like the USA) or Polaris (like Britain). The general codename for weapons of the cruise class built by the Americans is Tomahawk.

11 Max Hastings and Simon Jenkins, *The Battle for the Falklands*, p. 13.

12 *Ibid.*, p. 71.

13 *Ibid.*, pp. 79ff.

14 Tam Dalyell, *Mrs Thatcher's Torpedo* (London, 1983).

15 Patrick Cosgrave and George Ritchie, *The Future of NATO: The Threat from the North and the Case for Change* (London, 1985).

8. The End of the Beginning

1 See above, pp. 96ff.

2 David Butler and Dennis Kavanagh, *The British General Election of 1979* (London, 1980).

3 Nigel Lawson, *The New Conservatism* (London, Centre for Policy Studies, 1980). This is the text of a lecture given to the Bow Group on 4 August 1980.

4 John Erhman, *The Younger Pitt* (Vol. I, London 1966, Vol. II, London 1982). This as yet incomplete massive biography is among the Prime Minister's favourite historical reading.

5 Andrew Gamble, 'Thatcherism and Conservative Politics', in Stuart Hall and Martin Jacques (eds), *The Politics of Thatcherism* (London, 1983), pp. 109ff.

6 See above, p. 38.

7 Stuart Hall and Martin Jacques (eds), *op. cit.*, p. 9. This introduction is signed by Hall and Jacques.

8 Hugh Stephenson, *Mrs Thatcher's First Year* (London, 1980), p. 9.

Bibliography

Arnold, Bruce, *Margaret Thatcher: A Study in Power* (London, 1984).

Barnett, Joel, *Inside the Treasury* (London, 1982).
Behrens, Robert, *The Conservative Party from Heath to Thatcher* (London, 1980).
Blake, Robert, *The Office of Prime Minister* (Oxford, 1975).
— *The Conservative Party: from Peel to Churchill* (London, 1970).
— with John Patten (eds), *The Conservative Opportunity* (London, 1976).
Brittan, Samuel, *How to End the Monetarist Controversy* (London, 1982).
— *The Role and Limits of Government* (London, 1983).
Bruce-Gardyne, Jock, *Mrs Thatcher's First Administration: Confounding the Prophets* (London, 1984).
Burns, Terry, 'Economic policy and prospects', *Public Money*, 1981.
Butler, David, *Governing Without a Majority: Dilemmas for Hung Parliaments in Britain* (London, 1983).
— with Donald Stokes, *Political Change in Britain* (London, 1971).
— with Denis Kavanagh, *The British General Election of 1979* (London, 1980).

Calvert, Harry (ed.), *Devolution* (London, 1975).
Cosgrave, Patrick, *Margaret Thatcher: A Tory and her Party* (London, 1978).
— with George Richey, *NATO's Strategy: A Case of Outdated Priorities?* (London, 1985).
Conservative Members of Parliament, *Changing Gear: What the Government Should Do Next* (London, 1981).

Edwardes, Michael, *Back from the Brink* (London, 1983).

Finer, S. E., 'Manifesto Moonshine', *New Society*, 13 November 1975.
Franks, Lord (and others), *Falkland Islands Review: Report of a*

Committee of Privy Councellors, Cmnd 8787 (London, 1983).

Gamble, Andrew, *The Conservative Nation* (London, 1974).
— 'The rise of the resolute right', in *New Socialist* (Jan–Feb 1983).
— 'Thatcher: the second coming', in *Marxism Today* (July, 1983).
— 'Thatcherism and Conservative politics', in Stuart Hall and Martin
Jacques (eds) *The Politics of Thatcherism* (London, 1983).
Gilmour, Ian, *The Body Politic* (London, 1969).
— *Inside Right* (London, 1977).
— *Britain Can Work* (Oxford, 1983).
Goodhart, Philip, *The 1922* (London, 1973).
Government's Expenditure Plans 1980–1 to 1983–4, Cmnd 7841
(London, 1980).
Government's Expenditure Plans 1983–4 to 1985–6, Cmnd. 8789
(London, 1983).

Harris, Ralph, and Sewell, Brendon, *British Economic Policy 1970–4: Two
Views* (London, 1975).
— and Seldon, Arthur, *Over-ruled on Welfare* (London, 1979).
Hastings, Max, and Jenkins, Simon, *The Battle for the Falklands* (London,
1983).
Hayek, F. A., *The Road to Serfdom* (London ed., 1976).
— *New Studies* (London, 1978).
Hall, Stuart and Jacques, Martin (eds), *The Politics of Thatcherism*
(London, 1983).
Henderson, P. D., 'Mrs Thatcher's Old-style Dirigisme', in *Journal of
Economic Affairs* (London, January 1983).
Henessy, Peter, and Keith, Jeffrey, *States of Emergency* (London, 1983).

Joseph, Keith and Sumption, Jonathan, *Equality* (London, 1978).
Junor, Penny, *Margaret Thatcher: Woman, Mother, Prime Minister*
(London, 1983).

Kaldor, Nicholas, *The Economic Consequences of Mrs Thatcher* (London,
1983).
Keegan, William, *Mrs Thatcher's Economic Experiment* (London, 1984).

Lawson, Nigel, and Bruce-Gardyne, Jock, *The Power Game* (London,
1976).
— *The New Conservatism* (London, 1980).
— *What's Right with Britain* (London 1982).

Lewis, Russell, *Margaret Thatcher* (London ed., 1983).

Mount, Ferdinand, *The Subversive Family* (London, 1982).
Murray, Tricia, *Margaret Thatcher* (London, 1978).

Patten, Chris, *The Tory Case* (London, 1983).
Pliatzky, Leo, *Getting and Spending: Public Expenditure* (Oxford, 1982).
Pym, Francis, *The Politics of Consent* (London, 1984).

Riddell, Peter, *The Thatcher Government* (London, 1983).
Rose, Richard, *The Problem of Party Government* (London, 1974).

Seldon, Arthur (ed.), *The Emerging Consensus?* (London, 1981).
Speed, Keith, *Sea Change: the Battle for the Falklands and the Future of Britain's Navy* (Bath, 1982).
Stephenson, Hugh, *Mrs Thatcher's First Year* (London, 1980).

Thatcher, Carol, *Diary of an Election* (London, 1983).

Wapshott, Nicholas, and Brock, George, *Thatcher* (London, 1983).
Witonski, Peter (ed.) *The Wisdom of Conservatism* (1981 ed., North Carolina).
Williams, Philip M., *Hugh Gaitskell* (London, 1980).
— (ed.) *The Diary of Hugh Gaitskell, 1945–1956* (London, 1983).

Index